BLAKE STUDIES

Essays on his life and work

BLAKE STUDIES

Essays on his life and work

BY

GEOFFREY KEYNES Kt.

SECOND EDITION

OXFORD

At the Clarendon Press

1971

Oxford University Press, Ely House, London W. 1

GLASGOW NEW YORK TORONTO MELBOURNE WELLINGTON
CAPE TOWN SALISBURY IBADAN NAIROBI DAR ES SALAAM LUSAKA ADDIS ABABA
BOMBAY CALCUTTA MADRAS KARACHI LAHORE DACCA
KUALA LUMPUR SINGAPORE HONG KONG TOKYO

SECOND EDITION
REVISED AND ENLARGED

PRINTED IN GREAT BRITAIN

PREFACE

THIS volume entitled *Blake Studies* was first printed for the firm of Rupert Hart-Davis in 1949. As explained in the preface, I then intended it to be regarded as a series of appendices to the biographies of Blake by Alexander Gilchrist (1863) and Mona Wilson (1925). I disclaimed any place for it among the various interpretative volumes pioneered by Foster Damon (1924) and Northrop Frye (1947). The interest of the seventeen chapters then printed was chiefly biographical and textual with a bibliographical thread running through them. This book has been long out of print, but seems to be still in demand. Reprinting would obviously need some revision in the light of newer knowledge of Blake's life and work, and a few of the chapters would have to be greatly enlarged, notably Chapter III, 'The Engraver's Apprentice'. Here the episode of Blake's presence at the opening of the tomb of Edward I in Westminster Abbey in 1774 could be developed, following the lead of Paul Miner, who first detected the presence of a drawing of the King in his coffin attributable to Blake in the library of the Society of Antiquaries. The number of chapters has been increased to twenty-nine by the addition of various papers written in the years 1940 to 1970. Meanwhile my title, *Blake Studies*, has been borrowed for a periodical published bi-annually in 1969 and 1970 by the Departments of English, first of the University of Tulsa, Oklahoma, and later of Illinois State University. It is hoped that no confusion will arise from this titular duplication. My initial protest, made when the publication was first announced, was disregarded.

As before, the illustrations, increased from 48 to 55, have been chosen to illustrate the text rather than from among Blake's major works. Some were used in the first edition, others are new. I am indebted to Arnold Fawcus, Director of the Trianon Press in Paris, for the care with which he has made collotype prints from the often rather difficult subjects. I am grateful for permission to use them granted by the various private owners and institutions recorded in the list of illustrations.

I am again obliged to the Times Publishing Company for allowing me to reprint many of the papers which first appeared in *The Times Literary Supplement*; also to the *Bulletin of the New York Public Library* for permission to use Chapter XVII and to *The Book Collector* for Chapter XXIX. I am under obligations to several friends for assistance, notably Iain Bain, Raymond Lister, and G. E. Bentley, jr., and to Miss Joan Linnell Ivimy for the loan of documents preserved among the Linnell family papers.

GEOFFREY KEYNES

Brinkley, July 1970

CONTENTS

LIST OF ILLUSTRATIONS

I

WILLIAM AND ROBERT*

WILLIAM BLAKE, son of James Blake, hosier, and Catherine, his wife, was the third son in a family of five. His oldest brother, James, succeeded to the hosiery business after their father's death in 1784. James was a man of a frugal and un-adventurous mind and, as far as the evidence goes, seems to have played little part in William's life, although a long letter written to him during William's stay at Felpham in 1803 suggests that their relations may have been closer than the absence of other documentary evidence has been taken to indicate. The second son, John, was born in May 1755, but died in infancy. A second John, born in March 1760, was referred to by Blake in a verse letter written to Thomas Butts in November 1802, as—

> . . . my brother John, the evil one,
> In a black cloud making his mone,

and is stated by Frederick Tatham to have been a dissolute youth, who 'lived a few reckless days, enlisted as a soldier, and died'.[1] William's sister, Catherine, born in January 1764, was the only girl in the family. She lived in his house for a time, but this led to troubles between her and Mrs. Blake, so that the relations of brother and sister were not altogether happy. The fifth son of the family appears from the register at the church of St. James, Westminster,[2] to have been born on 19 June 1762 and christened Richard on 11 July. This child has always been identified with William Blake's favourite brother, Robert, or Bob, as he was known to his playfellow, J. T. Smith.[3] The change of name is unexplained and in addition there is uncertainty about Robert's age. It is probable that Richard Blake, correctly recorded in the register, did not live, and that Robert was born over five years later, though the register of his birth and christening has not been found. Tatham, in his account of William Blake, said that Robert died at the age of 24, implying that he was born in 1763. Adding to the uncertainty, Professor G. E. Bentley, jr., has discovered that a boy named Robert Blake, age 14, was

---

* First printed in *The Times Literary Supplement* (1943), xlii. 72, 84.
[1] *Blake Records*, p. 509.
[2] Ibid., p. 5.
[3] Smith's *Nollekens and His Times*, London, 1828, ii. 457.

entered at the Royal Academy as an engraver on 4 August 1782.[1] This boy must, therefore, have been born in 1768, and if he was William Blake's brother, younger by about ten years, he would have been aged 19 when he died in February 1787, an acceptable age in view of the immaturity of his output as an artist. In any case Robert was the only member of the family to play an important part in William's life. Tatham's account of him verges on the over-sentimental:

Robert, the youngest son [he wrote], was the affectionate companion of William; they sympathized in their pursuits and sentiments; like plants, planted side by side by a stream, they grew together and entwined the luxuriant Tendrils of their Expanding minds. They associated and excelled together, and, like all true lovers, delighted in and enhanced each other's beauties. . . . Robert was of amiable and docile temper, and of a tender and affectionate mind, and like many of those who appear born for early death, his short life was but as the narrow porch to his Eternal Lot; he died of consumption at 24 Years of age.[2]

Further details of Robert's brief existence are supplied by Blake's other biographers. After the death of James Blake, senior, in 1784, Robert lived with William and his wife at 27 Broad Street, Golden Square, next door to the hosiery business, and became his brother's pupil in drawing and engraving. For two and a half years they remained in happy intimacy which was not seriously disturbed by an incident such as that related by Gilchrist:[3]

One day a dispute arose between Robert and Mrs. Blake. She, in the heat of discussion, used words to him his brother (though a husband too) thought unwarrantable. A silent witness thus far, he could now bear it no longer, but with characteristic impetuosity—when stirred—rose and said to her: 'Kneel down and beg Robert's pardon directly, or you never see my face again!' A heavy threat, uttered in tones which from Blake, unmistakably showed it was *meant*. She, poor thing! 'thought it very hard', as she would afterwards tell, to beg her brother-in-law's pardon when she was not in fault! But being a duteous, devoted wife, though by nature nowise tame or dull of spirit, she *did* kneel and meekly murmur: 'Robert, I beg your pardon, I am in the wrong.' 'Young woman, you lie!' abruptly retorted he: '*I* am in the wrong!'

Early in 1787 Robert became seriously ill and soon afterwards died, being buried in Bunhill Fields on 11 February. He was nursed by his brother so assiduously that William is said to have gone without sleep for a fortnight, his

[1] Personal communication from Professor Bentley and *Blake Records*, p. 20.
[2] *Blake Records*, p. 509.
[3] Gilchrist's *Life of Blake* (ed. Todd, London, 1942), pp. 50–1. The source of the anecdote is not recorded.

exhaustion being such that after Robert's death he slept continuously for three days and nights. At the moment of Robert's death he 'beheld the released spirit ascend heavenward . . . clapping its hands for joy'.[1] Many years later, in 1800, Blake wrote to his friend, William Hayley: 'Thirteen years ago I lost a brother, and with his spirit I converse daily and hourly in the Spirit, and see him in my remembrance, in the regions of my imagination. I hear his advice, and even now write from his dictate.'[2] It is also related by John Thomas Smith, who had known Robert as a boy, in illustration of Blake's power of disuniting all other thoughts from his mind whenever he wished to indulge in thinking of any particular subject (or person, he might have added), that

after deeply perplexing himself as to the mode of accomplishing the publication of his illustrated songs, without their being subject to the expense of letter-press, his brother Robert stood before him in one of his visionary imaginations, and so decidedly directed him in the way in which he ought to proceed, that he immediately followed his advice, by writing his poetry, and drawing his marginal subjects of embellishments in outline upon the copperplate with an impervious liquid, and then eating the plain parts or lights away with *aqua fortis* considerably below them, so that the outlines were left as a stereotype.[3]

I have pointed out on another page that the first idea of such a process is likely to have been brought to Blake's notice as early as 1784, when his friend George Cumberland published an account of it. Nevertheless it is no doubt true that Blake's visionary mind was often filled with memories of his beloved brother and with such characteristic intensity that Robert's very presence seemed to be before him and to speak into his ears. In Blake's long poem, *Milton*, written and etched on copper in the years 1803 to 1808, are two plates representing symbolical naked figures, one being the mirror image of the other, which are marked respectively 'William' and 'Robert'. In either picture Milton, or Inspiration, in the form of a falling star, is entering the left foot of William and the right foot of Robert, thus illustrating many years after Robert's death William's lasting sense of their community of spirit. The left and right symbolism of the feet denotes the living William and the spiritual Robert.

Evidence enough has already been given to make clear the depth of the feeling which Blake entertained for his young brother. Intrinsically Robert Blake can have no great interest for posterity. Even if he had qualities that might have brought him to some degree of eminence, his early death prevented their flowering. Yet

[1] Gilchrist, op. cit., p. 51.   [2] *Complete Writings*, ed. Keynes, London, 1966, p. 797.
[3] Smith's *Nollekens and His Times*, London, 1828, ii. 461.

the reflected importance given him by his place in the life of William Blake make it worth while to put on record every particular of him that can be gathered. It is even possible that we possess a representation of his appearance traced by his brother's hand. In the Print Room of the British Museum is a careful pencil drawing by Blake of a nude youth posed as a model (Plate 1). The subject is a well-built boy of about sixteen or seventeen years standing sideways to the spectator with his hand resting on a mantelpiece or shelf. His rounded face is turned towards the observer and his aspect agrees well with the amiable character ascribed to Robert Blake by Tatham and J. T. Smith. This drawing was reproduced in my *Pencil Drawings of William Blake* (Nonesuch Press, 1927), and I then suggested that the subject may have been Robert. I have seen no reason since then to alter my opinion that the truth of this conjecture is quite likely. No other drawing by Blake from a living model is known, so that if he made any it seems that he did not keep them. A drawing of his brother would, however, be of enough importance to Blake to warrant its being preserved with the other drawings in his portfolio.[1] Other subjects associated with Robert were, as we shall see, carefully kept and have survived to the present day, so that our picture of him can be further elaborated.

A relic of great interest came to my notice some years ago, and was described for the first time in 1949. It is a folio sketch-book possessed by Robert when he was a young boy, and its pages are filled with the evidences of William's assiduous efforts to teach him the elements of drawing. On the front cover is inscribed in large letters 'Robert Blake's Book 1777'[2] and on the inside, mixed up with a sketch of a woman's head, 'Robt Blake'. Again, on the back cover is written 'Blake' in large Gothic characters at the top, 'Robertus' in the centre, and 'R. Blake' at the bottom, so that little doubt can remain as to the ownership of the book. William Blake's method of teaching his brother was to make a drawing of some part of the human body or of a whole figure to one side of a page, in order that Robert might make a copy alongside. Thus on the first page are no less than forty-one drawings of the lips and eight of the nose, the lips progressing from a few elementary lines to a full Cupid's bow. On the second page are more noses and lips together with an eye, on the third, hands and arms, on the fourth, a leg

---

[1] Professor Sir Anthony Blunt (*The Art of William Blake*, New York, 1959, p. 4 n.) makes the alternative suggestion that the drawing may have been made from a living model when Blake was a student at the Royal Academy in 1779. Obviously this is possible, but does not explain why he kept it in his portfolio for the rest of his life, the only one of its kind.

[2] If 1762 was the true date of his birth he was fifteen, but it now seems probable that he was in fact only eleven.

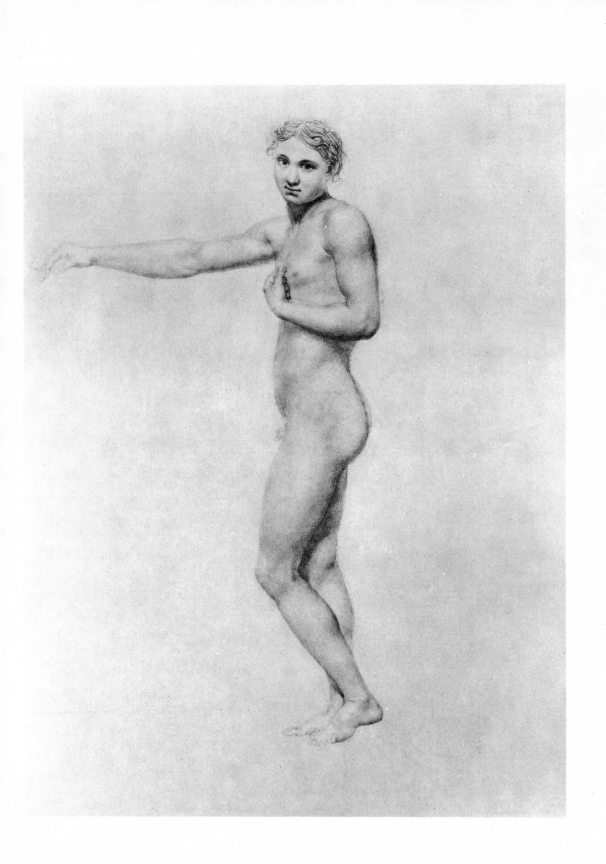

of Michelangelesque proportions, on the fifth, faces and grotesques in profile, on the sixth and seventh, full faces, on the eighth, more lips and eyes, on the ninth, dogs' heads and human ears, on the tenth, a woman's head, the hips and legs of a kneeling figure, and a very vigorously drawn heraldic eagle—though this is in the centre and was not copied by the pupil. By the eleventh page Robert had arrived at copying the outline of the whole human figure, with vertical and horizontal lines drawn to indicate the proper proportions of the parts. At the bottom of the page are excellent sketches of a seated woman, a male torso, and a small Hercules. On page 12 is a simple drawing of a woman in the dress of the period, and a head in a voluminous bonnet. It is not necessary to describe the contents of the whole volume in detail, thirty-eight pages in all being occupied by these drawings, several of which occupy a full page and were not copied by Robert. At the beginning Robert's copies are feeble puerilities; later he begins to catch something of the spirit of his brother's style: the older draughtsman was himself barely twenty years old, and was still in his artistic infancy, though many of his drawings, bearing a suggestion of his later mastery, form a valuable record of his beginnings as an artist.

The sketch-book contains in all fifty-six pages. A few are blank, and some towards the end have coloured drawings of birds and animals evidently copied by Robert from some book on natural history. Several of these are dated 1778, so that the whole book may be regarded as the workshop of the boy who posed as William Blake's model for the drawing now in the British Museum—if the conjectural identification be accepted. The book's history is partly recorded in a note written by a nineteenth-century owner inside the front cover. It is there stated that it was 'purchased some years since among the collection of Thomas Stothard, R.A., at one period a personal friend of the brothers'. It is possible that the sketch-book passed into Stothard's possession soon after Robert's death, being given to him as a memento of the young man that he had known and loved, for Stothard had been one of William's first professional acquaintances and they may have worked together as draughtsman and engraver respectively as early as 1779. He may therefore have associated with Robert for at least eight years. It was not until 1809 that Blake parted company with Stothard through their quarrel over their rival designs of 'The Canterbury Pilgrims', the story of which is well known. Stothard died in 1834, and his collections were sold at Christie's in June of the same year. The sketch-book was afterwards in the possession of Sir Alexander Spearman, being sold with his books at Puttick and Simpson's rooms on 9 January 1878. Its further history is not known until it appeared with the property of

George S. Hellman at the Anderson Galleries, New York (lot 51) on 25 November 1919. It was then acquired for the H. E. Huntington Library, California, and was included in the Blake exhibition held at the Grolier Club of New York during December 1919 and January 1920. Since that time the existence of the book seems to have been overlooked, and it was not described by the late C. H. Collins Baker when making his *Catalogue of Blake's Drawings and Paintings in the Huntington Library*, issued in 1938. Photostats of the whole book were supplied at my request by the Librarian of the Huntington Library, by whose courtesy I was enabled to make the present description.

Robert Blake's beginnings as an artist in 1777 did not give any great promise of future eminence. His association with his brother has, however, led to his being remembered as an original draughtsman of considerable power. Some of his drawings were kept by William and passed after his death in 1827 into the possession of Frederick Tatham. Several of these were seen by Gilchrist, who described them as 'naif and archaic-looking; rude and faltering, often puerile or absurd in drawing; but are characterised by Blake-like feeling and intention, having in short a strong family likeness to his brother's work. The subjects are from Homer and the Poets.'[1] Gilchrist describes particularly Robert's best-known drawing, now in the British Museum Print Room, of a group of people awestruck by an approaching cataclysm. This design was immortalized by William Blake, who used it for what is possibly his earliest experiment in relief-etching on copper, thereby improving Robert's design into a real work of art. Another sepia wash and pen drawing formerly in the collection of W. Graham Robertson[2] shews a huddled group of people cowering before an ancient man who threatens them with upraised arm. In my collection is a third drawing, undoubtedly from Robert's hand, though it had been supposed by its former owner, the late H. Buxton Forman, to be by William himself. It represents a Druid grove with two groups of male and female figures in long robes standing between two rows of trees, the branches forming a green roof over their heads (Plate 2). The figures are painted with bright water-colour washes and the composition, though it has some distinction, is not well drawn if judged by conventional standards. Robert Blake's archaic manner is, in fact, individual and original, and it is the more remarkable that his most distinguished composition, 'The King and Queen of the Fairies' (Plate 3), was for many years unrecognized, and was indeed passed by many authorities, including Gilchrist, as the work of his brother.

[1] Gilchrist, op. cit., p. 50.
[2] Sold with Robertson's Blake collection at Christie's, 22 July 1949, lot 81. Now in my collection.

Pl. 2

By far the most valuable manuscript of William Blake that has come down to us intact is the *Notebook* formerly known as *The Rossetti MS*. This book is fully described in the next chapter. It is enough to say now that it was clearly treasured by William primarily because it had belonged to Robert, who made sketches and drawings on some of the leaves at the beginning. Several of these are very slight drawings in pencil, but two are compositions in water-colour. The first of these, on page 9, represents a knight in armour rushing from beneath a Gothic cloister. On the right a woman in a long dress is flying away from him through a forest of slender tree trunks. This has been thought to be an illustration of a 'Gothic' novel, but its subject has not been identified. The second drawing is of two crowned fairies reclining in a rose-like flower. Over them hang two other bell-shaped flowers with a circle of little figures dancing beneath one of them. It has been called 'The King and Queen of the Fairies', and, on the assumption that it was by William, was adapted by Frederick Shields for the gilt cover design of the second edition of Gilchrist's *Life of Blake* published in 1880. It was also used in an altered form by William himself in plate 5 of *The Song of Los*, 1795, one of his illuminated books. In this the King and Queen are lying on two lilies under a dark starry sky. In all these drawings in the *Notebook* the stiff and angular lines of the figures are unmistakably those of Robert Blake, their style being quite different from that of William. 'The King and Queen of the Fairies' is a composition of imagination and great beauty, and suggests that Robert Blake at the time of his death was shewing, under William's influence, signs of developing into an artist of considerable power, even though he was still deficient in the niceties of accurate drawing, which were not fostered by a drawing master who himself did not believe in 'copying nature'. This design by itself is convincing evidence of the aesthetic feeling which bound Robert and William in a strange community of spirit both during their lives and after Robert's early death (Plate 3).

II

BLAKE'S NOTEBOOK

Students of the life and works of William Blake have long been aware of the existence of a manuscript volume containing a varied collection of his writings, interspersed with drawings and sketches. The book has been called at different times *The MS. Book, The Rossetti MS.*, or *Ideas of Good and Evil*, but its nature is best indicated by the title assigned to it here, *Blake's Notebook*. All serious students of Blake have realized the extraordinary richness of its contents, but few have been privileged to handle it themselves, and so to obtain at first-hand the full flavour of its associations. It is at once evident that Blake himself placed a high value on his *Notebook*, for it cannot have been economy alone that induced him to keep this apparently insignificant volume beside him for forty years, turning to it again and again to confide to its pages the most intimate outpourings of his genius, until it was filled from end to end. The book was turned this way and that in order that every corner might be used, and ultimately extra leaves had to be inserted to accommodate the later portions of the last poem which Blake tried to cram into it. During the last seven years of his life he added nothing more because the book was full, but it was preserved among his papers, and by a fortunate chance fell, twenty years after his death, into the hands of Dante Gabriel Rossetti. From that day, 30 April 1847, *Blake's Notebook* has been treated with the reverence it deserves, and in 1935 was reproduced in facsimile by the Nonesuch Press so that its beauty and its interest might be diffused over a wider circle.

The book consists of 58 leaves, measuring 19·6 × 15·7 cm. It has been paginated consecutively 1–116, and is made up of one gathering of 10 leaves, and four gatherings of 16 and 8 leaves alternately. The paper has no water-mark. A sheet, forming 2 leaves, of different and smaller paper is added at the end. The manner in which Blake used the book may be reconstructed from an examination of its contents, though the initial fact of interest to be noted is that it almost certainly belonged first, not to William Blake, but to his younger brother, Robert. On pages 5, 7, 9, 11, and 13 are sketches and drawings which have always, until recently, been assigned with the rest of the contents of the book to William Blake. But their lines are such that this belief cannot any longer be held. The figures delineated on these pages have an individual character quite different from

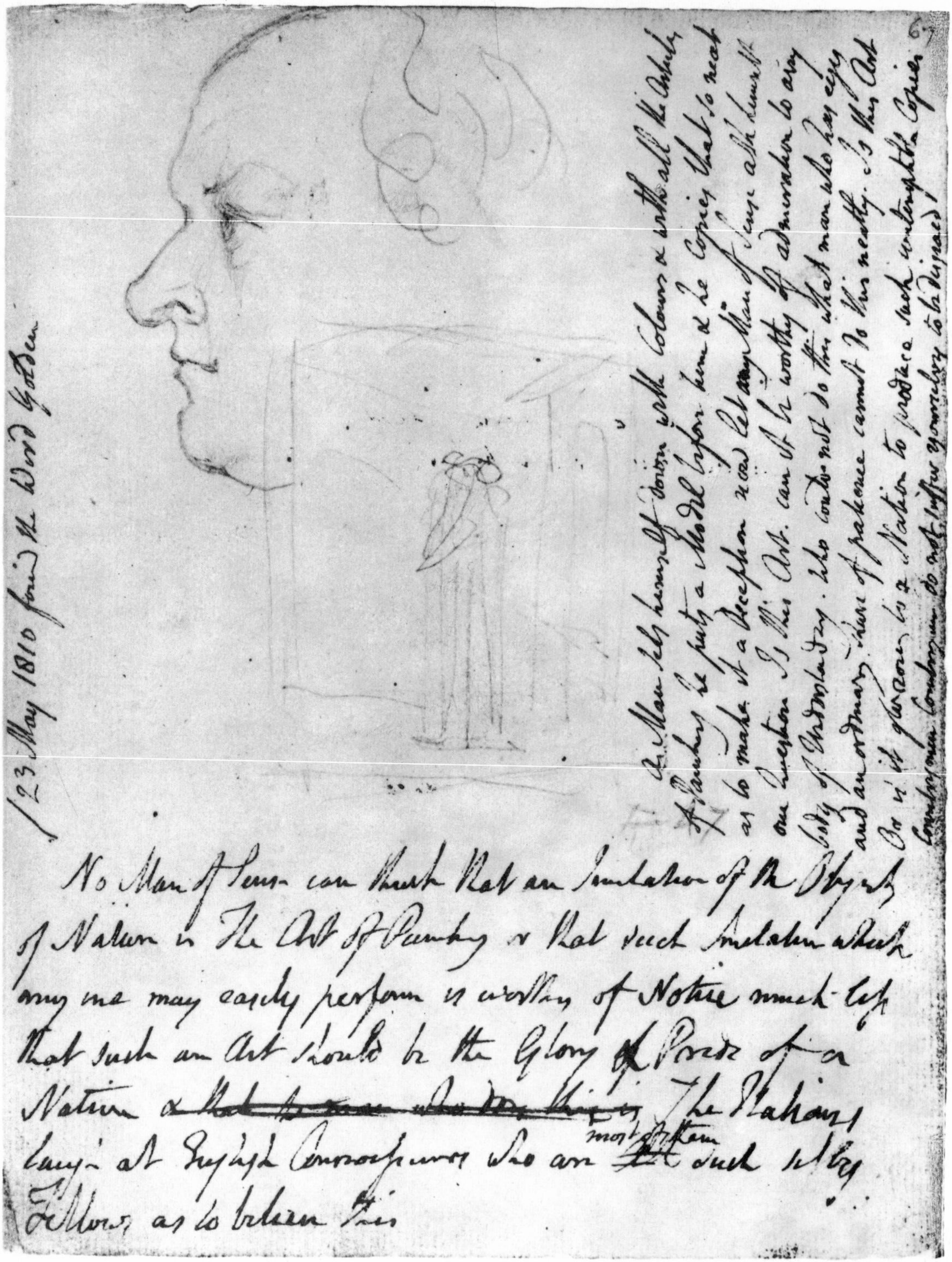

23 May 1810 from the Word Gotten

A Man sets himself down with Colours & with all the Apparatus
of Painting he puts a Model before him & he Copies that so neat
as to make a Deception now Let any Man of Sense ask himself
one Question Is this Art can it be worthy of admiration to any
body of Understanding. Who could not do this what man who has eyes
and an ordinary share of patience cannot to this nicely. Is this Art
Or is it glorious to a Nation to produce such contemptible Copies
[Countrymen Countrymen do not suffer yourselves to be disgraced]

No Man of Sense can think that an Imitation of the Objects
of Nature in The Art Of Painting or that such Imitation which
any one may easily perform is worthy of Notice much less
that such an Art should be the Glory & Pride of a
Nation & that [crossed out] The Italians
laugh at English Connoisseurs who are most of them such silly
Fellows as to believe this

PL. 4

that of figures drawn by William Blake, as comparison with any of the other drawings in the book will shew. They have, on the other hand, much in common with the amateurish drawing now in the British Museum which is authenticated as the work of Robert Blake and with others by him given a few years ago to the Tate Gallery.[1] This association with Robert Blake had not been noticed until I drew attention to it in the introduction to the Nonesuch facsimile of the *Notebook*.

Robert Blake's relation to his brother and the character of his drawings have already been described. The feeling that existed between them was evidently very deep, and this provides the clue to the motive that made William use and treasure the *Notebook* from the day of Robert's death until his own.

When Blake first began to use the book he filled the pages chiefly with rough sketches for a variety of subjects. These include ideas for several of the decorations in *Songs of Experience*, *The Marriage of Heaven and Hell*, *Europe*, and *America*, and for most of those in *Visions of the Daughters of Albion*. There is also a long series of drawings for 'emblems', which, according to the numbers attached to them, Blake arranged and rearranged several times, though he ultimately used only seventeen of them in the small book of engravings known as *The Gates of Paradise*, issued in 1793.[2] The drawings also include two profiles of Blake himself (pp. 66 and 67, plate 4), a head of his wife (p. 82) and an intimate domestic scene on page 4, which is supposed to represent Blake and his wife together. It is also on this page that the title 'Ideas of Good and Evil' has been scrawled; although it remains uncertain to what this should refer, it certainly was not meant as a title for the whole book. Perhaps it was intended to summarize the series of emblem drawings for which the book was first used.

Having used the volume as a sketch-book consecutively from his brother's beginnings until about the year 1793, Blake then turned it round, and began to write poems in it from the other end. This group of poems, including first drafts of several of the *Songs of Experience*, occupies pages 115–98 of the reversed book. It was then laid aside for a time until, during the period of his residence at Felpham, 1800–3, he again used it for a short series of poems and fragments which are written from the beginning of the book on pages 2–14. He picked it up again in 1807 to enter some desultory memoranda, including quotations from Aphra Behn and Dryden which had taken his fancy in reading Bysshe's *Art of Poetry*. Two years later he again began to fill the unused spaces, this time with the

---

[1] Two more in my collection have been described on p. 6.

[2] These are reproduced with the facsimile of *The Gates of Paradise* published by the Trianon Press for the William Blake Trust in 1968.

scurrilous doggerel on his friends and enemies and with the long prose pieces known as 'Public Address', in vindication of his engraving of 'The Canterbury Pilgrims', and 'A Vision of the Last Judgment', describing his large painting of that subject. These are written haphazardly wherever room could be found, and consist of fragments which are not consecutive but were jotted down in the heat of the moment as he thought of them. These are all to be assigned to the years 1808–11, when he was feeling annoyed and humiliated by his failure to obtain recognition through the exhibition of his pictures and his 'Canterbury Pilgrims'. By this time hardly a corner of the book remained unfilled, and it was laid aside for some years until, in 1818, Blake again took it up for the composition of his great philosophical poem, *The Everlasting Gospel*. This is in unconnected fragments scattered about in different parts of the book, and ultimately some of it was written on several separate leaves of paper. One of these was the last page of a folded leaf from a printed book carrying the catchword *And*,[1] on the first three pages of which Blake had written the draft of a prospectus of the 'Canterbury Pilgrims' engraving, presumably composed in 1809. These two leaves are now bound in at the end of the volume, but the remainder of *The Everlasting Gospel* has long been separated from it.

After Blake's death in 1827 the *Notebook* remained in the possession of his wife, by whom it is said to have been given to a brother of his young friend and disciple, Samuel Palmer. The next event in its history is recorded by Dante Gabriel Rossetti on the flyleaf at the beginning: 'I purchased this original M.S. of Palmer, an attendant in the Antique Gallery at the British Museum, on the 30th April, 1847. Palmer knew Blake personally, and it was from the artist's wife that he had the present M.S. which he sold me for 10^s. Among the sketches there are one or two profiles of Blake himself. D.G.C.R.' It has often been supposed that Rossetti was referring to Samuel Palmer, but this is clearly impossible, since he was never attached in any capacity to the staff of the British Museum. His brother William, however, was appointed to the Antique Gallery in 1848,[2] and the reference is clearly to him, though there is no further record of his having been a friend either of Blake or of his wife. The half-sovereign was actually supplied by Rossetti's brother, William, whose pocket was less depleted than his own.

[1] This is from page 16, 23, 42, or 46 of the quarto edition of Hayley's *Ballads*, 1802; Blake used waste sheets from this book for some years.

[2] See Mona Wilson's *Life of Blake* (Nonesuch Press, 1927), p. 35. Presumably Rossetti had met Palmer before he came to be employed at the British Museum.

Rossetti contemplated publishing part of the manuscript, and on 1 November 1860 wrote to William Allingham:

A man (one Gilchrist, who lives next door to Carlyle, and is as near him in other respects as he can manage) wrote to me the other day, saying he was writing a life of Blake, and wanted to see my manuscript by that genius. Was there not some talk of *your* doing something in the way of publishing its contents? I know William [Rossetti] thought of doing so, but fancy it might wait long for his efforts; and I have no time, but really think its contents ought to be edited, especially if a new *Life* gives a 'shove to the concern' (as Spurgeon expressed himself in thanking a liberal subscriber to his Tabernacle). I have not yet engaged myself any way to said Gilchrist on the subject, though I have told him he can see it here if he will give me a day's notice.[1]

Rossetti ultimately lent the volume to Gilchrist in 1861, and after Gilchrist's death in that year himself edited a selection from the manuscript which was printed in the second volume of Gilchrist's *Life of Blake*, 1863. He had already made a transcript (part of the paper is dated 1844, but the transcript must have been made some years later than this) of most of the poems, which he had bound up with the manuscript, heading it: 'Verse and Prose by William Blake (Natus 1757: obiit 1827). All that is of any value in the foregoing pages has been copied out. D.G.C.R.' He there introduced a number of alterations, correcting what he considered were imperfections in the metre, and supplying emendations, often quite unnecessary, though he did not in the printed selection adopt all the changes made in the first transcript. He wrote to Gilchrist: 'I am glad you approve of my rather unceremonious shaking up of Blake's rhymes. I really believe that is what ought to be done. . . .'

He changed his mind later, however, and in 1874 wrote to his brother that he would not then have made so many changes.[2] The harm, however, was already done; later editors followed Rossetti's text, and so corrupt versions were perpetuated. Further extracts were made by Swinburne for his *Critical Essay*, 1868, especially from *The Everlasting Gospel*, and W. M. Rossetti added to his brother's selections in his Aldine edition of Blake's poems, first published in 1874, though this text is scarcely better than its predecessor of 1863.

After Rossetti's death in 1882 *Blake's Notebook*, or *The Rossetti MS.* as it was henceforth to be known, was sold with his library at an auction held at his house, 16 Cheyne Walk, Chelsea. It was lot 483, offered on the third day, 7 July 1882,

---

[1] *Letters of D. G. Rossetti to William Allingham* (London, 1897), p. 237.
[2] Ibid., pp. 264–5.

and it made £110. Presumably it was then acquired by the book-collector, F. S. Ellis, with whose collection it was again sold at Sotheby's on 18 November 1885, on this occasion being bought by Ellis and Scrutton for £85. In the following year it was traded across the Atlantic, and came into the hands of the New York dealers Dodd, Mead and Co. From them it was bought by the late William Augustus White of Brooklyn, who added his signature on the flyleaf with date '26 January, '87'. From this date onwards successive Blake scholars were deeply indebted to W. A. White for his readiness to collaborate in elucidating the manuscript. About 1890 he sent the book to Quaritch in London in order that E. J. Ellis and W. B. Yeats might use it for their three-volume edition of the *Works*, published in 1893. A transcript was made for Ellis, but this again contained many inaccuracies. Ten years later White supplied Dr. John Sampson of Liverpool with material for a very much more accurate text of all the lyrical poems in the manuscript, which were incorporated in the Oxford editions of 1905 and later years. Finally, in 1924 he had the entire manuscript photographed for me, and I was thus enabled to prepare a new and carefully revised text for the Nonesuch edition of Blake's *Writings*, published in 1925. This text gave most of the alterations and deletions made by Blake and included almost every word capable of being deciphered.

After the late owner's death, the book passed to his daughter, Mrs. Frances White Emerson of Cambridge, Mass., who brought it again to England and allowed me to keep it for the greater part of a year. I was thus enabled to familiarize myself still further with the text and to satisfy myself that as perfect a text as I could make had been obtained. Some years later Mrs. Emerson put students of Blake still further in her debt by allowing the Nonesuch Press to reproduce the whole manuscript in collotype facsimile. This was published in 1935, and was accompanied by a reprint of the text I had prepared in 1925. Unfortunately, this was set up in France by a compositor who did not understand English, and the publisher's urgency deprived me of the opportunity of correcting the proofs myself. The proof-reader, although represented by the publisher as competent and working from an already printed text, nevertheless failed to eliminate some gross typographical errors for which I received the blame—not unnaturally, since my name appeared on the title-page as 'editor'. About the same time the late Max Plowman convicted me of making an omission when he borrowed my photographs of the manuscript and with great difficulty succeeded in deciphering some very dim pencil marks on page 116. The result of his labours is quoted on page 74 of the present volume. The actual discovery was not, as the reader will learn, one that adds anything to the glory of Blake's name, and the passage may even have been purposely obscured by him, but it does at least testify to the zeal of Blake students and editors in their unflagging quest for every vestige of his recorded mind.

Mrs. Emerson's final act of generosity was in December 1956, shortly before her death, when she entrusted me with the manuscript, instructing me to keep it as long as I wished and then to hand it over to the British Museum. This enabled me to incorporate further improvements in the text published by the Nonesuch Press in 1957.[1]

Rossetti had the manuscript bound in half-calf with his transcript at the end. This binding had become weak, and Mrs. Emerson had the volume rebound in levant morocco with interleaving to protect the pages from further damage by rubbing against one another. Much of the writing had already become very difficult to read, but *Blake's Notebook* is now preserved for posterity, both in its original form and in the Nonesuch facsimile, which gives a faithful representation of Blake's urgent genius.

[1] More recently Professor David Erdman has made further elucidation of obscured or deleted passages with the help of photographs taken under infra-red rays.

III

THE ENGRAVER'S APPRENTICE

THE story of Blake's apprenticeship to James Basire, engraver, of Great Queen Street, Lincoln's Inn Fields, has been told by Gilchrist, though it was incomplete in one important particular, namely the date at which the apprenticeship began. According to Gilchrist, Blake was aged 14 when he left the drawing-school of Henry Pars to become engraver's apprentice, that is to say, Gilchrist inferred, in 1771. In 1947 Mr. Ellic Howe, while engaged on researches in the records of the Stationers' Company, stumbled on the actual entry of Blake's bond in the Apprentice Register at Stationers' Hall and kindly communicated his discovery to me. The entry (reproduced here (page 15) by permission of the Worshipful Master of the Company) runs as follows, under the date 4 August 1772:

W^m. Blake Son of James of Broad Street Carnaby Market Hosier to James Basire of Great Queen Street Lincoln's Inn fields 7 y^{rs}. £52—10 paid by his Father.

Blake was born on 28 November 1757 and was therefore nearer fifteen than fourteen when he commenced engraver, so that his preliminary training as a draughtsman with Henry Pars lasted somewhat longer than has been supposed. His apprenticeship would have continued until the end of July 1779.

When the apprentices had done their task of engraving, the results were submitted to their master for his approval. Consequently most of their drawings and all their engravings were signed by him—*Basire del.* or *Basire delin. & sculp.*—with the result that the work of the juvenile artists and craftsmen cannot, as a rule, be identified with certainty. Gilchrist suggested that Blake's work done for Basire should be sought in the volumes of *Archæologia*, Basire's name being found on many of the plates executed for the Society of Antiquaries during Blake's apprenticeship, or in books such as *Memoirs of Hollis*, 1780, and Richard Gough's *Sepulchral Monuments of Great Britain*, Part I, 1786. The two Hollis volumes in fact contain nothing that can be attributed with any confidence to Blake. On the other hand there are strong reasons for believing that many of the plates illustrating Gough's *Sepulchral Monuments* were done by him. The main source of information is in Benjamin Heath Malkin's *A Father's Memoirs of his Child*, 1806,

... of Greenwich Gent. to ... ... who ... give ... ...
... ... 7 yr £100. Rec'd by his Father —

Josiah Curbing Son of Tho of Barnigate in the
City Kent Gent to Tho Smith of Sweetings Alley
Sa. 1 yr. 7 yr £100. Rec'd by his Father —

Wm Blake Son of James of Broad Street Carnaby
Market ... to James Basire of Lincoln Inn
Fields 7 yr £52..10 Rec'd by his Father

Jno Harris Son of Rich of Clerkenwell Close
Cooper to James Emonson ... St Johns Square
Clerkenwell Printer 7 yr. No Money.

Tho Hutchford Son of Tho of the Parish of
Stepton ... in the Co. of York Weaver to Jno
Gurr of Shoreditch Goldbeater 7 yr. ... £5
in charity by the Church Wardens of Stepton dale

Blake's entry in the Apprentice Register, Stationers' Hall

the facts having been derived from Blake himself. It is there related that Blake quarrelled with two other youths who came after him to Basire's workshop, and that their employer restored harmony by sending Blake out to make drawings of buildings and church monuments in London and the neighbourhood. Malkin emphasized that Blake's lasting enthusiasm for Gothic art was first aroused in this way, specifying work done by him in Westminster Abbey:

This occupation led him to an acquaintance with those neglected works of art, called Gothic monuments. There he found a treasure which he knew how to value. He saw the simple and plain road to the style of art at which he aimed, unentangled in the intricate windings of modern practice. The monuments of Kings and Queens in Westminster Abbey, which surround the chapel of Edward the Confessor, particularly that of King Henry the Third, the beautiful monument and figure of Queen Elinor, Queen Philippa, King Edward the Third, King Richard the Second and his Queen, were among his first studies. All these he drew in every point he could catch, frequently standing on the monument, and viewing the figures from the top. The heads he considered as portraits; and all the ornaments appeared as miracles of art, to his Gothicised imagination. He then drew Aymer de Valence's monument, with his fine figure on the top. Those exquisite little figures which surround it, though dreadfully mutilated, are still models for the study of drapery. But I do not mean to enumerate all his drawings, since they would lead me over all the old monuments in Westminster Abbey, as well as over other churches in and about London.

Malkin's evidence was supported by Blake's early friend, Thomas Stothard, who, according to another friend, J. T. Smith, 'often used to mention this drawing (the portrait of Queen Philippa) as Blake's and with praise'. Frederick Tatham also dwelt on this part of Blake's work:

If all his Drawings were enumerated from Westminster Abbey, as well as many other Churches in and about London, the Multitude would no doubt astonish the Calculator, for his interest was highly excited and his industry equally inexhaustible. These things he drew beautifully; ever attentive to the delicacies and timorous lineaments of the Gothic Handling, he felt and pourtrayed their beauties so well that his Master considered him an acquisition of no mean capacity.[1]

It has therefore long been accepted that Blake, having made these drawings, was also responsible for the splendid engravings published in the *Sepulchral Monuments*. In my *Bibliography of Blake* (1921) I listed (p. 197) the portraits of Henry III, Queen Eleanor, Queen Philippa, Edward III, Richard II, and Queen Anne, as having certainly been engraved by Blake, conjecturing that the engravings of the

[1] *Blake Records*, p. 512.

whole monuments with effigies were also by him. To these I would now add with confidence the six plates of the tombs of Aymer de Valence, Earl of Lancaster, John of Eltham, and William of Windsor. All are typical of his work.

Malkin's mention of the monument of Aymer de Valence, described in a paper by the antiquary, Sir Joseph Ayloffe, in 1780,[1] has led to an examination of drawings preserved in the library of the Society of Antiquaries, with the conclusion that representations of monuments in the presbytery of Westminster Abbey and coloured drawings of figures from wall-paintings believed to portray King Sebert[2] and Henry III, together with heads and ornaments on King Sebert's monument, were probably done by Blake. The drawings of the kings, signed *Basire del. 1775* (Plate 8), were included in the Blake exhibition at the Tate Gallery in 1913 (nos. 113, i and ii in the catalogue). The descriptions were written by the late A. G. B. Russell, who did not believe that the finished drawings were by Blake, though he allowed that they might have been done from his preliminary sketches. Sir Anthony Blunt, however, has accepted them as probably by him and the engravings already cited as clearly his work.[3]

More recently Mr. Paul Miner, of Wichita, Kansas, U.S.A., took the matter a long way further by drawing attention to the fact that the copper-plates for *Sepulchral Monuments* were bequeathed by Gough to the Bodleian Library, Oxford, and by ascertaining that the Library also housed many of the original drawings. In an article published in 1963[4] he established that Blake's pencil drawings for the portraits already mentioned are there, together with nine others made from the monuments and wall-paintings in the presbytery at the Abbey, some duplicating those at the Society of Antiquaries. The wall paintings, from which Blake is believed to have made the brilliantly coloured drawings of the two kings, were revealed after the tapestries hanging in front of them were removed in 1777. Basire was then commissioned to provide the drawings.

I have recently examined the album of drawings in the Bodleian Library and have listed the following as being probably by Blake. All are drawn on the same thick, yellowish laid paper with the watermark J WHATMAN in one half of the

---

[1] *An Account of Some Ancient Monuments in Westminster Abbey, By Sir Joseph Ayloffe, Bart. Read at the Society of Antiquaries March 12 1778. London, MDCCLXXX.* This is part of *Vetusta Monumenta, Volumen Secundum, Londini, 1789.* The eight plates illustrating the monuments of Aveline, King Sebert, and Anne of Cleves are most probably all by Blake.

[2] Or Sigebert, *fl.* 637, King of the East Angles.

[3] *The Art of William Blake*, New York, 1959, p. 3 n.

[4] *Bulletin of the New York Public Library*, December 1963, pp. 639–42. Four of the drawings are reproduced with photographs of the actual effigies.

sheet and in the other half a coat of arms with a 'bend', surmounted by a fleur-de-lis and with GR below:[1]

1. Henry III, his effigy on the tomb, sepia water-colour and pen work, unsigned. $9\frac{1}{4} \times 3\frac{5}{8}$ in.
2. —— his head and shoulders, large scale, pencil, signed *Basire del.* $13\frac{5}{8} \times 11\frac{5}{8}$ in.
3. Queen Eleanor, her effigy on the tomb, sepia water-colour and pen work, unsigned. $12\frac{1}{8} \times 4\frac{1}{4}$ in.
4. —— her head and shoulders, large scale, pencil, signed *Basire del.* $13\frac{3}{8} \times 11\frac{1}{2}$ in.
5. —— her effigy on the tomb, sepia water-colour, signed *B.d.* $10\frac{1}{2} \times 5$ in.
6. Edward III, his effigy on the tomb, sepia water-colour, signed *Basire d.* $10\frac{1}{4} \times 4\frac{3}{4}$ in.
7. —— his effigy alone, sepia water-colour, signed *Basire d.* $10\frac{1}{4} \times 4\frac{3}{4}$ in.
8. —— his head and shoulders, large scale, pencil, unsigned. $13\frac{3}{8} \times 11\frac{1}{2}$ in.
9. Queen Philippa, her head and shoulders, large scale, pencil, signed *Basire del.* $13\frac{1}{4} \times 11\frac{5}{8}$ in.
10. Aveline, wife of Edmund Crouchback, Earl of Lancaster, her effigy, pen drawing with wash frame, signed *Basire del.* (Plate 5). $15 \times 10\frac{7}{8}$ in.
11. Edmund, Earl of Lancaster, pen drawing with wash frame, signed *Basire del.* $15\frac{1}{8} \times 10\frac{7}{8}$ in.
12. Aymer de Valence, Earl of Pembroke, his effigy, pen drawing, signed *Basire del.* $14\frac{3}{4} \times 10\frac{1}{4}$ in.
13. John of Eltham, his effigy, sepia drawing, signed *Basire del. 1777.*
14. Children of Edward III, their monument, sepia drawing, signed *Basire del. 1777.*
15. Richard II and Queen Anne, their effigies on the tomb, sepia water-colour, signed *B.D.* $13\frac{1}{2} \times 6\frac{7}{8}$ in.
16. Queen Anne, her head and shoulders, pencil, signed *Basire del.* (Plate 6). $13\frac{3}{4} \times 11\frac{3}{8}$ in.
17. Richard II, his head and shoulders, large scale, pencil, signed *Basire del.* (Plate 7). $13\frac{3}{4} \times 11\frac{1}{4}$ in.
18. Richard and Queen Anne, their effigies on the tomb, sepia water-colour, signed *B.D.* $11\frac{1}{4} \times 10$ in.
19. Kings Sebert and Henry III, brilliant water-colours, signed *Basire del.*, a duplicate of the drawing at the Society of Antiquaries (Plate 8).

1 Dated by Heawood, *Watermarks, c.* 1768.

Pl. 7

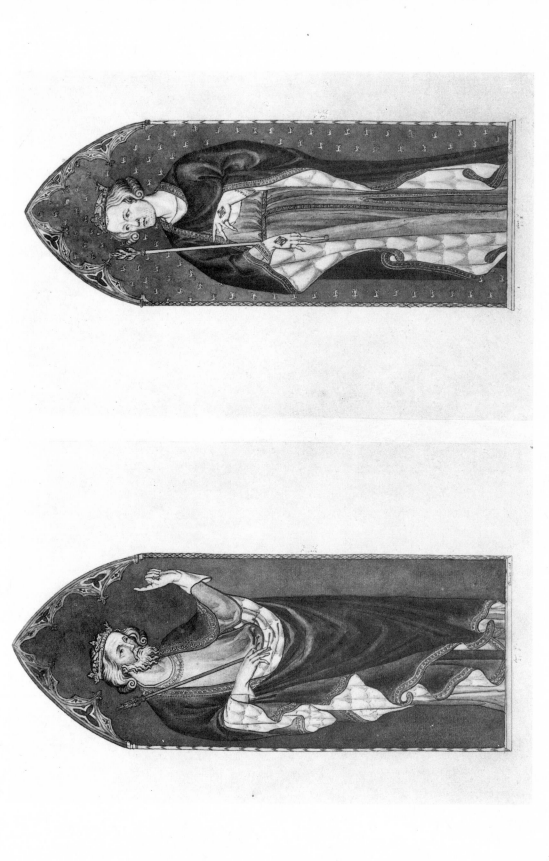

The body of Edward y^e 1st as it
appeard on first opening the Coffin.

The body as it appeard
when some of the vestmen
were removed.

I

II

EDWARD I.

In his account of Blake's time as apprentice Gilchrist slipped in an account of an incident that took place early in 1774:

During the progress of Blake's lonely labours in the abbey, on a bright day in May 1774, the society for which, through Basire, he was working, perpetrated by royal permission, on the very scene of those rapt studies, a highly interesting bit of antiquarian sacrilege: on a reasonable pretext, and with greater decency, than sometimes distinguish such questionable proceedings. A select company formally and in strict privacy opened the tomb of Edward the First, and found the embalmed body 'in perfect preservation and sumptuously attired', in 'robes of royalty, his crown on his head, and two sceptres in his hands'. The antiquaries saw face to face 'the dead conqueror of Scotland'; had even a fleeting glimpse— for it was straightway re-enclosed in its cere-cloths—of his very visage: a recognizable likeness of what it must have been in life. I cannot help hoping that Blake may (unseen) have assisted at the ceremony.

This reference suggested to Mr. Paul Miner that it would be worth finding out whether any drawings of Edward I in his coffin had survived at the Society of Antiquaries. He was much interested to discover that there was in the library an unsigned sheet with two pencil drawings of the King in his tomb, evidently made as a preliminary record of what was visible when the covering was removed (Plate 9). The measurements of the coffin are given (6 ft. 7 in. long, 2 ft. 7 in. wide at the top) and the drawings, numbered I and II, are inscribed above:

I. The body of Edward yᵉ 1ˢᵗ as it/appeard on first opening the Coffin
II. The body as it appeard/when some of the vestmen[ts] were remov'd.

In December 1959 Mr. Miner sent me a reproduction of the drawing with the question: 'Could the inscriptions on this sheet be in Blake's hand?' After careful consideration I gave the opinion that the writing was not his and the matter dropped, apart from a brief mention of the drawings in the article already mentioned. In 1968 I came to a reconsideration of this question, and it occurred to me to compare the writing on the drawings with a photostatic copy of Blake's earliest manuscript composition beginning: 'then She bore pale Desire.'[1] It then became obvious to me that the two hands on the drawings of 1774 and in the manuscript, accepted as written not later than 1778 and probably before 1777, are identical, and that my opinion, given in good faith, had unfortunately misled Mr. Miner. There can no longer be any doubt that the drawings of Edward's

[1] Now in the Berg Collection, New York Public Library.

body are by Blake, who must have been an interested participator in the historical event in Westminster Abbey.

Sir Joseph Ayloffe, who was in charge of the operation attended by the Dean, wrote a detailed account of the opening of the coffin, which he read to the Society of Antiquaries on 12 May 1774.[1] He first described the events leading up to the opening of the tomb, relating that the King died on 7 July 1307 during his successful campaign against the Scots. When dying he directed that his body should be embalmed and taken round by his troops as they moved through the countryside. After it had reached its final resting-place the tomb was opened at intervals by his successors to make sure that the embalmment was effective and his body still in sound condition. This examination was carried out by Edward II and Edward III, but was not done again until Sir Joseph was given permission to repeat it in 1774. His description is worth quoting, since it tells us exactly what Blake saw:

The tomb of King Edward the First, built in the form of an altar-table, stands at the West end of the North side of the Confessor's chapel, and at the head of his father King Henry the Third's monument, from which it is separated by the stair-case and entrance, leading from the ambulatory into the chapel. It is in length, from out to out, nine feet seven inches; in height, from the floor of the chapel to the upper edge of the cover-stone, three feet seven inches; and is composed of only five slabs of Purbeck marble, each of them three inches in thickness. Two of these slabs form the sides, two the ends, and one the cover.

This tomb, which is quite plain, except that the under edge of the cover-stone is chamfered, or sloped off diagonally towards its upper edge, is raised upon a basement of free-stone, which, extending every way near two feet beyond the tomb itself, forms an ascent to it of two steps above the pavement of the chapel. Each of these steps is six inches in height. On the South side, and at each end, it stands open to the chapel: but on the North side it is defended from the ambulatory by a grating of strong iron-work. The smaller upright bars of this grating terminate at the height of five feet, in a fleur de lis; and the two standards, or end bars, finish in a small busto of an elderly man with a long visage. A like busto is also placed in the front part of the frame of the baldoquin, or canopy, built over the tomb. The workmanship of each of these busto's is very rude. And yet they have so much resemblance of the face of King Edward the First, as exhibited on

---

[1] This was published in *Archæologia* (1775), iii. 376, and was printed as a separate large quarto pamphlet in 1775, entitled: *An Account of the Body of King Edward the First As it appeared On Opening his Tomb in the Year 1774. By Sir Joseph Ayloffe, Bart. V.P.S.A. and F.R.S. Read at the Society of Antiquaries May 12, 1774. Printed in the Year MDCCLXXV.* There are no illustrations.

his coins, broad seal, and statue at Caernarvon castle, that there is not much room to doubt of their having originally been intended to represent that monarch.

★ ★ ★

On opening the tomb, the cover-stone was found to be uncemented to the end and side slabs; and towards the upper edge of the latter were observed some small chasms, or holes, which seemed to have been made by the insertion of an iron crow, or some such instrument, and to have been afterwards filled up with fine plaister. The joint between the top and sides, although made extremely close, was also drawn with the same material. As soon as the two ends of the cover-stone were raised upon three courses of blockings prepared for that purpose, there appeared within the tomb a plain coffin of Purbeck marble, laid on a bed of rubble stone, which had been built up to such a height from the floor, as was necessary for bringing the upper side of the coffin-lid into contact with the under side of the covering stone of the tomb. This coffin, from out to out, is in length six feet seven inches, and in depth one foot and four inches. The breadth, at the shoulders, is two feet seven inches; in the middle, two feet three inches; and at the feet, one foot and ten inches. The thickness of each side of this coffin, as also that of its lid, which is cut out of a block of Purbeck marble, is three inches. The lid hath not ever been cemented to the sides of the coffin, but appeared to be so closely and neatly fitted to them, that scarce any dust could penetrate through the crevice. The outside of this coffin is stained with a yellowish paint, or varnish, and is much smoother than the outside of the tomb, partly owing to its having been less exposed to the air, and partly owing to the imposition of the varnish. On lifting up the lid, the royal corpse was found wrapped up within a large square mantle, of strong, coarse, and thick linen cloth, diaper'd, of a dull, pale, yellowish brown colour, and waxed on its under side.

The head and face were entirely covered with a *sudarium*, or face-cloth, of crimson sarcenet, the substance whereof was so much perished, as to have a cobweb-like feel, and the appearance of fine lint. This *sudarium* was formed into three folds, probably in imitation of the napkin wherewith our Saviour is said to have wiped his face when led to his crucifixion, and which, the Romish church positively assures us, consisted of the like number of folds, on each of which the resemblance of his countenance was then instantly impressed.

When the folds of the external wrapper were thrown back, and the *sudarium* removed, the corpse was discovered richly habited, adorned with ensigns of royalty, and almost intire, notwithstanding the length of time that it had been entombed.

Its innermost covering seemed to have been a very fine linen cerecloth, dressed close to every part of the body, and superinduced with such accuracy and exactness, that the fingers and thumbs of both the hands had each of them a separate and distinct envelope of that material. The face, which had a similar covering closely fitted thereto, retained its exact form, although part of the flesh appeared to be somewhat wasted.

It was of a dark-brown, or chocolate colour, approaching to black; and so were the hands and fingers. The chin and lips were intire, but without any beard; and a sinking or dip, between the chin and under lip, was very conspicuous. Both the lips were prominent; the nose short, as if shrunk; but the apertures of the nostrils were visible. There was an unusual fall, or cavity, on that part of the bridge of the nose which separates the orbits of the eyes; and some globular substance, possibly the fleshy part of the eye-balls, was moveable in their sockets under the envelope. Below the chin and under jaw was lodged a quantity of black dust, which had neither smell nor coherence; but whether the same had been flesh, or spices, could not be ascertained.

One of the joints of the middle finger of the right hand was loose; but those of the left hand were quite perfect.

Next above the before-mentioned cerecloth was a dalmatic, or tunic, of red silk damask; upon which lay a stole of thick white tissue, about three inches in breadth, crossed over the breast, and extending on each side downwards, nearly as low as the wrist, where both ends were brought to cross each other. On this stole were placed, at about the distance of six inches from each other, quatre-foils, of philligree-work, in metal gilt with gold, elegantly chased in figure, and ornamented with five pieces of beautiful transparent glass, or paste, some cut, and others rough, set in raised sockets. The largest of these pieces is in the centre of the quatrefoil; and each of the other four is fixed near to the angle: so that all of them together form the figure of a quincunx. These false stones differ in colour. Some are ruby; others a deep amethyst: some again are sapphire; others white; and some a sky-blue.

The intervals between the quatrefoils on the stole are powdered with an immense quantity of very small white beads, resembling pearls,[1] drilled, and tacked down very near each other, so as to compose an embroidery of most elegant form, and not much unlike that which is commonly called, The True-lover's Knot. These beads, or pearls, are all of the same size, and equal to that of the largest pin's head. They are of a shining, silver-white hue; but not so pellucid as necklace-beads and mock-pearls usually are.

Over these habits is the royal mantle, or pall, of rich crimson sattin, fastened on the left shoulder with a magnificent *fibula* of metal gilt with gold, and composed of two joints pinned together by a moveable *acus*, and resembling a cross

[1] Several of the gentlemen present at opening the coffin thought them to be real seed pearls; but all of them, being exactly of the same size, hue, and shape, militate against that opinion.

garnet hinge. This *fibula* is four inches in length, richly chased, and ornamented with four pieces of red, and four of blue transparent paste, similar to those on the quatrefoils, and twenty-two beads or mock-pearls. Each of these pastes and mock-pearls is set in a raised and chased socket. The head of the *acus* is formed by a long piece of uncut transparent blue paste, shaped like an acorn, and fixed in a chased socket.

The lower joint of this *fibula* appears to be connected with the stole, as well as with the chlamys; so that the upper part of each of the lappets or straps of the stole, being thereby brought nearly into contact with the edge of the royal mantle, those straps form, in appearance, a guard or border thereto.

The corpse, from the waist downward, is covered with a large piece of rich figured cloth of gold, which lies loose over the lower part of the tunic, thighs, legs, and feet, and is tucked down behind the soles of the latter. There did not remain any appearance of gloves: but on the back of each hand, and just below the knuckle of the middle finger, lies a quatrefoil, of the same metal as those on the stole, and like them ornamented with five pieces of transparent paste; with this difference, however, that the centre-piece in each quatrefoil is larger, and seemingly of a more beautiful blue, than those on any of the quatrefoils on the stole.

Between the two fore-fingers and the thumb of the right hand, the king holds a scepter with the cross made of copper gilt. This scepter is two feet six inches in length, and of most elegant workmanship. Its upper part extends unto, and rests on, the king's right shoulder.

Between the two fore-fingers and the thumb of his left hand, he holds the rod or scepter with the dove, which, passing over his left shoulder, reaches up as high as his ear. This rod is five feet and half an inch in length. The stalk is divided into two equal parts, by a knob or fillet, and at its bottom is a flat ferule.

The top of the stalk terminates in three bouquets, or tiers of oak-leaves, of green enamel, in *alto relievo*, each bouquet diminishing in breadth as they approach towards the summit of the scepter, whereon stands a ball, or mound, surmounted by the figure of a dove, with its wings closed, and made of white enamel.

On the head of the corpse, which lies within a recess hollowed out of the stone-coffin, and properly shaped for its reception, is an open crown or fillet of tin, or latton, charged on its upper edge with trefoils, and gilt with gold; but evidently of inferior workmanship, in all respects, to that of the scepters and quatrefoils.

The shape and form of the crown, scepters, and fibula, and the manner in which the latter is fixed to the mantle, or chlamys, exactly correspond with the representation of those on the broad-seal of this king, as exhibited by Sandford in his Genealogical History of the Kings and Queens in England.

On a careful inspection of the fingers of both hands, no ring could be discovered. However, as it cannot be supposed that the corpse was deposited without that usual attendant ensign of royalty, we may with great probability conjecture, that, on the shrinking of the fingers, which must have been the consequence of length of time, and the operation of the anti-ceptics applied to them; the royal ring had slipped off from the finger, and buried itself in some part of the robes, none of which were disturbed in order to search for it.

The feet, with their toes, soles, and heels, seemed to be perfectly entire; but whether they have sandals on them or not is uncertain, as the cloth tucked over them was not removed.

On measuring the body by a rod, graduated into inches divided into quarters, it appeared to be exactly six feet and two inches in length. So that, although we may with some degree of propriety adopt the idea of those Historians, who tell us, that the king was taller than the generality of men; yet we can no longer credit those, who assert, that he was taller by the head than any other man of his time. How far the appellation of *Long Shanks*, usually given to him, was properly applicable, cannot be ascertained, since the length of the *tibæ* could not be truly measured, and compared with that of the *femora*, without removing the vestments, and thereby incurring a risque of doing injury to the corpse.

*   *   *

I have already mentioned, that, previous to the removal of the top stone of king Edward's tomb, the dean of Westminster, who was present from the opening to the shutting it up, had taken every possible precaution that no damage might be done either to the royal body, or its sarcophagus. The like vigilance was observed by him during the time the coffin continued open: so that the corpse did not receive the least violation or injury; neither was it despoiled of any of its vestments, regalia, or ornaments. On the contrary, all things were suffered to remain in the same condition, situation, and place, wherein they were found. After the spectators had taken a sufficient view, the top of the coffin, and the covering-stone of the tomb, were restored to their proper places, and fastened down by a strong cement of terrice before the dean retired from the chapel.

Dr. Richard Gough was present at the opening of the tomb and provided an eye-witness confirmation of Ayloffe's description in a letter to another antiquary, Thomas Pennant, dated 11 May 1774.[1] He called the whole episode 'a high treat'

---

[1] Bodleian Library, MS. Gough Gen. Top. 43, f. 238. Gough described the opening of the tomb in another letter to Dr. Michael Tyson dated 7 May 1774, adding in a postscript: 'I proposed Basire to go, but Mr. Barrington did not think it necessary. So little did we expect to find what we did find. The rude sketches I scrawled of the sceptres will not convey an idea of them. We must not be too severe on the hasty manner in which the whole was conducted; considering who we had to deal with, and that we were neither Hugenots nor Roundheads' (J. Nichols, *Literary Anecdotes of the Eighteenth Century*, vol. viii, 1814, p. 612).

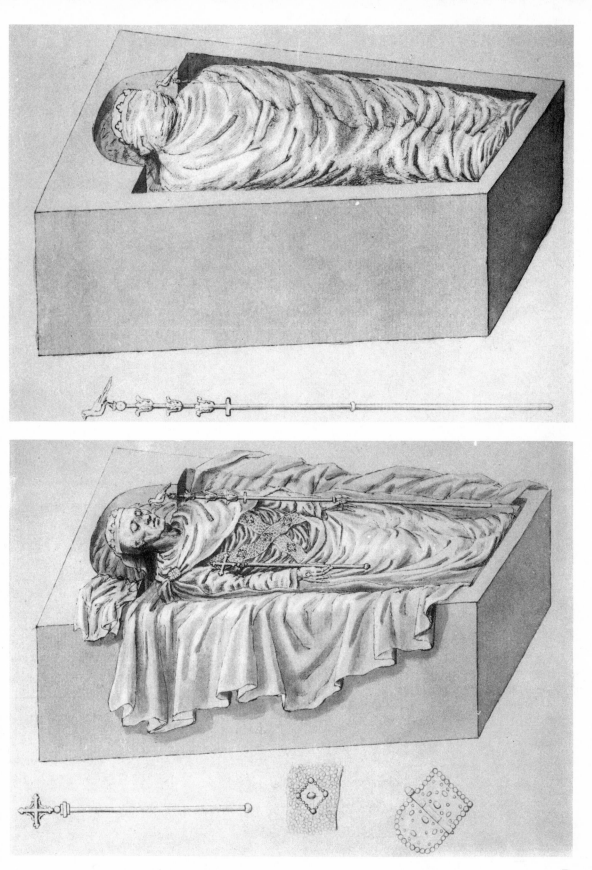

for the members of the Society of Antiquaries and mentioned that they were given the opportunity for 'about one hour's view and discussion' before the tomb was closed up for ever. He described the body as having 'the face cover'd by a mask of fine linnen reduced to a brown tint, but so close as to exhibit the whole face in perfect preservation (the skin dried to the bone) & to make me regret we had not a draughtsman as I proposed'. No doubt he expected to see some well-known professional artist and did not notice the nameless apprentice peering as best he could between the crowd of distinguished gentlemen surrounding the tomb.

When I visited the library at the Society of Antiquaries to see the preliminary drawings inscribed by Blake, I found that the album of drawings contained also two careful sepia water-colours of King Edward, first as he appeared, wrapped in his cerements, and secondly when he had been exposed by turning them aside (Plate 10). These drawings, not mentioned by Mr. Miner, shew in minute detail the vestments described by Sir Joseph Ayloffe. Below are separate drawings of the pearl-encrusted stole and quatrefoil, of the gilt fibula, and of the two wands held by the King in either hand.

The drawings are not signed or dated and were not engraved, but they have the same general characters as many of the other sepia water-colours attributed to Blake. Since the preliminary sketch is certainly by him, it seems logical to believe that the detailed drawings are also his work. Ayloffe's account states that the coffin was open only for a very short time, just long enough for 'the spectators to take sufficient view'. Clearly the most important spectator of them all was the engraver's apprentice, who looked closely and for long enough to imprint on his memory the exact appearance of the King and his vestments, so that he could ensure accuracy of detail in his finished work.

Malkin, Tatham, and Gilchrist were certainly right to insist on the importance of this early work in Westminster Abbey and elsewhere. It determined Blake's high valuation of Gothic art, gave him the deep historical sense so often evident in his writings, and provided ample memories for use in his paintings throughout his life, and, forty years after his visits to the Abbey, for the 'visions' of historical and imaginary persons drawn for John Varley's benefit. The apprentice was necessarily at a very impressionable age and his mind registered his visual experiences in sharp and wiry detail.

Prints in other books can sometimes be attributed to Blake's pencil as well as his graver, and an example of this was illustrated by Mr. Ruthven Todd in his book, *Tracks in the Snow*, 1946. A print was used as a tailpiece to vol. iii of Jacob

Bryant's *New System, or An Analysis, of Ancient Mythology*, London, 1774–6. It shows a dove bringing a sprig to the Ark, shaped like a crescent moon and floating on the waters under a semicircle of rainbow. Volumes i and ii of the *New System* also have engraved tailpieces, and those from volumes i and iii are reproduced here. The later one was, as already said, certainly designed by Blake. The earlier one was not so certainly, though probably, also from his hand. Even if drawn by another, the design of intertwined serpents would have appealed to the fancy of a boy who in later years was to use so constantly the symbol of the serpent in his own designs (Plate 11).

A characteristic of Blake's mind, the continuity of his ideas over a long period of years, is illustrated in a later chapter by the history of the Job theme. Mr. Ruthven Todd in his book illustrates it again when he draws attention to the fact that the crescentic Ark of his boyhood's design remained in the mind's eye of the artist until he incorporated it in his symbolic system and used it twice in *Jerusalem*, plates 24 and 44, some forty years later. A further search through the numerous plates in volume ii of the *New System* reveals several other possible sources of ideas which came to fruition during Blake's maturity. Several writers, including the late Laurence Binyon, have commented on the strangely impressive use made by Blake in *Jerusalem* of the man-headed bulls some years before the granite bulls of Ninevah, now in the British Museum, had been discovered by Layard's excavations. It seemed to Binyon to be almost second sight on Blake's part, who could never have rested his bodily eye on anything of the kind. But on plate 16 of the *New System* we find a series of illustrations of this very idea derived from Greek sources (Plate 11). It would not be difficult for the imagination of the mature artist to develop this figure, first absorbed by the boy's mind, into the terrific images of *Jerusalem*.[1]

Another symbol encountered several times in the Prophetic Books (*The Four Zoas, Milton*, and *Jerusalem*) is the Mundane Egg, signifying the Universe as perceived by the senses. On plate 4, volume ii of the *New System* this is illustrated in the most literal fashion, one of the eggs being entwined by a serpent—*Ophis et Ovum Mundanum* (Plate 11)—again an image likely to appeal to Blake.[2]

---

[1] On plate 33 of *Jerusalem* the man-headed animals drawing the plough are more like lions than bulls. It is on plate 46 that the creatures, harnessed by serpents to the Chariot of Time, assume a more bull-like form.

[2] Professor G. M. Harper (*The Neoplatonism of William Blake*, London, 1961, p. 296) thinks it unlikely that Blake was influenced by having seen this image as a youth, since the Mundane Egg did not have symbolic importance until he was writing *The Four Zoas* twenty years later. Nevertheless Blake's visual memory was so exceptionally good that images seen long before might still exert some influence in

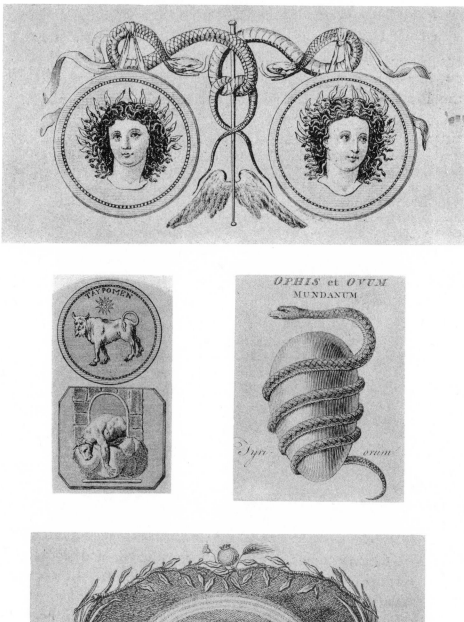

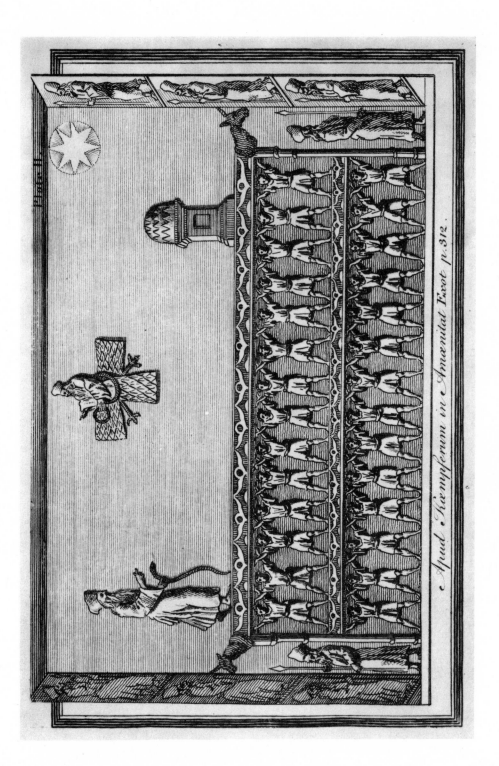

Apud Kæmpferum in Amœnitat Exot p. 312.

W. Blake del. & sculp.

Bryant states (*New System*, vol. i, p. 480) that according to orphic theology the Mundane Egg was produced by Hercules, who was sometimes symbolized by a serpent. Both these figures were taken by Bryant from Vaillant's *Coins of the Colonies* (vol. ii, pp. 331, 136).

Lastly, and most remarkable of all, on plate 2, volume ii is illustrated 'Zor-Aster Archimagus before an altar with a particular covering like a Cupselis or hive: taken from Kaempfer's Amoenitates Exoticae' (Plate 12). Beneath is a frieze of figures with arms upraised and crossed, a theme which was to appear in 1795 in one of the designs for Young's *Night Thoughts*, in 1809 in the third illustration to Milton's 'Hymn on the Nativity',[1] in the water-colour drawing of 'David delivered out of Many Waters' from the Butts Collection, and finally in the supreme design of 'When the Morning Stars sang together' designed about 1820 and engraved as plate 14 in *Illustrations of the Book of Job*.[2]

These plates from the *New System* are reproduced here not as works of art, nor even as having been necessarily engraved by Blake during his apprenticeship. They are given as evidence of images which Blake certainly *saw* during his boyhood, and afterwards reproduced and transformed for his own purposes by passing them through the furnace of his creative imagination.

A minor detail of the Ark tailpiece, the palm leaves with which the lower part of the design is framed, Blake used again a few years later in one of his earliest signed engravings, the frontispiece to Commins's *Elegy Set to Music*, 1786 (Plate 13). This, his first original book illustration, shows a young sailor springing eagerly from his boat to meet his wife and child, the sentiment and characterization of the figures being strongly reminiscent of Stothard's work. Stothard had not begun making book illustrations, many of which Blake engraved, until 1779, the year in which Blake's time with Basire ended, so that his influence can scarcely have been felt by the apprentice. But in 1784 Blake set up in business with his fellow apprentice, Parker, as print sellers and dealers, and they even published in that year a pair of prints after designs by Stothard, whose early friendship with Blake and his brother Robert has already been described.

---

conjunction with a later stimulus such as the Neoplatonic writings of Thomas Taylor. In her recent book, *Blake and Tradition*, Princeton (and London), 1968, Miss Kathleen Raine implies that Blake's study of Bryant's book was continued over a long period and was the source of many more symbols than are mentioned here.

[1] Reproduced in *Milton's Hymn*, edited by the present writer for the Cambridge University Press, 1923.

[2] On plate 75 of *Jerusalem* is a frieze of angels, perhaps also derived from this source; but the figures have wings alternately raised and lowered, so that they do not intersect like the arms in the other designs.

Another glimpse of Blake, the apprentice, may be gained from a glance at his first independent print; the first, that is, that can be identified. Students of his work have long been familiar with the print of 'Joseph of Arimathea among the Rocks of Albion'. This is signed as 'Engraved by W. Blake 1773 from an old Italian Drawing, Michael Angelo pinxit'. We now know that in 1773 Blake had been apprenticed only a few months to Basire, and, even had the time been somewhat longer, it seemed incredible that so mature a work as this fine and impressive print could have been produced by a boy of barely sixteen years. The puzzle has been resolved by my discovery in 1942 of a unique and previously unknown print of the first state of this plate. Blake must have kept a pull from the plate in his portfolio, and many years later he wrote at the bottom, 'Engraved when I was a beginner at Basire's from a drawing by Salviati after Michael Angelo' (Plate 14). The drawing by Salviati (i.e. Gioseffo Porta, 1535–85) has not been identified, but the source of the figure is Michelangelo's fresco of the Crucifixion of St. Peter in the Cappella Paolina at the Vatican.[1] The apprentice's rendering of it, with a background of sea and rocks supplied from his imagination, is undistinguished, though remarkable for a beginner. Although the style is somewhat tame, it is nevertheless not so monotonous and pedestrian as the plates done for his master's eye and to please his customers. It was twenty years later, or more, that Blake again took up his juvenile plate, rubbed the surface down and almost completely re-engraved it, adding strength to the figure and dramatic intensity to the background so that the print was transformed into the mature and characteristic work of art which had seemed so curiously precocious. The boy had chosen the subject because it was from a picture by his idol, Michelangelo, but in the intervening years the young man had been reading Jacob Bryant and the Druidical mythologists, and so he was able to fit the figure into the beginnings of his own mythology, and add the information that 'This is One of the Gothic Artists who Built the Cathedrals in what we call the Dark Ages Wandering about in sheep skins & goat skins of whom the World was not worthy; such were the Christians

[1] Perhaps Blake's memory was at fault, since it is possible that he had seen the large engraving of this figure after Michelangelo, which is attributed with some confidence to the French engraver, Béatrizet. Blake collected engravings as a boy and might even have possessed this print. Both Blake's versions and Béatrizet's are reproduced in my book on *Blake's Separate Plates*, Dublin, 1956. Blake's figure seems to have evident relationship to the conventionalized representation of a Druid priest current during the late seventeenth and mid eighteenth centuries, best seen in the frontispiece to William Stukeley's *Stonehenge*, 1740. Robert Blake's drawings of what appear to be Druid ceremonies mentioned in the first chapter date William's interest in Druid mythology back to at least 1784. The early version of what later became 'Joseph of Arimathea' suggests that this perhaps had its beginnings as early as 1773.

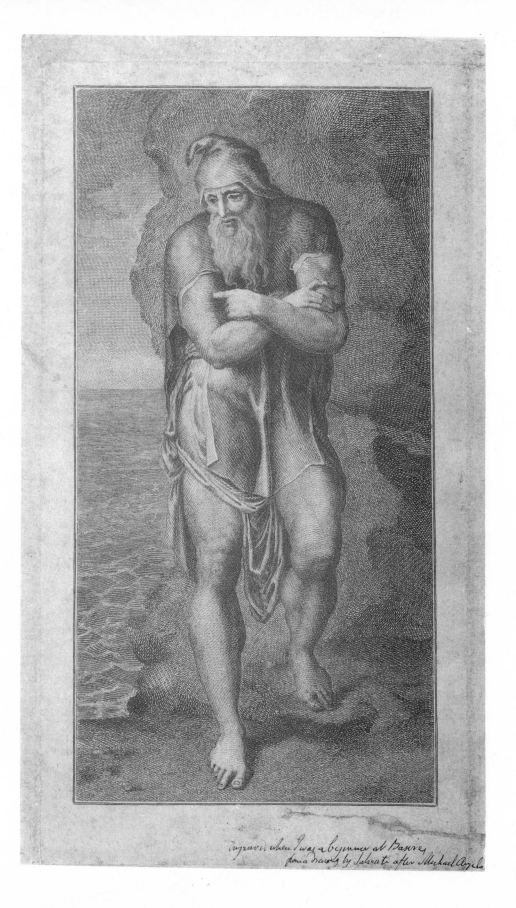

Engraved when I was a beginner at Basires
from a drawing by Salviati after Michael Angelo

PL. 14

in all Ages'. It is interesting to notice that Michelangelo's figure is represented with 'the classical foot', that is, with feet having second toes considerably longer than the great toes. This peculiarity was seized upon by the apprentice, who always afterwards drew feet shewing these proportions. The idiosyncrasy was certainly deliberate, for Blake usually drew human hands and feet with particular care, and he directed attention to them when he wrote much later in his life in the description of his picture of the Last Judgement: 'I intreat, then, that the Spectator will attend to the Hands & Feet, to the Lineaments of the Countenances; they are all descriptive of Character, & not a line is drawn without intention, & that most discriminate & particular.'[1]

Blake's reading during his years of training was certainly extensive among the poets from Spenser to Chatterton, as may be inferred from his own compositions printed as *Poetical Sketches* in 1783. His enthusiasms in art and artists he has also expressed clearly enough in his *Descriptive Catalogue* and other writings. There is, however, little or no evidence as to what he may have read in art criticism, except for one interesting relic which has been for many years in my own library. This is a copy of Fuseli's translation of the Abbé Winkelmann's *Reflections on the Painting and Sculpture of the Greeks*, London, 1765. On the flyleaf Blake has written his name, now his earliest surviving signature, and his professional address as engraver's apprentice. The abbreviated form 'Lincoln's Inn' for 'Great Queen Street, Lincoln's Inn Fields' might arouse suspicions that it was really one of his legal namesakes (see p. 33) who had been reading Fuseli's Winkelmann, were it not that the signature resembles the artist's later signatures much more closely than those of the other Blake of which I have seen many examples.

[1] *Complete Writings*, ed. Keynes, 1966, p. 611.

This book seeks to analyse the ideas of Art and Beauty current among the
Greeks, particularly in relation to their exaltation of the naked human form above
all other kinds of beauty. Among their followers the author admires Blake's idols,
Michelangelo and Raphael, beyond most other artists. There are innumerable
passages in this book which may have sown in Blake's mind seeds of some of the
ideas that afterwards grew to the size, sometimes, of obsessions. Blake's dogma,
'Art can never exist without Naked Beauty displayed',[1] finds its justification in
many of Winkelmann's pages; also his distaste for drawing from models, his
preference for general forms of beauty and ideal images, and his use of garments
which emphasize rather than obscure the human form.[2] It is true that in his last
years Blake came to condemn Greek art, because 'Grecian is Mathematic Form',
whereas 'Gothic is Living Form'. This was the result of lumping Greece and Rome
together as 'Warlike States', which 'never can produce Art'.[3] Yet in the *Descriptive
Catalogue* of 1809 he had written:

Painting and Sculpture as it exists in the remains of Antiquity and in the works
of more modern genius, is Inspiration, and cannot be surpassed; it is perfect and
eternal. Milton, Shakespeare, Michael Angelo, Rafael, the finest specimens of
Ancient Sculpture and Painting and Architecture, Gothic, Grecian, Hindoo and
Egyptian, are the extent of the human mind. The human mind cannot go beyond
the gift of God, the Holy Ghost.

So it is probable that the youthful Blake owed much to Greek inspiration under
the guidance of Winkelmann and Fuseli, and that this was not counteracted by
Jacob Bryant's 'low opinion of the Greeks',[4] whose ponderous text had perhaps
made less impression on the boy's mind than the copper-plates upon which he
was employed.

To conclude these observations on Blake's apprenticeship it may be remarked
that James Basire's good training, with his own application to the work, placed
him in the first rank among the journeyman engravers of his time. Examination
of his plates shews that he could vary his technique at will and equal the best
exponents of any of the different methods then in fashion. Blake, the rebel and
creator, could always give way to the successor of Blake, the faithful apprentice,
when economic necessity pressed its claims.

---

[1] The Laocoön plate, *Complete Writings*, 1966, p. 776.
[2] Coleridge also noticed this peculiarity in his letter to Tulk. See p. 82.
[3] On Virgil, *Complete Writings*, 1966, p. 778.
[4] See Todd's *Tracks in the Snow* (1946), pp. 31–3.

IV

POETICAL SKETCHES[1]

WILLIAM BLAKE's *Poetical Sketches* were first printed in 1783 in a slender octavo of thirty-eight leaves when their author was aged 26. The poems had mostly been written during his boyhood, beginning, according to the unsigned 'Advertisement', with his twelfth and extending to his twentieth year. Information about the printing of the book was given by John Thomas Smith in his account of Blake published at the end of his book, *Nollekens and His Times*, 1828. Smith had known the Blake family as a boy and, according to his own statement, had been a playfellow of Robert. This fact tends to confirm indirectly the suggestion made on page 2 that Robert's true age when he died was 19. Smith was born in 1766 and so would have been of very nearly the same age as Robert, if this suggestion is correct.

Smith's father had been assistant to the sculptor Joseph Nollekens, and the son was for three years a pupil in the same studio. Later he was a topographical draughtsman and author of antiquarian books, and in 1816 was appointed Keeper of Prints and Drawings in the British Museum, a post which he held until his death in 1833. Smith had passed his life in the society of artists and his account of Blake is an important source of information about his life. In the course of this he stated that he and Blake were both guests at the parties attended by many interesting people at the house of 'the Rev. Henry Mathew', 27 Rathbone Place. Smith's memory was, however, at fault as to their host's name. He was, in fact, the Revd. Anthony Stephen Mathews (1733–1824), minister of Percy Chapel, Charlotte Street, from 1766 to 1804.[2] Smith said that Blake came to know Mrs. Mathews through his friendship with Flaxman and Stothard, and that it was Flaxman and their hostess who together defrayed the cost of printing the *Poetical Sketches*. There is good reason for believing in Flaxman's disinterested generosity, for Blake's letters shew that he regarded him with the deepest gratitude and affection, Flaxman having undoubtedly been one of his earliest and closest friends. A rift occurred later, but this is not relevant to the present inquiry.

[1] First printed in *The Times Literary Supplement* (1945), xliv. 120, 132.

[2] This correction was made by the late H. M. Margoliouth in his article in *Notes & Queries*, 14 April 1951, p. 163.

POETICAL

SKETCHES.

_____

By W. B.

_____

LONDON:

Printed in the Year M DCC LXXXIII.

Blake's childhood and the contemporary influences which helped to shape the poems in *Poetical Sketches* have been critically examined by Miss Ruth Lowery in her book, *Windows of the Morning* (Yale University Press, 1940), and she was inclined to rate Blake's debt to Flaxman as very high indeed. Partly she based her conclusions on a document which had come to light in an American collection and runs as follows:

Mr. Blake with Compts. sends Mr. Flaxman a Draft. for £100 and begs to have a Receipt.

ESSEX STREET
9 Mch.

The watermark in the paper gives the maker as G. Jones but the date has been cut away. Miss Lowery states that 'G. Jones is Griffith Jones, of Hertfordshire, who, between 1804 and 1810, made paper at the Nash Mills, now owned by John Dickinson and Company, Limited. Preserved there are the original moulds upon which G. Jones made paper, and a minute comparison and measurement of the watermark identified 1806 as the date when the sheet of paper was made' (*Windows of the Morning*, p. 50). Miss Lowery therefore concluded that in 1806 Blake was owing Flaxman a considerable sum of money, part of which was probably advanced for the printing of *Poetical Sketches* twenty-three years before. There is, however, more than one good reason for rejecting this conclusion as untenable. In the first place, Miss Lowery chose to ignore the fact that the document is not in the handwriting of William Blake, though there is some superficial resemblance to his hand. Secondly, it is known, as Miss Lowery herself stated, that a firm of lawyers named Blake did business in Essex Street during most of the years between 1783 and 1828, though there is not the slightest reason for supposing that William Blake was related to, or was even acquainted with, his namesakes. The transaction between Flaxman and the lawyer Blake can, in fact, be identified by reference to a paper by Mr. Edward Croft Murray, F.S.A., on 'An Account Book of John Flaxman'.[1] From this it appears that Robert Blake of 14 Essex Street, Strand, acted as intermediary between Flaxman and a Committee of Wykehamists in the affair of erecting the monument to Dr. Joseph Warton in Winchester Cathedral. A payment for £100 is stated to have been made on 9 March 1804, so that evidently the dating of the watermark was only approximate.

---

[1] Published in the Walpole Society's vol. xxviii, 1939–40, p. 70. Attention was drawn to this by Dr. C. F. Bell in a letter to *The Times Literary Supplement*, 31 March 1945. The Account Book is in the British Museum, Add. MS. 39784. BB.

The only financial transaction between William Blake and Flaxman of which there is complete evidence relates to a payment made to Blake on 14 December 1799, on account of three copper-plate engravings of a Statue of Britannia. These were in illustration of Flaxman's *Letter to the Committee for Raising the Naval Pillar or Monument*, London, 1799, and Blake's receipt (now in the library of Haverford College, Haverford, Pa.) shews that he received 8 guineas for the engravings, with 12*s.* 8*d.* added for the copper. This document is entirely in Blake's hand, and is signed by him. It is improbable that Flaxman would have paid Blake this relatively small sum if he was already creditor since 1783 for a much larger amount.

The cost of composition cannot in any event have been large, and the number of copies printed was certainly small—fifty would seem to be a reasonable guess in view of the fact that only twenty-two copies are known to have survived to the present time. It may be assumed that the printing was done in London since all the people concerned lived there, and the eighteenth-century press-work scales in London are known, so that the approximate cost of printing fifty copies of the book can be calculated, given the necessary expert knowledge. This knowledge has been applied by Mr. Ellic Howe and the result is set out below in detail:

POETICAL SKETCHES

	£	s.	d.
9½ sheets of demy, 76 pp. of which 4 blank—			
Approximately 85,000 ens @ 4*d.* per 1,000	1	10	0
Author's corrections (if any), say 5 hrs.	0	1	8
Make up 76 pp. incl. 2 blanks and set title page ⎫ Lead out verses as required, say 6 pp. per hour ⎭	0	4	0
Impose 9 formes @ 8 pp. + 1 @ 4 pp.	0	4	0
Press work @ 6*d.* per token, 2 men at press, 9 sheets	0	9	0
Warehouse work = fold and stitch, etc.	0	4	0
	£2	12	8
Add. 100% for overheads (contemporary practice)	2	12	8
Paper = say 5 sheets of demy per copy: 50 copies = ½ ream	0	10	0
Profit on paper	0	2	0
	£5	17	4

Total cost, say, £6. 0*s.* 0*d.*, or nearly 2*s.* 5*d.* per copy.

The typography of *Poetical Sketches* suggests that it was entrusted to a small and not particularly competent shop. The late W. E. Moss noticed that the type and layout of the *Poetical Works* of Scott of Amwell, printed for J. Buckland, 1782, is almost identical with that of *Poetical Sketches*. Furthermore four of the engravings in this book were made by Blake after Stothard, and this might have brought Blake into contact with the printer shortly before his poems were to be set up in type. Again, however, as in *Poetical Sketches*, there is no printer's imprint, and Blake did not work again for the publisher Buckland so that this line of investigation leads us no further.

No part of the original manuscript of the pieces published in *Poetical Sketches* has survived, so that the printed pages are the sole authority for the text. This authority would be good if it could be asserted that Blake himself had certainly seen and corrected proofs of the book, but it seems unlikely that he did so, for he would not have passed a number of typographical errors which annoyed him so much afterwards that he was at some trouble to correct them in the copies given to his friends. The statement in the 'Advertisement' that since the time of their composition the author of the poems 'has been deprived of the leisure requisite to such a revisal of these sheets, as might have rendered them less unfit to meet the public eye', clearly refers to the poems themselves and not to the printed proof-sheets, since the 'Advertisement' was certainly written before the poems were printed, not afterwards. It is possible, as has been suggested, that Blake resented the opening of the second paragraph of the 'Advertisement'— 'Conscious of the irregularities and defects to be found in almost every page, his friends . . .'; nevertheless he usually allowed copies of the books to reach these friends without removing the offending leaf, and it may be that more has been made of this cause of offence than it really deserves.

Study of other manuscripts from Blake's hand shows that his punctuation was apt to be perfunctory or even misleading, and it is evident that the printer of *Poetical Sketches* was sometimes uncertain how to deal with it. This has provided several interesting problems for Blake's editors, notably in three places:

(1) In 'To Winter' page 4, lines 6–7, the text reads,

> . . . his storms are unchain'd, sheathed
> In ribbed steel, I dare not lift mine eyes;

Here the sense seems to demand an interchange of comma and semi-colon,

> . . . his storms are unchain'd, sheathed
> In ribbed steel; I dare not lift mine eyes,

(2) In 'Fair Elenor', page 8, the text reads,

> As the deer wounded Ellen flew over
> The pathless plain; as the arrows that fly
> By night; destruction flies, and strikes in darkness,
> She fled from fear, till at her house arriv'd.

This clearly demands a full-stop after the 'darkness', and in my Nonesuch edition I further emended the punctuation to read,

> . . .; as the arrows that fly
> By night, destruction flies, and strikes in darkness.

Blake commonly, however, used the semi-colon in an unconventional way, and the second emendation is perhaps unnecessary.

(3) In 'Blind-Man's Buff', page 28, lines 11–20, the text reads,

> Such are the fortunes of the game,
> And those who play should stop the same
> By wholesome laws; such as all those
> Who on the blinded man impose.
> Stand in his stead as long a-gone
> When men were first a nation grown;
> Lawless they liv'd—till wantonness
> And liberty began t'increase;
> And one man lay in another's way,
> Then laws were made to keep fair play.

Loose construction and careless punctuation have both contributed to ambiguity of meaning. In the Nonesuch text (1925) I tried to give the passage its greatest amount of meaning,

> . . . laws, such as—all those
> Who on the blinded man impose
> Stand in his stead; as, long a-gone
> When men were first a nation grown,
> Lawless they liv'd—till wantonness
> And liberty began t'increase,
> And one man lay in another's way;
> Then laws were made to keep fair play.

If this amount of interference is distasteful, readers may amend it as they please.

The remaining irregularities in punctuation are less important and need not be discussed. Unimportant also are various archaic or irregular spellings and minor misprints which do not leave the sense in doubt. Of much greater interest are a number of other errors which Blake himself took the trouble to correct in ink. There are twenty-two copies of *Poetical Sketches* known at the present time. Several bear inscriptions shewing that they belonged to Thomas Butts, George Cumberland, John Flaxman, Ann Flaxman, William Hayley, John Linnell, William Long, Samuel Palmer, and Charles Tulk. The last has an inscription, 'To Charles Tulk Esq.—from William Blake', the only one, so far as I know, with evidence that it was given by Blake himself. Nevertheless some of them do contain one or more corrections in ink which appear to have been made by the author's hand, and these are naturally of the greatest importance in establishing the text. But before these corrections are specified, attention may be directed to lines 15–18 of 'An Imitation of Spenser' (p. 24):

> Midas the praise hath gain'd of lengthen'd cares,
>   For which himself might deem him ne'er the worse
> To sit in council with his modern peers,
>   And judge of tinkling rhimes, and elegances terse.

One of Blake's most acute editors, Dr. John Sampson, assumed without discussion that *cares* was here a misprint for *ears*. Miss Lowery pointed out that in no copy of the book so far examined had Blake made this correction, and it would be dangerous to assume that Blake really wrote *ears* when he has corrected other apparently more trivial mistakes. In 1949 I was able to set all doubts at rest by the discovery that in the Graham Robertson copy (Q in the census), in which there are a number of other corrections undoubtedly in Blake's hand, the *c* of *cares* has been altered by a stroke of the pen to *e*. The correction is inconspicuous, and may have been overlooked in other copies.

In the same category is the reading on the last page of the book in the prose piece entitled 'Samson': 'Let us detain thee while I make ready a kid, that thou mayest sit and eat, and tell us of thy name and warfare.' Here W. M. Rossetti suggested *wayfare* for *warfare*, but so far this has not the support of Blake's correction.

Attention was first attracted to the author's corrections during a discussion in *The Times Literary Supplement* of the first stanza of the celebrated 'Mad Song', which is printed in *Poetical Sketches* (p. 15) as follows:

> The wild winds weep,
>   And the night is a-cold;
> Come hither, Sleep,
>   And my griefs unfold:

But lo! the morning peeps
Over the eastern steeps,
And the rustling beds of dawn
The earth do scorn.

In the issue of *The Times Literary Supplement* for 9 October 1919 the late Professor H. J. C. Grierson (as he then was) published a letter pleading for the common-sense alteration of *beds* in the penultimate line to *birds*, and deprecating purely aesthetic conclusions such as that of Professor Saintsbury (supported by Dr. John Sampson), who maintained in his *History of English Prosody*, 1910 (vol. iii, p. 11) that the 'entire imagery of the poem is *atmospheric*, and the phrase "*beds* of dawn" for the clouds whence sun and moon issue is infinitely fine'. To this letter I added another in the issue of 23 October pointing out that the alteration of *beds* to *birds* was not first made, as was usually supposed, by D. G. Rossetti in his selection of Blake's poems printed in the second volume of Gilchrist's *Life* (1863 and 1880), but had been made in 1847 by Robert Southey when reprinting the poem in *The Doctor* (vol. vi). Southey had been acquainted with Blake, and expressed great admiration for his poetic talents. Furthermore I was able to draw attention for the first time to the fact that Blake had himself made the correction in the copy of *Poetical Sketches* which had belonged to Thomas Butts. This book was then in the possession of the late T. J. Wise and is now in the Ashley Library in the British Museum. I afterwards found the same correction in two other copies, and Miss Lowery added a third—namely, the Graham Robertson copy, later in the possession of Mr. Kerrison Preston.[1] The reading 'birds of dawn' may therefore be accepted as fully established. Sir Herbert Grierson also drew attention[2] to the fact that Blake may have taken 'rustling' from Macpherson's *Ossian*, where it is a recurrent epithet applied to the sound of birds' wings.

Mr. Preston afterwards informed me that his copy contains another important correction in the same stanza of the 'Mad Song' which has not been noticed before, though I now find it had also been made by Blake in the Butts copy. This is the alteration of *unfold* in the fourth line to *infold* with obvious advantage to the meaning. The emendation had already been made by some of Blake's editors to *infold* or *enfold*, though without Blake's authority. The page of *Poetical Sketches* shewing these corrections by Blake is reproduced opposite by Mr. Preston's permission. The true reading of the first stanza of the 'Mad Song' is therefore now established as follows:

[1] Now in the Westminster Public Library with the rest of Mr. Preston's Blake library.
[2] In a letter to *The Times Literary Supplement*, 7 April 1945.

MAD SONG.

THE wild winds weep,
 And the night is a-cold;
Come hither, Sleep,
 And my griefs unfold:
But lo! the morning peeps
 Over the eastern steeps,
And the rustling birds of dawn
The earth do scorn.

Lo! to the vault
 Of paved heaven,
With sorrow fraught
 My notes are driven:
They strike the ear of night,
 Make weep the eyes of day;
They make mad the roaring winds,
 And with tempests play.

Like a fiend in a cloud
 With howling woe,
After night I do croud,
 And with night will go;
I turn my back to the east,
From whence comforts have increas'd;
For light doth seize my brain.
With frantic pain.

      SONG.

> The wild winds weep,
>   And the night is a-cold;
> Come hither, Sleep,
>   And my griefs infold:
> But lo! the morning peeps
>   Over the eastern steeps,
> And the rustling birds of dawn
>   The earth do scorn.

In the first (three-volume) Nonesuch edition of Blake's writings I was able to add a second correction made by the author in the third stanza, line 3, of 'To Winter' (p. 4), printed in 1783, as,

> He withers all in silence, and *in* his hand
> Unclothes the earth, and freezes up frail life.

Here he has deleted the second *in*, again with clear advantage to sense and metre.

In the fourth printing (1939) of the Nonesuch one-volume edition I added three more corrections made by him in John Linnell's copy of *Poetical Sketches*, these being:

(1) In 'An Imitation of Spenser', page 24, stanza 2, line 5, printed as,

> And love of Folly needs none others curse,

altered to 'none *other* curse'.

(2) In 'King Edward the Third', page 44, lines 18–19:

> . . .; while Reason, in her
> Frail bark, . . .

altered to 'in *his* Frail bark'.

(3) In the same, page 46, penultimate line, printed as,

> Shall flee away, and leave them all forlorn;

altered to 'leave *him* all forlorn'.

Miss Lowery adds four more corrections. Two are from the Tulk copy of *Poetical Sketches* now in the Huntington Library, California:

(1) In the 'Song', 'Love and harmony combine', page 12, stanza 4, line 4, printed as,

> There is love: I hear her tongue

altered to 'I hear *his* tongue'. This change Dr. Sampson had already made in 1905, though without Blake's authority.

(2) In 'Fair Elenor', page 7, stanza 2, lines 1–2, printed as,

> . . . and sunk upon the steps
> On the cold stone her pale cheeks . . .

altered to 'her pale *cheek*'. The second of these is found also in the Graham Robertson copy, which provides two more:

(3) In 'Fair Elenor', page 9, stanza 16, line 1, printed as,

> O Elenor, I am thy husband's head,

altered to read,

> O Elenor, *behold* thy husband's head.

This change was also made in Mrs. Flaxman's copy of the book, and in the Butts copy.

(4) In 'To the Evening Star', page 5, line 2, printed as,

> Now whilst the sun rests on the mountains, . . .

whilst is altered to *while*.

This completes the sum of the author's corrections so far detected in various copies of *Poetical Sketches*. The changes demonstrate in an interesting way the necessity for examining carefully every extant copy of a work such as this, printed without the author's supervision and distributed privately to his friends. Only in this way can the text be brought to a state corresponding as nearly as possible to the author's intention.

CENSUS OF COPIES

In my *Bibliography of Blake*, Grolier Club, 1921, I compiled a census of as many copies of *Poetical Sketches* as I could discover, these amounting to fourteen. Miss Lowery added four more in the *Transactions of the Bibliographical Society*, vol. xvii, 1936, p. 354. This list, together with the added copies that increase the number to twenty-two, is now revised and brought up to date.

(A) British Museum (C. 59, v. 30). Bound in calf, edges trimmed. Possibly one of Samuel Palmer's copies; see copy G below. Acquired for the British Museum in June 1890, from Quaritch for £42. Then unbound.

(B) Butts copy. In original blue-grey wrappers, untrimmed, as issued. Sold at Sotheby's, 2 May 1906 (lot 801, £60). Acquired by the late T. J. Wise, and now in the Ashley Library at the British Museum (Ashley 2366). Contains four corrections in Blake's hand.

(C) Tulk copy. Inscribed 'Charles Tulk Esq.—from William Blake'. Bound in citron morocco, gilt, by the Club Bindery. Sold in 1906 (B. F. Stevens, £109). Resold with the Hoe Library pt. 1, at the Anderson Galleries, New York, 26 April 1911 (lot 389, $275). Now in the H. E. Huntington Library, San Marino, California. Contains corrections in Blake's hand.

(D) George Cumberland copy, with his signature on the title-page. Bound in half-calf, with a print of 'The man sweeping the interpreter's parlour' inserted as frontispiece, and with Cumberland's book-plate, engraved by Blake, inside the cover. The frontispiece is inscribed, 'The Parable of the relapsed sinner & her 7 Devils', but not in Blake's hand. Given by Cumberland to John Linnell, and sold at Sotheby's with Linnell's books 3 June 1918 (lot 3, Pickering, £60). Acquired by the late Beverly Chew. Sold at the Chew sale at the Anderson Galleries, New York, 8 December 1924 (lot 28, Rosenbach, $900). Later in the library of John J. Emery. Exhibited at the Philadelphia Museum of Art, 1939, No. 1.

(E) William Long copy, inscribed on the title-page 'To Mr. Long from J. Flaxman'. Now bound in green morocco by Macdonald. It was offered to me by T. Thorp of Guildford for £60 in December 1919, and was then bound in half-calf with several dramatic works. Afterwards acquired by Col. Hughes, Philadelphia, and sold with his books by the American Art Association, 24 April 1924 (lot 58, $525). Acquired by George C. Smith, jr., and sold with his library at the Parke-Bernet Galleries, New York, 2 November 1938 (lot 9, Gabriel Wells, $350). Acquired by E. W. Keese and sold at Sotheby's, 14 March 1961 (lot 503, Hollings, £1,300). Now in U.S.A. Contains corrections in Blake's hand. (William Long, 1747–1818, was a surgeon, and a friend both of Flaxman and Hayley; see copy S.)

(F) Mrs. Ann Flaxman copy, with three additional songs inscribed, but not in Blake's hand, on the flyleaves. These are, 'Song 1st by a Shepherd', 'Song 2nd by a Young Shepherd', 'Song 3d by an Old Shepherd'. The second of these is a variant version of 'Laughing Song' from *Songs of Innocence*. The first and third were first printed by R. H. Shepherd in B. M. Pickering's edition of *Songs of Innocence and of Experience*, 1868. This copy of *Poetical Sketches* is bound in contemporary red morocco, yellow edges, and has at the top of the title-page the inscription 'present (*del.*) from Mrs. Flaxman May 15 1784'; the recipient is not indicated. Other inscriptions on the flyleaves are, 'Reed's Sale 1807', and 'ex Bibliotheca Heberiana, fourth portion, sold by Evans, 9 Dec., 1834'. There is a book-plate inscribed 'J.H.A. 1834', perhaps that of J. H. Anderdon. Later history unknown until it was sold at Sotheby's from an anonymous source, 22 March 1910 (lot 448, Edwards, £52). It was lent to me by Francis Edwards, and I published a full description in *Notes and Queries*, 24 September 1910. Now in the Alexander Turnbull Library, Wellington, New Zealand. There are numerous corrections in the text and in the margins in both pen and pencil. Most of these are the same as were made by Blake in other copies, but some seem to be suggestions made by friends, perhaps the Flaxmans.

(G) Samuel Palmer copy, containing a pencil note by John Linnell stating that it was one of three copies found by him at Palmer's house. It was then unbound. Now bound in half-morocco, trimmed. Sold at Hodgson's in 1906 (Maggs, £16. 5s.). Afterwards acquired by Prof. G. H. Palmer, and now in the Library of Wellesley College. (The other two copies found in sheets in March 1890 are H and N below.)

(H) John Pearson copy, bound in green morocco, gilt, by F. Bedford, untrimmed. Sold at Sotheby's, 7 November 1916 (lot 40, Dobell, £51). Acquired by Herschel V. Jones, and sold with his library at the Anderson Galleries, New York, 2 December 1918 (lot 121, G. D. Smith, $445). In 1936 in the Carl H. Pforzheimer Library, New York.

(I) T. G. Arthur copy, bound in red morocco, gilt, by Lortic frères, untrimmed. Title-page and Advertisement leaf repaired. Sold at Sotheby's 15 July 1914 (lot 46, G. D. Smith, £56). Sold by G. D. Smith on 8 November 1918, to A. E. Newton for $400. Sold with the Newton Library at the Parke-Bernet Galleries, New York, 16 April 1941 (lot 124, Papantonio, $225). Present owner not traced. Exhibited at the Philadelphia Museum of Art, 1939, No. 2.

(K) R. A. Potts copy, bound in calf, gilt, by F. Bedford. Pp. 49–70 in facsimile. Sold at Sotheby's, 20 February 1913 (lot 71, £8. 5s.). Sold again at Sotheby's, 22 July 1918 (Protheroe, £10); at Sotheby's, 17 December 1919 (G. D. Smith, £8); at the Anderson Galleries, New York, 28 April 1921 ($10). In 1936 said to be in the possession of Francis J. Underhill. Offered for sale in London by Raphael King, cat. 34, January 1940, for £65. Now in the U.S.A.

(L) A copy sold at Sotheby's, 'The Property of a Lady', on 2 May 1911 (lot 321, Quaritch, £49). Stated to be bound in contemporary red straight-grained morocco, gilt, gilt edges. Acquired by H. T. Butler, and sold with his library at Hodgson's, 14 June 1934 (lot 439, Robinson, £92). Acquired by Lord Rothschild, and now with his library in Trinity College, Cambridge. The late owner was suspicious of the binding, because the end-papers do not appear to be original. An inscription on the title-page has become illegible owing to washing.

(M) H. Buxton Forman copy, bound in blue morocco, gilt, by Roger de Coverly, with a sonnet by Buxton Forman in his hand on the flyleaf and corrections in the text copied by him from copy B. Sold at the Anderson Galleries, New York, 15 March 1920 (pt. 1, lot 35, $410). Present owner not traced.

(N) Thomas Gaisford copy, bound in green morocco, gilt, by F. Bedford, untrimmed. Sold with the Gaisford Library at Sotheby's, 23 April 1890 (lot 184, Quaritch, £48). Acquired by B. B. Macgeorge. Sold with the Macgeorge Library at Sotheby's, 9 July 1924 (lot 109, Quaritch, £118). Offered by Quaritch, November 1924, for £135. Acquired by Willis Vickery, and sold with his library at the Anderson Galleries, New York, 3 March 1933 (Beyer, $975). Acquired by Professor Chauncey B. Tinker; now in Yale University Library.

(O) W. E. Moss copy, bound in red morocco, gilt, by Fazakerley. Sold with the Moss collection at Sotheby's, 2 March 1937 (lot 141, Sawyer, £80). Now in U.S.A. Owner not traced.

(P) Stirling copy, bound in green morocco, gilt, by Rivière, untrimmed. Pp. 57–70 in facsimile. Acquired by General Archibald Stirling of Keir from Quaritch, about 1900, and now in the Stirling Collection, Glasgow University.

(Q) Graham Robertson copy, bound in green morocco, gilt, by Zaehnsdorf, gilt edges. Title-page mended, and Advertisement leaf in facsimile. First recorded as sold with the library of Maurice Johnson at Sotheby's, 21 March 1898 (C. Brown, £6. 17s. 6d.). Sold again at Hodgson's, 20 November 1901 (Quaritch, £12. 10s.). Bought from Quaritch by W. Graham Robertson, and given by him to Mr. Kerrison Preston. Now in the Preston Blake Collection, Westminster Public Library. Contains corrections in Blake's hand.

(R) W. A. White copy, unbound, untrimmed, and unopened. Now in the Rosenbach Foundation, Philadelphia. Exhibited at the Philadelphia Museum of Art, 1939, No. 3.

(S) William Hayley copy, bound, edges trimmed. A faded and cropped inscription on the title-page has been read as, 'To William Haley from J. Flax[man]'. It was presumably this copy that was mentioned by Flaxman in a letter to Hayley, 26 April (1783), 'I have left a pamphlet of poems with Mr. Long, which he will transmit to Eartham; they are the writings of a Mr. Blake you have heard me mention: his education will plead sufficient excuse to your liberal mind for the defects of his work' (*Letters of W. B.*, ed. A. G. B. Russell, 1906, p. 51). The book was in the Kemble-Devonshire Collection of Drama, formed about 1825, and is now in the H. E. Huntington Library, California. The information about the inscription was given to Miss Lowery by the Assistant Curator of Rare Books in 1934.

(T) John Linnell copy, bound in half-calf together with copy K of *A Descriptive Catalogue*. Inscribed, 'John Linnell 38 Porchester Terrace Bayswater 1846', and 'To James T[homas] L[innell] 1866'. From Linnell's son, James, it passed to his grandson Herbert, and finally was sold in 1937 by his great-grandson, John Linnell, to Lessing J. Rosenwald, Philadelphia. It is now in the Lessing J. Rosenwald Collection, Library of Congress. This copy contains five corrections in Blake's hand, as recorded above.

(U) Hornby Library copy, bound in calf, gilt, by F. Bedford. Pp. 49–70 in facsimile. Similar to copy K above. Now in the H. F. Hornby Library, City of Liverpool Public Libraries.

(V) Locker-Lampson copy, in blue-grey wrappers, untrimmed, in green morocco case. Acquired by Dr. James B. Clements and sold with his library at the Parke-Bernet Galleries, New York, 9 January 1945 (lot 70, C. A. Stonehill Inc. $2000). Present owner not traced.

(W) University College, London, copy. Bound in green morocco by Douglas Cockerell, 1904. It has the usual corrections on pp. 4 and 15, probably in Blake's hand. There are other corrections but none of these is in Blake's hand and they have no authority.

There are a few other sale records of unidentifiable copies not included here. Alexander Gilchrist stated in the *Life* (1863) that he had found the book so rare that he had had to use a borrowed copy. Miss Lowery noted that Sotheby's catalogue for 16–20 July 1886 lists an uncut copy said to have been formerly Gilchrist's property. As Gilchrist died in 1863, the catalogue statement is presumably inaccurate. Perhaps it was the borrowed copy which had remained among his books.

V

ENGRAVERS CALLED BLAKE[1]

THE study of William Blake's output as an engraver of supreme originality and imagination leads inevitably to a consideration of his work as a journeyman engraver, which from the end of his apprenticeship to Basire in 1779 formed an important part of the sources of his very modest livelihood. Many of these engravings, made as book illustrations after draughtsmen such as Stothard, Flaxman, and Fuseli, or done for the publishers of decorative prints, have little or no importance in the history of art except in so far as it was Blake's hand that made them. Yet the more conventional side of his profession was not without influence on his creative work and possesses also its biographical interest. Students of Blake have therefore been at pains to detect and list all the engravings that could be attributed to him, and indeed many unsigned prints which could not possibly be his have also been fathered on him, sometimes in order to give a spurious interest and value to goods of no intrinsic merit whatever. Mrs. Trimmer's series of miserable prints in illustration of the Bible are examples of this tendency. Another source of confusion has lain in the possibility that there may have been another, or more than one other, engraver of the same name working in London at the same time. It was noted by A. G. B. Russell in 1912 in his *Engravings of William Blake* that there were three plates in existence bearing the lettering: *Blake sc. 'Change Alley*. One is the frontispiece of a thin volume entitled: 'The Poetry of Various Glees, Songs, &c. as performed at the Harmonists. London: Printed at the Philanthropic Reform, London-Road, St. George's Fields, 1798'. The second is a ticket of admission to a concert held on 28 May 1800 in aid of the funds for erecting a naval monument at Greenwich after a design by Flaxman. (William Blake did in fact execute three very trivial engravings for a pamphlet in favour of the same project, a statue of Britannia Triumphant 230 feet high on Greenwich Hill, but this is only a coincidence.) The third is a ticket of admission to the opening of the West Middlesex Water Works on 4 December 1809. Russell accepted these as the work of William Blake, and suggested that 'Change Alley was the address of the printer with whom he worked on these occasions.

[1] First printed in *The Times Literary Supplement* (1942), xli. 36.

The Harmonists' volume is in my collection. The other two prints are in the British Museum. In my *Bibliography of Blake*, 1921, I was able to add the information that 'Blake, Mr., Engraver, No. 6 Exchange-alley, Cornhill—4 copies' appeared in the list of subscribers to Bell's *Shakespeare*, an elaborately illustrated work in twenty volumes, published 1786–8. This seemed to point strongly to the fact that Blake of Exchange-alley was not the same as William Blake the artist and poet, who could have had no possible use for four copies of Bell's *Shakespeare* in 1788. Confirmation of this was provided by Miss Mona Wilson who noted that the London directory for 1795 recorded 'W. S. Blake, Engraver' at 16 Exchange Alley (*Life of W. B.*, 1927, p. 318). An undated print of the period shewing 'A View of Sydney Harbour', now in the British Museum, is signed W. S. Blake, without any address. No. 6 Exchange Alley in the Bell's *Shakespeare* subscription list is probably a misprint for No. 16. Nevertheless the compilers of the catalogue of the very important Blake exhibition held at Philadelphia in 1939 again listed another copy of the Harmonists' volume among the works of William Blake, and added two more items of the same kind. One was a card of introduction to the Harmonic Society, undated, but presumably about 1798, with the same lettering as before. The other was the card of L. Parroissien, who taught 'Latin, French & English grammatically, with Writing & Accompts', at the Academy, Great Ilford, Essex. This was again undated, but was lettered: *Blake Sculpt. Abchurch Lane*, thus introducing a new address, though it may be noted that Exchange Alley and Abchurch Lane are very near one another, both running into Lombard Street on opposite sides. A more recent addition to my collection is a large engraved sheet, 58·4 × 45 cm., giving an Address to *General Washington, Published by W. S. Blake, 16 Change Alley, Friday June 17 1800*, with head- and tail-pieces and a separate typographical explanation of the plate. The Address is not signed and may be by the engraver and publisher himself.

Further evidence of a conclusive kind can be added. The late W. E. Moss informed me that he had discovered two more specimens of the work of the ' 'Change Alley' Blake. Both are masonic certificates printed on vellum. One is a general form which could be used by any lodge by filling in its name and number. This specimen happened to have been used by the Secretary of the Lodge of Loyalty in Guernsey in 1818, but the engraving was probably made much earlier. It is lettered: *Bro Blake sculp. 'Change Alley*. The other certificate was specially engraved for the Lodge of Harmony No. 612 in the Island of Guernsey between the dates 1809 and 1814, when the Lodge was given another number. It is lettered: *Bro R. W. Isemonger delint. Bro Blake sculp.* Lastly, I have a note of another trade card lettered: *I. Rowe*|*Engraver and Printer*|*10 Change Alley*|*Apprentice & Successor to the late Mr. Blake.*

Reference has already been made (see p. 15) to Mr. Ellic Howe's discovery of Blake's being bound apprentice to James Basire in 1772. Another entry in the same Apprentice Register had previously caught his eye a page or two earlier, since it was twice signed 'Wm. Blake'. From this it appears that on 5 February 1771 Thomas Powell, apprentice of John Bannister, was 'Turned by Consent of proper Parties to Wm. Blake of Butcher Hall Lane Newgate Street, Engraver, Citizen, & Clothworker.' This entry was signed by all three parties to the trans-action, and Wm. Blake signed in addition the statement: 'I Promise to make the said apprentice free of the Sta$^{rs.}$ Co. at the End of his Term.' Either, therefore, there was yet another master-engraver called William Blake working in the city at about the same period as the subject of this book was serving his apprenticeship, or it may be that W. S. Blake was already established in business at Butcher Hall Lane as early as 1771.

However this may be, it is now possible to state definitely that a journeyman engraver named William Staden Blake was working from about 1780 to 1810 in the neighbourhood of Lombard Street, first in Abchurch Lane, then at No. 16, and later at No. 10, Exchange Alley. He was a Mason, and was succeeded after his death by his apprentice, I. Rowe, and so may now be allowed a separate identity from his more distinguished namesake. His work is of honest insignificance, a quality which, it must be confessed, often characterizes the genuine labours of William Blake, when he was engaged in earning his bread and butter. Finally, it is quite possible that William Blake and W. S. Blake were acquainted with one another, the connecting link being the amateur engraver and print collector, George Cumberland. Already in 1784 Cumberland was thinking, and no doubt talking, about a method of writing poems on copper, an account of which he communicated to Henry Maty's *New Review*;[1] this is printed in vol. vi, 1784, p. 318, and Cumberland there stated that 'the inventor in January last, wrote a poem on copper by means of this art; and some impressions of it were printed by Mr. Blake, in Exchange-alley, Cornhill, which answered perfectly well, although it had cost very little more time than common writing. Any number of impres-sions, in proportion to the strength of biting-in may be taken off.' A letter[2] written by George Cumberland to his brother Richard in the same year describes the same process, though it is evident that he proposed only to etch his poem on

[1] First noticed by Miss Mona Wilson, *Life of Blake* (1927), p. 23.
[2] Printed in full at pp. 231–2 below.

copper without attempting to reverse the writing, so that the print would have to be read with the aid of a mirror. In my collection are two books of his own prints made up by Cumberland himself. Each contains a print of his poem, 'To the Nightingale', but neither, being a counter-proof, is in reverse and needs no mirror. Perhaps Blake made Cumberland aware of this method of overcoming the difficulty.

In his prose burlesque known as *An Island in the Moon*, written about 1787, Blake appears to have been satirizing various contemporary figures, and he makes an unmistakable reference to Cumberland's method of printing as follows:

. . . them illuminating the manuscript.
'Ay,' said she, 'that would be excellent.'
'Then', said he, 'I would have all the wording engraved instead of printed, and at every other leaf a high-finished print—all in three volumes folio,—and sell them for a hundred pounds apiece. They would print off two thousand.'[1]

The number, two thousand, was the same as George Cumberland had mentioned in his letter to his brother.

By December 1795 Blake and Cumberland were corresponding as friends, and they may well have been acquainted for some years before this. Blake, however, makes no mention in his writings of the namesake who had printed Cumberland's plates in 1784, though he refers to several of the better-known engravers of his time. Mr. Ruthven Todd has drawn attention[2] to the fact that the names of 'William Blake' and 'W. S. Blake (Writing Engraver)' both appeared in 1797 on a list of signatories to a testimonial to one Alexander Tilloch, who claimed to have devised a method of engraving which would prevent the forging of bank-notes; but even this does not necessarily mean that the two Blakes had met. Direct communication between the 'engravers called Blake', whether as friends or rivals, must therefore for the present remain conjectural.

Inspired, perhaps, by my example in writing about W. S. Blake, Professor G. E. Bentley, jr., has published an article (*Notes & Queries*, May 1965, pp. 172–8) on 'A Collection of Prosaic Blakes'. He has added more information about W. S. Blake and given accounts of no less than twenty-two other William Blakes living in London at the same time, though none of them was an engraver.

[1] *Blake's Complete Writings*, 1966, p. 62. The manuscript is defective just before this passage.; 'Them' was formerly read as 'thus'.
[2] *The Times Literary Supplement*, 10 February 1945.

VI

BLAKE'S ILLUSTRATIONS TO YOUNG'S *NIGHT THOUGHTS*[1]

WILLIAM BLAKE, in the year 1795, was living at Hercules Buildings, Lambeth. For eight years he had been labouring at the composition and decoration of his series of books in 'illuminated printing', in which the text and designs were etched on copper plates, the prints from these being then colour-printed or painted by hand with ordinary water-colour. The idea of combining text and decoration was, indeed, far from new, and had been carried out in past ages in innumerable illuminated manuscripts, though it had fallen into disuse since the invention of printing more than three hundred years before. Blake had unhesitatingly rejected the ordinary mode of printing, and had evolved a method which, in some of its technical details, was entirely new. It is probable that his first experiments were made in 1788 with the tiny plates of the brief didactic works, *There is No Natural Religion* and *All Religions are One*. In 1789, having gained in skill and confidence, he began to make the twenty-eight plates of the *Songs of Innocence*. During the next six years he executed eight more books, including *The Marriage of Heaven and Hell*, *Songs of Innocence and of Experience*, *Europe*, and *America*. The tentative beginnings of *There is No Natural Religion* had proved to be the root from which Blake's genius had grown and flowered, until in the pages of *America*, on a scale many times larger than that of his first attempts, he had rivalled in beauty the manuscripts of medieval times, and surpassed most of them in imaginative power. The colouring of the earlier copies of the *Songs of Innocence* is simple and even pallid in effect. In the later books he gave freer rein to his instinct for magnificence of colouring. This did not reach its climax until many years later, during the period 1815–20, when he was colouring superb examples of *Europe*, *America*, *Jerusalem*, and other books; but by 1795 the tendency was becoming evident.

No doubt Blake's sanguine temperament had filled his mind with rosy dreams of selling hundreds of copies of his illuminated books. He was to be his own printer and publisher, and so was to obtain an easy means of livelihood while achieving

[1] Part was first printed as an Introduction to *Blake's Illustrations to Young's Night Thoughts*, Harvard University Press, 1927, with thirty reproductions.

the recognition that his genius desired and the propagation of the doctrines by which mankind was to be redeemed. Disappointment, however, was to be his lot. His books were sold in such small numbers that in more than one instance only a single copy is now known to have survived. It was becoming clear, therefore, by 1795 that public favour must be sought by some different means. Hitherto he had illustrated and printed only his own poems, with a success which posterity has now no hesitation in acclaiming. At the same time he had made original copper-plate engravings for only two works by other writers, namely a frontispiece for Thomas Commins's *Elegy Set to Music*, 1786, a sentimental and insipid ballad, and six plates for Mary Wollstonecraft's *Original Stories from Real Life*, 1791. This and other work as a journeyman engraver had brought him into relationship with some of the publishers, but whether the idea of enlarging the scope of his scheme of book decoration to include the poems of other writers originated in his own brain or another's, there is now no means of determining with certainty. Since his own compositions had failed to attract any attention, perhaps Blake wished to try the effect of a fine edition of the work of some popular favourite, putting grand marginal decorations on almost every page. If it were of a large enough size, it could scarcely fail to make some impression on the minds of his contemporaries. Certainly no scheme could seem grandiose enough to appal his imagination. In 1795 his artistic exuberance was at its height; not only were there his own illuminated books as evidence of his pre-eminence, but he had also made the series of stupendous colour-prints, including 'Nebuchadnezzar', 'Newton', 'God Creating Adam', and a number of paintings stood to his credit. It is difficult to believe, however, that Blake's undirected impulse would have seized upon the *Night Thoughts* of Dr. Edward Young as suitable material on which to exercise his powers of illustration, though it is possible that he had chanced to read Young's prose work entitled *Conjectures on Original Composition*, which was first published in 1759. This contains many sentences which Blake must strongly have approved, such as: 'Genius often then deserves most to be praised when it is most sure to be condemned; that is, when its excellence, from mounting high, to weak eyes is quite out of sight'; or again: 'So boundless are the bold excursions of the human mind, that, in the vast void beyond real existence, it can call forth shadowy beings and unknown worlds, as numerous, as bright, and perhaps as lasting, as the stars . . . when such an ample area for renowned adventure in original attempts lies before us, shall we be as mere leaden pipes, conveying to the present age small streams of excellence from its grand reservoir in antiquity, and those, too, perhaps, muddied in the past?'

The *Night Thoughts* had been published in nine parts, or *Nights*, in the years 1742–5, and they had soon achieved an immense popularity which it is not easy at the present day to understand. The language has a pompous quality that only partially cloaks the lack of profundity in the thoughts expressed. Fewer, perhaps, of the present generation have read the book than have enjoyed an irreverent charade illustrating the letter Y—an elderly figure in spectacles and nightcap seated with forefinger to forehead in semi-darkness. Nevertheless Young's poetry earned the admiration of a great modern critic,[1] and it is possible that he may yet share in the fashionable reinstatement of the great figures of the Augustan age of literature.

In 1795 the eighteenth century had not yet been passed, so that the flavour of the *Night Thoughts* may be supposed to have been still palatable. Clearly Richard Edwards, publisher and bookseller, of 142 Bond Street, was of this opinion. Blake had not, as far as is known, done any work before this for Edwards; but when the two men met, their ideas from their different standpoints seemed good to one another, the artist eager to exercise his talents, the publisher anxious to turn this new-found genius to good commercial account. It may be guessed that Henry Fuseli acted as intermediary. Already for some years he had been Blake's friend and admirer, and had found him 'damned good to steal from'. He also had a far wider acquaintance than the more eccentric Blake among the literary and artistic figures of his time. When the idea of adorning Young's *Night Thoughts* with marginal designs had once been launched, Blake no doubt worked at it with feverish energy. His work began to be talked about, and some of the echoes of these conversations may be heard in the pages of the diary written by the landscape painter Joseph Farington, R.A. On 19 February 1796 he notes that 'West, Cosway, and Humphry spoke warmly of the designs of Blake the engraver, as works of extraordinary genius and imagination. Smirke differed in opinion, from what he had seen; so do I.' Later, on 24 June 1796, he records several facts of interest: 'Fuseli called on me last night and sat till 12 o'clock. He mentioned Blake, the Engraver, whose genius and invention have been much spoken of. Fuseli has known him several years and thinks he has a good deal of invention, but that "fancy is the end and not a means in his designs". He does not employ it to give novelty and decoration to regular conceptions, but the whole of his aim is to produce singular shapes and odd combinations.

'Blake has undertaken to make designs and to encircle the letter-press of each page of Young's "Night Thoughts". Edwards, the Bookseller, of Bond Street, employs him, and has the letter-press of each page laid down on a large half-sheet

---

[1] George Saintsbury, in *A Short History of English Literature*, pp. 560, 561.

of paper. There are about 900 pages. Blake asked 100 guineas for the whole. Edwards said that he could not afford to give more than 20 guineas, for which Blake agreed. Fuseli understands that Edwards proposes to select about 200 from the whole, and to have that number engraved as decorations for a new edition.'

In these sentences lies the first indication of the immense scale on which Blake was working and of the minute scale on which he was to receive his reward. The scheme seems almost to obey the law of inverse squares—a principle which might have deterred a more worldly artist; but Blake was no doubt thinking, as always, more of his artistic fame than of his pecuniary reward, and his faith in his own powers carried him forward.

The pages of the first editions of the *Night Thoughts*, 1742–5, were taken as the centre of each design. These pages were inlaid, out of centre, toward the top and left-hand margin, in sheets of Whatman drawing paper, which have the date 1794 in the watermark. The Whatman sheet was then itself inlaid in an edging of stronger paper, on which was drawn a ruled and tinted framework. The whole page thus constituted measures 21 × 16 inches. Blake's designs to the number of 537 appear to have been drawn with a brush in Indian ink and were then coloured with a varying degree of elaboration. The intense application with which Blake worked is shewn by the fact that this immense number of water-colour drawings was completed and forty-three of them were engraved on copper in less than two years, so that the first instalment of the printed work was ready for publication in the autumn of 1797. The engraved plates bear dates ranging from 21 June 1796 to 22 March 1797, so that the time taken seems to have been about equally divided between the water-colour drawings and the engravings.

The publisher prepared the way by issuing early in 1797 the following prospectus:[1]

EDWARDS'S
MAGNIFICENT EDITION
OF
YOUNG'S NIGHT THOUGHTS

Early in JUNE will be published, by subscription, part the first of a splendid edition of this favourite work, elegantly printed, and illustrated with forty very spirited engravings from original drawings by BLAKE.

These engravings are in a perfectly new style of decoration, surrounding the text which they are designed to elucidate.

---

[1] Transcribed from a copy in the possession of the late P. J. Dobell in 1914.

The work is printed in atlas-sized quarto, and the subscription for the whole, making four parts, with one hundred and fifty engravings, is five guineas;— one to be paid at the time of subscribing, and one on the delivery of each part;— The price will be considerably advanced to non-subscribers.

Specimens may be seen at Edwards's, No. 142 New Bond Street; at Mr. Edwards's, Pall-Mall; and at the Historic Gallery, Pall-Mall: where subscriptions are received.

This fine 'atlas quarto' consists of fifty-six separate leaves, printed on both sides, and forty-three of the pages have a large engraved design surrounding the text. This part includes only the first four 'Nights' of the poem. A prefatory 'Advertisement', dated 22 December 1796, declares that 'no apology can be necessary for offering to the publick an embellished edition of an English classick, or for giving to the great work of Young some of those advantages of dress and ornament which have lately distinguished the immortal productions of Shakespeare and Milton'. The publisher, it is stated, though 'not uninfluenced by professional, acted also under the impulse of higher, motives', seeking to make the arts 'subservient to the purposes of religion'. 'In every page the reader finds his attention held captive by poetry in its boldest and most successful exertion: everywhere is his imagination soothed with pleasing, or enlarged with grand imagery: everywhere does he see fancy binding flowers round the altar of truth, while reason in awful pomp is presenting her sacrifice to heaven.' After much more in the same vein, the writer asserts that the publisher 'has shrunk from no expense in the preparing' of the book. 'It has been regarded by him, indeed, not as a speculation of advantage, but as an indulgence of inclination—as an undertaking in which fondness and partiality would not permit him to be curiously accurate in adjusting the estimate of profit and loss.' The more curious accuracy of the present day cannot help noticing that Blake had been paid at the rate of about ninepence for each of his water-colour designs, with, probably, an additional guinea for the engraving of each plate. In spite of this, the writer of the Advertisement considers that 'of the merit of Mr. Blake it is unnecessary to speak', though he adds that 'to the eyes of the discerning it need not be pointed out; and while a taste for the arts of design shall continue to exist, the original conception, and the bold and masterly execution of this artist cannot be unnoticed or unadmired'. This ingenious, if disingenuous, preface is attributed by Alexander Gilchrist to Blake's friend, Fuseli. It seems far more probable that it was written by Edwards himself. The leaf of 'Explanations of the engravings' at the end may have been compiled by Fuseli, for it was certainly not written by Blake.

Unhappily the literary and artistic public of 1797 failed to appreciate the moral exaltation predicted for them by the writer of the preface as they contemplated Young in the embrace of Blake. No contemporary reviews of the book have come to my notice, though some doubtless appeared; whether these were appreciative or unfavourable does not now matter. The venture was a failure, and the three later parts were never published; nor, so far as is known, were the plates for them ever engraved. Blake's disappointment must have been intense, but his mind was not yet touched with the bitterness and resentment that filled it in later years, so that he was probably able to find consolation enough by turning to other work. Almost immediately afterwards, indeed, he embarked on a somewhat similar series of a 116 designs for Gray's poems. These he made no attempt to publish. They had been commissioned by John Flaxman in 1797 as a gift for his wife.[1]

It must be admitted that contemporary judgement, based on the merits of the engravings alone, was not far wrong. Blake's inspiration was weighed down by his technique, which still adhered to the conventions learned during his apprenticeship. Although he expresses much beauty of line, the general effect is sometimes arid and monotonous. The designs cover too large an area to be able to keep more than a part of the emotional content with which they left Blake's mind.

Some copies of the book were splendidly painted with water-colour washes. These were certainly not all done by Blake himself, nor is there any reason to suppose that Mrs. Blake had any hand in them, though this attribution has occasionally been made. Presumably Blake coloured one or more examples himself, the publisher keeping one to serve as a pattern for a professional colourist. How many copies were done is not known, nor is it certain (except in one instance) which are to be regarded as originals from Blake's hand. One such is likely to be the example from the collection of Thomas Butts, sold at Sotheby's in 1852. This was later in the Monckton Milnes, Crewe, and A. E. Newton libraries. About 1942 the late W. E. Moss compiled a census of the coloured copies known to him, with comments on the construction of the book. He listed fifteen copies, with two more perhaps to be identified with others already listed. He believed his own copy had been coloured by Blake, and suggested that the publisher, Richard Edwards, had the majority done by his brother, Thomas, a skilled colourist.[2]

Since 1942 two more coloured copies have come to my notice. One was sold in 1945 at the Parke-Bernet Galleries, New York (John Gribble Library, lot 28,

[1] See a letter from Mrs. Flaxman discovered by Dr. Mary K. Woodworth, *Notes and Queries*, ccxv (1970), 312–13.

[2] This paper, now in the Bodleian Library, Oxford, was published in the *Blake Newsletter*, ed. Morton D. Paley, University of California (1968), ii. 2. 19–23.

16 April) and again in 1947 (P. F. Webster Library, lot 5, 28 April). The other one, of exceptional interest, had been bought in Geneva by a lady for £5[1] and was offered at Sotheby's on 3 March 1958 (lot 47, Traylen, £680). The book contained a note on the flyleaf: 'This copy was coloured for me by Mr. Blake. W. E.' The first owner was probably William Esdaile (1758–1837), a banker and collector of prints and drawings. The inscription seems to provide unequivocal evidence that this one, at any rate, was coloured by Blake himself. It is now in the Paul Mellon Collection.[2]

The two enormous volumes containing the water-colour designs remained in the possession of Richard Edwards, whose signature was on the flyleaf of the first volume. Some correspondence concerning them was lent to me by the late James Bain in 1925, and from this it appears that Richard Edwards afterwards sold them to his brother Thomas, already mentioned, who had a book-shop in Halifax. They were offered in a catalogue of his stock when he was retiring from business in 1826, but failed to find a customer. They were offered again with Thomas Edwards's remaining stock at Sotheby's in May 1828 (lots 940 and 1130), but were again not sold. The drawings consequently remained with the Edwards family at Halifax until 1874. In that year they were put into the hands of an agent, Thomas Birtwhistle, a stationer of Halifax, by whom they were brought to London in April; they were then to be seen 'any morning before 11 at Anderton's Hotel, Fleet Street'. On 3 June 1874 Birtwhistle wrote to James Bain, bookseller of the Haymarket: 'The owner of Blake is away but has left the sale of the Book in my hands. I could not without writing him take your price, but if you think fit to say 425£, I can make it satisfactory. It is very likely if I write he may hold out for the other 25£, as he has a great opinion of the work and is in no need of cash.' The bargain was thus brought to a satisfactory conclusion and the books became the property of James Bain.[3] They were destined to remain for many years at his shop in the Haymarket, partly

[1] Information from Mr. Anthony Hobson of Sotheby's.

[2] Nineteen coloured copies have been listed by Professor G. E. Bentley, jr., in the *Blake Newsletter*, (1968), ii. 41–5, including this one.

[3] At some time during Bain's ownership a set of reproductions of the water-colours seems to have been projected. Messrs. Francis Edwards of Marylebone High Street recently had a lithographic full-size reproduction of No. 191 of the series, and in my collection is a coloured version of this design in miniature, in which the page of Young's text is replaced by a statement that it is a 'specimen of Blake's Designs in illustration of Young's Night Thoughts. Being a reproduction, on a reduced scale, of No. 191 of the original set of Five hundred and thirty-seven Water-colour Drawings.' Nothing further, however, was heard of this. No reproductions were made until 1927, when 500 copies of a set of thirty were printed by the Harvard University Press for the Fogg Museum of Art, Cambridge, Mass., with an introduction by myself.

(8)

What Title, or what Name endears thee more?
Cynthia! Cilene! Phœbe!---or doſt hear
With higher guſt, fair *P----d* of the Skies?
Is that the ſoft Enchantment calls thee down,
More powerful than of old *Circean* charm?
Come; but from Heavenly Banquets with thee bring
The Soul of Song; and whiſper in mine ear
The Theft divine; or in propitious Dreams,
(For Dreams are Thine) transfuſe it thro' the breaſt
Of thy firſt Votary;---But not thy Laſt;
If, like thy Nameſake, Thou art ever Kind.

And Kind Thou wilt be; Kind on ſuch a Theme;
A Theme ſo like thee; a quite *Lunar* Theme,
Soft, modeſt, melancholy, female, fair!
A Theme that roſe all-pale, and told my ſoul,
'Twas Night; on her fond Hopes perpetual Night!
A Night which ſtruck a damp, a deadlier damp,
Than that which ſmote me from *Philander*'s tomb.
Narciſſa follows, e'er His tomb is clos'd.

Woes

(14)

Is Cord, is Cable, to man's tender Tie
On earthly bliss; it breaks at every Breeze.

O ye blest scenes of *permanent* Delight! 180
Full, above measure! lasting, beyond bound!
Could you, so rich in rapture, fear an End,
That ghastly Thought would drink up all your Joy,
And quite unparadise the realms of Light.
Safe are you lodg'd above these rowling Spheres;
The baleful influence of whose giddy Dance,
Sheds sad Vicissitude on all beneath.
Here teems with Revolutions every Hour;
And rarely for the better; or the best,
More mortal than the common births of Fate. 190
Each *Moment* has its Sickle, emulous
Of *Time*'s enormous Scythe, whose ample Sweep
Strikes Empires from the root; each *Moment* plays
His little Weapon in the narrower sphere

Of

Fountain of Animation! whence defcends
Urania, my celeftial Gueft! who deigns
Nightly to vifit me, fo mean; and *now*
Confcious, how needful Difcpline to Man,
From pleafing Dalliance with the Charms of *Night,*
My wand'ring Thought recalls, to what excites
Far other beat of Heart; *Narciffa's* Tomb!

   Or is it feeble Nature calls me back?
And breaks my Spirit into Grief again?
Is it a *Stygian* Vapour in my Blood?
A cold, flow Puddle, creeping thro' my Veins?
Or is it *thus* with all Men?—Thus, with all.
What are we? how unequal? now we foar,
And now we fink; to be *the fame,* tranfcends
Our prefent Prowefs. Dearly pays the *Soul*
For Lodging-ill; too dearly rents her Clay.
Reafon, a baffled Counfellor! but adds
The Blufh of Weaknefs, to the Bane of Woe.
The nobleft Spirit fighting her hard Fate,
In this damp, dufky Region, charg'd with Storms,

                        But

[40]

" And Fruits promiſcuous, ever-teeming *Earth*,   790.
" That Man may languiſh in luxurious Scenes,
" And in an *Eden* mourn his with'ring Joys?
" Claim Earth and Skies Man's Admiration, due
" For *ſuch* Delights! Bleſt Animals! too Wiſe
" To *wonder*; and too Happy to *complain*!

" OUR *Doom decreed* demands a mournful Scene;
" Why not a Dungeon dark, for the *Condemn'd?*
" Why not the Dragon's ſubterranean Den,
" For Man to howl in? Why not his Abode,
" Of the ſame diſmal Colour with his Fate?   800.
" A *Thebes*, a *Babylon*, at vaſt Expence
" Of Time, Toil, Treaſure, Art, for Owls and Adders,
" As congruous, as, for Man, this lofty Dome,
" Which prompts proud Thought, and kindles high Deſire,
" If from her humble Chamber in the Duſt,
" While proud Thought ſwells, and high Deſire inflames,
" The poor *Worm* calls us for her Inmates there;
" And, round us, *Death*'s inexorable Hand
" Draws the dark Curtain cloſe; undrawn no more.

" *Undrawn*

[42]

Of Matter, never dignify'd with Life,
Here lie proud Rationals ; *The Sons of Heav'n !*
The Lords of Earth ! The Property of Worms !
Beings of Yesterday, and no To-morrow !
Who liv'd in Terror, and in Pangs expir'd !
All gone to rot in Chaos ; *or, to make*
Their happy Transit into Blocks, *or Brutes,*
Nor longer sully their CREATOR's *Name.*

LORENZO! hear, pause, ponder, and pronounce.   840.
Just is this History ? If *such* is Man,
Mankind's Historian, tho' Divine, might weep.
And dares LORENZO smile ?--- I know thee Proud ;
For once let Pride befriend thee ; Pride looks pale
At such a Scene, and sighs for something more.
Amid thy Boasts, Presumptions, and Displays,
And art Thou then a Shadow ? Less than Shade ?
A Nothing ? Less than Nothing ? To *have* been,
And *not to be,* is lower than Unborn.
Art thou *ambitious?* Why then make the Worm   850.
Thine Equal ? Runs thy Taste of *Pleasure* high ?
Why patronize sure Death of ev'ry Joy ?

Charm

perhaps because their owner liked them too much to be willing to part from them easily, partly because they served as a centre of attraction for many customers who might otherwise have gone elsewhere to buy their books. Eventually, however, a worthy purchaser was found in the person of the late Marsden J. Perry, an American bibliophile, who in 1908 disposed of his Blake collection to William Augustus White of New York, already the owner of a large collection of Blake's illuminated books. Not long before his death in 1927 Mr. White gave them to his daughter, Mrs. Frances White Emerson, who generously sent them to me in the following year with instructions that I should keep them as long as I wished before passing them on to the Department of Prints and Drawings at the British Museum. The transfer was effected about the end of the year 1928.

While Alexander Gilchrist was writing his *Life of Blake*, published in 1863, the drawings for *Night Thoughts* were still out of sight at Halifax. When they had been brought to London in 1874, their fame soon spread, for they were a marvellous and unexpected discovery for the slowly growing band of critics, connoisseurs, and artists who were helping to raise Blake's name out of the obscurity into which it had fallen. J. Comyns Carr was one of the critics who soon afterwards expressed his admiration for the designs, and his articles in the *Cornhill* (1875) and *Belgravia* (1876) contained the first descriptions of them that were published.

The volumes were included in the exhibition held at the Burlington Fine Arts Club in 1876, and a few years later a large number of the designs were described by Frederic Shields, the descriptions being printed in 1880 as an appendix to the second edition of Gilchrist's *Life*. Since that time many students of Blake's work have seen them at Bain's shop or at Mr. White's house, or, more recently, on exhibition at the British Museum, and the verdict has been unanimous that, although unequal, as is to be expected in so immense a series, the designs as a whole take a high place in the full range of Blake's artistic output. Five of them are reproduced here (Plates 15–19).

Very many are of great beauty, and some of them shew Blake's imagination working at its highest level, while embodying much of his own symbolism. On a first consideration it might seem strange that Blake should have solved so successfully the problem of illustrating Young's elusive thoughts. But actually few books could have served him better, for, as Comyns Carr wrote in 1876, 'the poet says so much and means so little', that the artist is left with the widest possible range for the selection of his subjects. He may remain with Young on earth and illustrate quite literally some ordinary incident; he may seize an empty simile and give it, to the astonishment of its creator, a vivid corporeal existence; he may catch the merest breath of an allusion and, flying out far beyond the world of the bewildered poet, clothe it in the airy graces of his imagination until it assumes a beauty undreamt of while it remained in the realm of words; or he may take a vague metaphor and embody it in a design of terrifying grandeur which it had wholly missed in its original setting. All these things Blake has done many times over. He has taken the clay of Young's mind and with deft fingers has moulded it into the image of true poetry.

VII

BLAKE AND THE WEDGWOODS[1]

D<small>R</small>. E<small>RASMUS</small> D<small>ARWIN</small>, F.R.S., of Lichfield, grandfather of Charles Darwin, is not now regarded as a poet of distinction; yet his poem *The Botanic Garden*, the second part of which is entitled 'The Loves of the Plants', is well known for various reasons, one being the association of the book with the names of Josiah Wedgwood and William Blake. 'The Loves of the Plants', although it is called Part II, was published first, as a quarto volume, in 1789, and in this edition it is a very scarce book. Part I, 'The Economy of Vegetation', was published two years later, in 1791, and is usually associated with the second or third edition of 'The Loves of the Plants'. Both volumes contain a number of engravings, one of those in Part I being an engraving by Blake after a wash drawing by his friend Henry Fuseli, entitled 'The Fertilization of Egypt'. Blake did not engrave directly from Fuseli's work, but made another wash drawing for himself containing additional features. The two drawings may be seen together today in the Print Room of the British Museum. In the engraving the dog-headed Anubis stands astride the Nile with his arms raised towards the Dog-star. In the background, the spirit of fertility, a winged and bearded figure, hovers with outspread arms. This figure, a characteristic product of Blake's mind, is only vaguely shewn in Fuseli's drawing, and a peculiar musical instrument known as a *sistrum*, lying beside the left foot of Anubis, is not in either drawing. Blake, however, signed the plate only as engraver, the invention being ascribed to Fuseli. Four other plates in the same volume give representations of the figures on the Portland Vase, the now famous Roman funeral vessel of deep blue glass, decorated with figures in opaque white glass. It had recently been purchased by the Duke of Portland from the Barberini family for 1,000 guineas, and very skilful replicas had been made at Etruria by Josiah Wedgwood. The four unsigned plates in Dr. Darwin's volume illustrate one side of the whole vase (Plate 20), the designs in the two compartments (one on either side), and those on the bottom and the handles. They are somewhat coarsely executed, in the dot-and-lozenge technique used by Basire and his pupils, but give an excellent idea of the design of the vase. In my *Bibliography of Blake* published by the Grolier

[1] The greater part first printed in *The Times Literary Supplement* (1926), xxv. 909.

Club of New York in 1921, I noted that 'the engravings of the Portland Vase . . . are unsigned, but are in my opinion certainly by Blake; the style of engraving is typical of his work, and this attribution is supported by the fact that the reduced engravings of the same subject in the octavo edition of 1799 were engraved (and one signed) by him'. Confirmation of this attribution is to be found in letters still extant written by Dr. Darwin and Joseph Johnson, the publisher. Darwin had evidently had more than one letter from Johnson, since there were difficulties about making use of plates previously engraved by Bartolozzi, for on 9 July 1791 Darwin wrote to Josiah Wedgwood the following letter[1] preserved among the Wedgwood papers now deposited at Keele University:

Dear Sir,

Mr Johnson's engraver now wishes much to see Bartolozzi's plates of the vase, & will engrave them again if necessary—I told Johnson in my own name, *not in yours*, that I thought the outlines too hard, & in some places not agreeable.

Now if you could be so kind as to send Bartolozzi's prints to Mr Johnson St. Paul's Churchyard,—or let him know if He can have them at your house in Greek Street—as he said he can not anywhere procure them. He promises to take great care of them, the name of the engraver I don't know, but Johnson said He is capable of doing anything well.

I am sorry to give you so much trouble on this account, but always apply to you in all difficulties in matters of taste.

* * *

Your affect. friend & ser^t
E. Darwin

On the 23rd of the same month Johnson wrote to Darwin a letter first detected in 1930 among the Darwin family papers by Mr. C. W. Thomas of the University of Wisconsin:

London, July 23, 1791

Dear Sir,

It is not the expense of *purchasing* Bartolozzi's plates that is any object; they *cannot be copied* without Hamilton's consent, being protected by act of parlt.

Blake is certainly capable of making an exact copy of the vase, I believe more so than Mr. B[artolozzi], if the vase were lent him for that purpose, & I see no other way of its being done, for the drawing he had was very imperfect—this you will determine on consulting Mr. Wedgwood, & also whether it should be copied as before, or reduced & brought into a folding plate.

[1] First printed in a letter from myself to the Editor of *The Times Literary Supplement*, 3 July 1930.

The Portland Vase.

1. London, Published Dec.ʳ 1.ˢᵗ 1791, by J. Johnson, S.ᵗ Paul's Church Yard.

I have no wish in this case but to do what you desire. It is not advisable to publish before the winter, yet I will do it as soon as the work is ready if you desire it.

The reason Mr. H[amilton] assigns for not allowing his plates to be copied is that he is a considerable sum out of pocket, the sale not having indemnified him for his expenses.

I believe that if Dr. P[riestley] had been found by the high-church mob he would have been murdered. We hope that part of his library and some Ms. have been saved from the wreck by the activity of his son & some of his friends.

I am Sr.,

Yr. obedt.,

J. JOHNSON

I could wish for particular instructions for the engraver.

It seems certain, therefore, that Blake obtained access to the Portland Vase itself, or had the loan of a Wedgwood replica, during the autumn of 1791. The plates were rapidly completed and were published, according to the imprints, on 1 December of the same year. Blake did not, so far as is known, have any direct dealings with either Darwin or Wedgwood at this time. Joseph Johnson, however, was his close friend, and had employed him constantly for book illustrations since 1780. In 1791 he had intended to publish Blake's poem *The French Revolution*, but only the first part of this has survived, and that only in a single copy, probably a proof. Johnson's reference to Dr. Priestley's misfortunes at the end of his letter is characteristic, for he was the friend of many of the more radical spirits of his time besides Blake.

Mr. Thomas, when he communicated Johnson's letter to me, remarked that he had previously been struck by the resemblance between these engravings of the Portland Vase and Michelangelo's figures on the Medici tomb at Florence. Blake's early admiration for Michelangelo is very well known, and the influence is at work in his mind even when his hand is tracing the outlines of the Portland Vase.

The designs on the Vase may have had another interest for Blake, since they illustrate the symbols of the Eleusynian mysteries as described in Thomas Taylor's *Dissertation on the Eleusynian and Bacchic Mysteries*, c. 1791, a book with which Blake is likely to have been familiar. Miss Kathleen Raine has traced a connexion between the mysteries and Blake's poems, *The Little Girl Lost* and *Found*.[1]

★ ★ ★

Although the engravings done for Dr. Darwin in 1791 are unlikely to have brought Blake into direct relationship with Josiah Wedgwood the elder, it has

[1] *Blake and Tradition*, Princeton, 1968, i. 126–33.

long been known that Blake must have had dealings with one of the younger Wedgwoods some twenty-five years later, about the year 1816. The existence of eighteen plates of Wedgwood ware drawn and engraved by Blake has been recorded by more than one authority. A set of proofs of the engravings was in the collection of John Linnell and is now in the Print Room at the British Museum. A set of four earlier proofs, one with a watermark in the paper dated 1816, is also in the Print Room, and four proofs were in the collection of W. Graham Robertson.[1] The latter were formerly in the possession of Blake's friend Frederick Tatham, who wrote on one of them the following note:

Mr. Flaxman introduced Blake to Mr. Wedgwood. The Designs of the Pottery were made by Mr. Flaxman & engraved by Blake for some work. Wedgwood's last sale of pottery was about 35 or 37 years ago when I purchased several specimens. These were white that I purchased & were of very elegant shapes, some too elegant for use.

These proofs were probably known to Gilchrist, who attributed the work to the years 1781–3, when Blake first made Flaxman's acquaintance; but the date 1816 in the paper shewed that the engravings were really made at a much later time in Blake's life. No information concerning his later relations with the Wedgwoods, or the catalogue for which the engravings of pottery were presumed to have been made, was to be found in the books on Wedgwood and his wares. Investigation, however, of the mass of records preserved in the Wedgwood Museum at Etruria, made at my request by the late John Cook, the Curator, in 1926, produced interesting results. These were placed at my disposal by the late Frank Wedgwood, who also gave me a complete set of the engravings (Plate 21).

Blake's dealings with the firm were probably begun during the first half of the year 1815. He had sent a preliminary drawing by July, and a copy of an answering letter from Josiah Wedgwood the younger is the earliest record that has been found; it is as follows:

ETRURIA, *29 July, 1815*

SIR,—I return the drawing you have been so good to send me, which I entirely approve in all respects. I ought to have mentioned when the Terrine was sent you that the hole for the ladle in the cover should not be represented & which you will be so good to omit in the engraving.

I presume you would make a drawing of each article that is to be engraved, & if it will be agreeable to you to complete the drawings before the engraving is begun, I think it may enable me to make the best arrangement of the articles on

[1] Sold with the Graham Robertson Collection at Christie's, 22 July 1949 (lot 90, Sawyer, 30 gns.).

889

888

160

891

114

120

112

115

is this stand right?
in drawings it is dish stand

Blake d & sc

the copper plates, but if this is not quite as agreeable to you as going on with the drawing & engraving together, I will only beg you to make two or three drawings, & I will in that case in the mean time consider of the arrangement. I have directed a Terrine to be sent you, presuming you will prefer having only one vessell at a time. If you would have more, be so good as to let Mr. Mowbray at my house know, who has a list of more articles.

I am, Sir,
Your mo. obt. svt.,
Josiah Wedgwood

Mr. Blake, 17 South Molton St.

Blake's error in representing the hole for the ladle in the Terrine may have discouraged him for a time; and it was nearly seven weeks later that he wrote the following note to Wedgwood:

17 South Molton Street
8 September, 1815

Sir,—I send Two more drawings with the First that I did, altered, having taken out that part which expressed the hole for the ladle.

It will be more convenient for me to make all the drawings first, before I begin Engraving them, as it will enable me also to regulate a System of working that will be uniform from beginning to end. Any remarks that you will be pleased to make will be thankfully reciev'd by, Sir,

Your humble Servant,
William Blake

No more of this polite correspondence seems to have survived; but the visionary artist was now fairly launched upon his very mundane task of making the numerous drawings that Wedgwood needed. During the last five months of the year Wedgwood's London agent was providing Blake with specimens from which to work, and the following entry occurs in the records of transactions which were sent regularly to Etruria:

October 23, 1815. For Mr. Blake for designs:
China form fruit basket, without handles & stand.
oval Cream Bowl—No. 888 of Book of Drawings.
oval rose-top Soup Terrine with listel band on cover, No. 2 Book of Drawings.
Butter boat, 2 handles, loose stand.

Among the articles mentioned in Mr. Wedgwood's last list for Mr. Blake to make designs from are the following eight, which have been either sent to him, or set out for him, agreeably to the preceding list recd., 8th Aug.; should the patterns be meant for the same, we of course imagine that only one of each is meant

for him—if otherwise, be pleased to mention it or enquire of Mr. Wedgwood
whether any other patterns are intended than those in his list recd. the 8th Aug.:

> oval Salad.
> square Do.
> round Do.
> new high oval sauce terrine and std.
> round cream bowl form Do   & Do.
> low oval Butter Boat.
> new oval Do.
> Butter Boat 2 handles fixed & std.

please to mention likewise whether the oval rose-top soup terrine with listel
band on cover, palm handles, No. 5 Book of Engravings, as noted in Mr.
Wedgwood's Mem. of 29 July, is still to be sent to Mr. Blake to make a Design
from, as it appears that he recd. No. 5 Book of Drawings from us in the first
Instance instead of No. 5 Book of Engravings. If Mr. Blake is to have the latter,
please to send us one up together with the others hereon noted.

The work was now proceeding faster; and two days later Blake sent his patient
wife to fetch yet more materials:

> 25 Oct. 1815. Mrs. Blake: 1 W.H. Basin 20 in.
> 1 Nurse Lamp with bason
> top & lip 1st Size.

By December great progress had been made:

> 5 December, 1815: Mr. Blake states that he intends very soon sending us some
> of the Drawings—he has Articles sufficient to go on with for the present.
> 13 Decr. 1815: Mr. Blake has left a packet of Drawings (forwarded herewith)
> from some of the articles, & states he shall very soon have completed Designs
> from all that he has.

No further references to Blake have been found in the agent's records, and it is
possible that by the end of the year the task of making the drawings had been
completed. The engravings were still to be made, and it seems to be clear that
these were all done during the year 1816. A set of twelve very early proofs was at
Etruria.[1] These are again on paper dated 1816, and have many pencil notes and
marks for corrections. Several of the articles illustrated had to be completely erased
and others engraved in their places. Blake's eighteen plates, most of them signed
Blake d. & sc., illustrated altogether 185 excellent examples of Wedgwood's pottery,

---

[1] Most of the Wedgwood archive has been transferred to the library of Keele University.

all designed for domestic purposes: none of them deserves Tatham's stricture, 'too elegant for use'. The reward that Blake received for his work has not been ascertained with certainty, but Wedgwood's ledgers shew under the date 11 November 1816, the entry:

William Blake, Engraver, London, £30 on account of engraving.

No other entry has been found, so that this may represent the whole amount that was paid.

The engravings are skilfully executed, but even Blake could not be expected to invest domestic utensils with much of his own feeling. The finished plates do not appear to have been included in any catalogue distributed by Wedgwood's to their customers, but to have been intended only for their own use. The whole set consists of thirty-one prints, the last thirteen not being executed by Blake. Numbers nineteen and twenty are signed by J. T. Wedgwood; the remainder are unsigned. Complete sets survived only at Etruria. One set, printed in 1820 (now in my collection by the kindness of the late Frank Wedgwood), was stitched into wrappers of rough brown paper and provided with a manuscript index. Other sets, printed in 1838 and 1840, shew many alterations, and various plates have been added. By 1838 an index had been printed. Eight of Blake's copper-plates have actually survived to the present day, but they have been altered and partly re-engraved. In the centre of one of them Blake's figure has been erased and a 'Wedge bed pan' has been put in its place.

It cannot be pretended that this letter from Blake has any literary merit. Its biographical interest, however, is considerable. No letter of his written between the years 1809 and 1818 was hitherto known to exist. After the failure of his exhibition in 1809 he lived for ten years in a state of extraordinary obscurity, and the extant records of his life are very scanty. It has been shewn by Professor G. E. Bentley, jr.,[1] that his chief source of income during the years 1814 to 1817 was from engraving Flaxman's outlines for *The Works Days and Theogony of Hesiod*, published in 1817. It is known also that he elaborated during 1815 three or four very splendid copies of his illuminated books and that the composition of his supreme symbolic work, *Jerusalem*, was proceeding at this time. These new records of the Wedgwood episode afford a glimpse of how the artist-poet provided some of the necessities of life. The plates of *Jerusalem* are temporarily laid aside and Blake is earning his bread in his room at 17 South Molton Street littered with *terrines*, *salads*, and *butter-boats*.

[1] *The Library* (1965), 5th ser. xx. 315–20.

VIII

A DESCRIPTIVE CATALOGUE[1]

BLAKE's exhibition of his own pictures, held in the shop of his brother James in Broad Street, Golden Square, in 1809, has for long been one of the best-known events in his life, and one of the most frequently described. The exhibition was patronized by few visitors, but these few included Charles Lamb, Robert Southey, Seymour Kirkup, and Crabb Robinson, whose remarks on it, particularly those of Crabb Robinson, have provided an unusually bright illumination of the incident— bright, that is, for any event at this period of Blake's life, notable in the main for its numerous dark places. Our knowledge of the exhibition is further extended by the existence of Blake's *Descriptive Catalogue*, in which he described and commented, sometimes at considerable length, on the nine frescoes and seven water-colour drawings which he chose to shew.

This catalogue was first reprinted with Gilchrist's *Life* in 1863, and was given again in the Nonesuch editions of Blake's writings, 1925, 1927, and 1957, the first of these containing reproductions of all the pictures, eleven in number, traced at the present time. Most writers on Blake have quoted from the *Catalogue* which, as Miss Mona Wilson has said in her *Life of Blake*, 'is not merely a commentary on the sixteen exhibits; it is a manifesto eulogizing Raphael and Michael Angelo at the expense of Titian and Correggio, Rubens and Rembrandt' (*Life*, 1927, p. 207). The opening date of the exhibition is fixed by the existence of a single-leaf typographical advertisement (see facsimile opposite), dated by Blake on the verso 15 May 1809, and in the *Catalogue* itself he announced that it would close on 29 September. Only two examples of the advertisement leaf are known to exist; one is now in the Bodleian Library (acquired in 1893). Gilchrist mentioned an example then (1863) in the possession of Alex. C. Weston, and this was included in the Burlington Fine Arts Club Exhibition in 1876; it was stated to bear the same date in Blake's hand and to be directed to Ozias Humphry, the miniaturist. This is no doubt identical with the copy now in the H. E. Huntington Library, California. It has been said that another is in the library of the Royal Academy, but a search there has proved this to be an error.

---

[1] First printed in *The Times Literary Supplement* (1942), xli. 456.

EXHIBITION

OF

𝕻aintings in 𝕱resco,

Poetical and Historical Inventions,

BY. WM. BLAKE.

THE ANCIENT BRITONS—Three Ancient Britons overthrowing the
Army of armed Romans; the Figures full as large as Life—
From the Welch Triades.

In the last Battle that Arthur fought, the most Beautiful was one
That return'd, and the most Strong another: with them also return'd
The most Ugly, and no other beside return'd from the bloody Field.

The most Beautiful, the Roman Warriors trembled before and worshipped:
The most Strong, they melted before him and dissolved in his presence:
The most Ugly they fled with outcries and contortion of their Limbs.

THE CANTERBURY PILGRIMS from *Chaucer*—a cabinet Picture in
Fresco—Thirty Figures on Horse-back, in a brilliant Morning Scene.

Two Pictures, representing grand Apotheoses of NELSON and PITT,
with variety of cabinet Pictures, unchangeable and permanent in
Fresco, and Drawings for Public Inspection and for Sale by Private
Contract, at

No. 28, Corner of BROAD STREET, *Golden-Square.*

"Fit Audience find tho' few" MILTON.

Admittance 2s. 6d. each Person, a discriptive Catalogue included. *Containing*
Ample Illustrations
on Art

Watts & Co. Printers, Southmolton St.

A

DESCRIPTIVE CATALOGUE

OF

PICTURES,

Poetical and Historical Inventions,

PAINTED BY

WILLIAM BLAKE,

IN.

WATER COLOURS,

BEING THE ANCIENT METHOD OF

FRESCO PAINTING RESTORED:

AND

DRAWINGS,

FOR PUBLIC INSPECTION,

AND FOR

Sale by Private Contract,

At No 8 Corner of Broad Street Golden Square

LONDON:

Printed by D. N. Shury, 7, Berwick-Street, Soho,
for J. BLAKE, 28, Broad-Street, Golden-Square.

1809.

The only 'copy' to be found there is a manuscript made by J. H. Anderdon, perhaps from the original now in the Bodleian, and inserted in his extra-illustrated set of the Royal Academy catalogues.

With this relatively large amount of information about the exhibition already available, it is all the more surprising that it should have been possible to announce in 1942 the discovery of further printed matter relating to it. In the course of work on a catalogue of Blake's pictures and drawings, Mr. Ruthven Todd noticed that when the painting of 'The Canterbury Pilgrims' was sold with the Thomas Butts collection at Foster's auction rooms in 1853 it was stated in the sale catalogue to be accompanied by 'the artist's explanations'. The lot was bought by Sir William Stirling-Maxwell for 10 guineas, and inquiries addressed to his son, the late Sir John Stirling-Maxwell, who still owned the picture, resulted in the loan of a small volume containing a bound copy of *A Descriptive Catalogue*[1] together with a printed leaf, hitherto unrecorded, advertising the *Catalogue*.

The leaf measures 13·9 × 16·5 cm., and has been folded down the centre for insertion in the book. (The sheet on which it has been mounted bears a watermark date 1820.) The text runs as follows:

A DESCRIPTIVE CATALOGUE
OF
BLAKE's EXHIBITION,
At No. 28, Corner of
BROAD-STREET,
GOLDEN-SQUARE.

THE grand Style of Art restored ; in FRESCO, or Water-colour Painting, and England protected from the too just imputation of being the Seat and Protectress of bad (that is blotting and blurring) Art.

In this Exhibition will be seen real Art, as it was left us by *Raphael* and *Albert Durer, Michael Angelo,* and *Julio Romano;* stripped from the Ignorances of *Rubens* and *Rembrandt, Titian* and *Correggio* ;

BY WILLIAM BLAKE.

The Descriptive Catalogue, Price 2s 6d. containing Mr. B's Opinions and Determinations on Art, very necessary to be known by Artists and Connoisseurs of all Ranks Every Purchaser of a Catalogue will be entitled, at the time of purchase, to view the Exhibition.

These Original Conceptions on Art, by an Original Artist, are Sold only at the Corner of BROAD STREET.

Admittance to the Exhibition 1 *Shilling; an Index to the Catalogue gratis.*

Printed by Watts & Bridgewater, Southmolton-street.

In this advertisement Blake expressed his prejudices against the art of Rubens and Rembrandt, Titian and Correggio, and in favour of Raphael and Albert Durer,

[1] Copy O described below. Now in the Stirling Collection, University of Glasgow.

Michelangelo and Julio Romano, prejudices due largely to his own lack of familiarity with the pictures of the artists he condemns. His views, shewing a remarkable degree both of ignorance and insight, are developed at considerable length in the *Descriptive Catalogue*. His reference to 'bad (that is blotting and blurring) Art' is also repeated in the *Catalogue*, where under Number VI, 'A Spirit vaulting from a cloud to turn and wind a fiery Pegasus—Shakespeare', he wrote: 'This picture was done many years ago, and was one of the first Mr. B. ever did in Fresco; fortunately or rather providentially he left it unblotted and unblurred, although molested continually by blotting and blurring demons; but he was also compelled to leave it unfinished for reasons that will be shewn in the following.'

In the other advertisement leaf it was announced: 'Admittance 2s. 6d. each Person a descriptive Catalogue included'. In the more recently discovered leaflet it is stated that the Catalogue costs 2s. 6d., and that: 'Every purchaser . . . will be entitled, at the time of purchase, to view the Exhibition'. But, lest this charge should seem excessive, the last line of the advertisement adds: 'Admittance to the Exhibition 1 Shilling; an Index to the Catalogue gratis'. Even this inducement was insufficient to attract many patrons, for the exhibition received little or no attention except for a virulent attack in Leigh Hunt's paper, *The Examiner*, published on 17 September, not long before it closed. Thomas Butts was, it seems, the only purchaser of any of the pictures exhibited, seven of them, and probably more, being afterwards in his collection.

The two advertisement leaves appear to have been printed in the same shop in South Molton Street, where Blake also had his single apartment, though the name of the firm is given as 'Watts and Co.' on one, and as 'Watts and Bridgewater' on the other. The *Descriptive Catalogue* itself was printed by D. N. Shury, Soho. The offer of 'an Index to the Catalogue gratis' suggests that there may be yet another separate leaf to be discovered, though this would probably be merely an offprint of the index given on the fourth leaf of the *Catalogue*.

Full bibliographical details of the first advertisement and the *Catalogue* are to be found in my *Bibliography of Blake*, Grolier Club, New York, 1921. Since that date, however, a number of additional copies of the *Catalogue* have come to light, and this opportunity may be taken of providing a revised census of copies. Nineteen copies are recorded. Some of these have the address of the exhibition added on the title-page in Blake's hand, and a correction in the text on page 64. The careful addition of the address to so many copies, and the emphasis on the address in the two advertisement leaves, suggests that Blake was fearful lest its not being well enough known should discourage visitors. It is interesting to notice that Blake still had a spare copy of the *Catalogue* by him as late as 1824, which he gave to young Frederick Tatham in June of that year.

(A) British Museum Reading Room. Acquired 29 March 1864. Press-mark C.31, h.21. Bound in morocco, gilt, 18 × 11 cm. No manuscript addition on title-page.

(B) British Museum Print Room. Inscribed 'Presented by William Smith Esq., 1856'. Bound in cloth, morocco spine, 18 × 10·5 cm. With manuscript addition on title-page.

(C) G. L. Keynes. Probably to be identified with a copy offered by Messrs. Lowe Brothers, Birmingham, for 7*s*. 6*d*. in a catalogue issued in February 1915. It was sold in 1916 by Messrs. Maggs Brothers for £13 to the late William Bateson, F.R.S., who gave it to me in 1922. Stitched in its original blue wrappers, untrimmed, 19 × 11·5 cm. With manuscript addition on title-page, and correction on p. 64. This seems to be the only copy which has remained, except for some repairs to the wrapper, exactly as it was issued in 1809.

(D) H. E. Huntington Library, California. From the T. G. Arthur Library, sold at Sotheby's, 15 July 1914 (lot 45, G. D. Smith, £24. 10*s*.). Bound in brown morocco, gilt edges, by Bedford.

(E) Thomas Boddington copy, sold at Sotheby's, 4 November 1896 (lot 96, W. Browne, 5 gns.). Bound in morocco. Probably the same copy sold for William Cowan at Sotheby's, 4 December 1912 (lot 849, Quaritch, £4). Bound in morocco, gilt edges, 19 × 11 cm. With manuscript addition on title-page. Not traced.

(F) Beckford-Hamilton Palace copy. Sold at Sotheby's, 4 July 1882 (Quaritch, £9). Traded to America, and bought later by G. D. Smith who sold it to Felix Isman. Sold again in 1932 to A. S. W. Rosenbach, from whom it was acquired by Chauncey B. Tinker, Yale University. Bound in green morocco, gilt, marbled edges. With manuscript addition on title-page, and correction on p. 64. Exhibited at the Grolier Club, 1905 (no. 36 in the catalogue).

(G) Fitzwilliam Museum, Cambridge, presented by the late Charles Fairfax Murray. Bound with the original wrappers in blue morocco, gilt, untrimmed, 19 × 11·5 cm. With manuscript addition on title-page.

(H) Bodleian Library, Oxford, bequeathed by Francis Douce in 1835. Bound in half-calf, 18 × 11 cm. With manuscript addition on title-page, and correction on p. 64.

(I) Robert Balmanno copy. Afterwards in the E. W. Hooper Collection, and bequeathed by Hooper to his daughter, Mrs. Greely S. Curtis, jr., Boston,

Mass. Given to the Houghton Library, Harvard University, by Mrs. Ward Thoron in 1951. Bound with an uncoloured copy of *Songs of Innocence* (*Census*, Keynes and Wolf, copy U), and *The Prologue and Characters of Chaucer's Pilgrims*, 1812, 19 × 11·5 cm. The flyleaf of the volume has a watermark dated 1818.

(J) B. B. Macgeorge copy, sold at Sotheby's, 1 July 1924 (lot 124, Dobell, £9. 10*s*.). Offered by Messrs. Maggs Brothers in a catalogue in November 1924, for £21. Afterwards in the collection of Willis Vickery, and then in that of the late A. Edward Newton, sold at the Parke-Bernet Galleries, New York, 17 April 1941 (lot 149, T. J. Gannon, $275). Bound in red morocco, gilt edges, by Rivière. With manuscript addition on title-page, and correction on p. 64. Now in the Paul Mellon Collection.

(K) Lessing J. Rosenwald. John Linnell's copy, bound with a copy of *Poetical Sketches*, and inscribed on the flyleaf 'John Linnell, 38, Porchester Terrace, Bayswater, 1846'. Below is written 'To James T. L., 1866', i.e. given by Linnell to his son, James T. Linnell. Now in the Lessing J. Rosenwald Collection, Library of Congress, Washington, D.C.

(L) W. A. White copy. Bound in green morocco by Zaehnsdorf, untrimmed, with the original wrappers preserved. With manuscript addition on title-page, and correction on p. 64. Sold at Sotheby's, 14 July 1895 (Quaritch, 3 gns.), and acquired by W. A. White. Bought after his death by A. S. W. Rosenbach, who disposed of it in 1929 to Lessing J. Rosenwald. Now in the Lessing J. Rosenwald Collection, Library of Congress, Washington, D.C.

(M) A. S. W. Rosenbach. From the library of W. E. Moss, sold at Sotheby's, 2 February 1937 (lot 196, Rosenbach, £50). The pages, 19 × 11 cm., are inlaid throughout on larger leaves. Bound in brown morocco, gilt, by Bedford. Manuscript addition on title-page.

(N) E. J. E. Tunmer, sold at Sotheby's, 15 June 1937 (lot 346, Robinson, £37). Offered for sale by Messrs. Robinson, Pall Mall, in March 1938, for £60. Acquired by Otis T. Bradley, New York. Sold at the Parke-Bernet Galleries, New York, 6 November 1944 (lot 78) and again, 4 October 1946 (lot 46). Bound in cloth, edges untrimmed. Perhaps the same copy, bound in 'old cloth', sold at the Parke-Bernet Galleries, 29 January 1952 (lot 51). Acquired by Dr. B. Juel-Jensen and later resold. Not traced.

(O) Sir John Stirling-Maxwell, Bt. From the collection of Thomas Butts, sold at Foster's, 29 June 1853, with the tempera of 'The Canterbury Pilgrims' (lot 93, Stirling, £10. 10*s*.). Then in the collection of Sir William Stirling-Maxwell; now in Glasgow University Library. Bound in red quarter-roan and cloth, with the leaflet here first described, top edges gilt, others untrimmed, 18·4 × 11 cm., book-plate of William Stirling of Keir, i.e. Sir William Stirling-Maxwell. With manuscript addition on title-page, and correction on p. 64.

(P) Tatham copy. Inscribed on the title-page, in Tatham's hand, 'Frederick [Ta]tham | from the Author | June 12, 1824'. Carries the signature 'J. Mitford' and the note: 'Burton opened 5 Ap 67.' No inscription by Blake on the title-page and no correction on p. 64. Sold with the Phillipps collection of printed books, Sotheby's, 25 November 1946 (lot 27, Quaritch, £85). Next in the collection of Arthur Randle and resold at Sotheby's, 1 October 1948 (lot 34, Rosenbach, £95). Now in the collection of Mrs. Landon K. Thorne, New York. Bound in calf, and lettered *Blake's Catalogue of Pictures*.

(Q) Inserted in the J. H. Anderdon extra-illustrated volume of the Royal Academy catalogues, now in the library of the Royal Academy, is a cutting from an undated bookseller's catalogue, offering a copy of *A Descriptive Catalogue . . .* 'calf neat . . . 6s. Presentation copy from the Author and MS. Memoranda by Mr. M., &c., &c.' The only 'Mr. M.' who would have been likely to receive a copy from Blake would appear to be Benjamin Heath Malkin, author of *A Father's Memoirs of His Child*, 1806. This cannot be identified with any copy listed above.

(R) Robert Arthington of Leeds copy, sold at Sotheby's, 17 May 1866 (lot 21, £1. 9s.). Possibly later in the possession of A. Anderdon Weston, and to be identified with a copy described above.

(S) Charles Lamb bound his copy with Elia's *Confessions of a Drunkard*, Southey's *Wat Tyler*, and the *Poems* of Rochester and Lady Winchelsea. It was bought with others of Lamb's books from Edward Moxon by Charles Welford, of Bartlett and Welford, and taken to the United States. In 1848 it was included in a 'Catalogue of Charles Lamb's Library for sale by Bartlett and Welford', as: 'Tracts Miscellaneous, 1 thick volume 12mo . . . 12 tracts with the MS list of Contents.' Then sold at auction by Carley, Keese, and Hill of New York, 4 October 1848, no. 376, to Campbell ($4·25). Not traced further.

Robert Southey probably possessed a copy, and Crabb Robinson records that he purchased four, but none of these has been identified.

IX

WILLIAM BLAKE WITH CHARLES LAMB
AND HIS CIRCLE[1]

IT is always interesting to speculate on the contacts and reactions upon one another of great contemporaries, and to wonder why this one or that could not see the merits of the other, which to us at the distance of a 100 or 200 years seem so plain or even transcendent. So it has appeared to me to be worth while to string together the rather scrappy evidences (which are all that we possess) connecting William Blake with some of his contemporaries, and no contemporaries could be more appropriate for the Charles Lamb Society than Lamb himself and some of his immediate friends and acquaintances.

The following are some unpublished lines by Blake:

> A Woman Scaly and a Man all hairy
> Is such a match as he who dares
> Will find the woman's scales will
> scrape off the man's hairs.

These strange lines are unpublished because they have only been recently deciphered by the late Max Plowman among the dim pencillings found in Blake's manuscript notebook. The lines taken by themselves sound senseless, and many would be reluctant to accept them as the serious utterance of a great poet and artist. Let it, however, be understood that the lines were written down in a private notebook, most of the contents of which were not intended for publication, so that we are really eavesdropping and violating the privacy of Blake's chamber. Nevertheless, these apparently idle words can be given meaning if they are correlated with the habit of Blake's mind and his symbolic system. The 'Man all hairy' may be Orc, the Spirit of Revolt in man's nature, a personification who plays an important part in all Blake's symbolic works.[2] The 'Woman Scaly' is the evil side of sex and materialism, a covering of scales being always an attribute of Blake's Satan, the opponent of the Imagination and of the world of the Spirit, which had so much

---

[1] A paper read to the Charles Lamb Society, 9 October 1943.
[2] See *America*, Preludium (*Complete Writings*, ed. Keynes, 1966, p. 196).

more meaning and value for Blake than any of our mundane and material affairs. The words quoted express, therefore, the results of a conflict between two great opposed forces, material and spiritual, the kind of conflict with which Blake's mind was obsessed and which gave rise to much of his greatest, albeit most obscure, utterances. Orc might have won the battle against a mere scaly Satan; but a Woman Scaly, Blake feared, would scrape off the hairs of Orc, and so emasculate the Spirit of Revolt.

These new lines by Blake are quoted not for mystification, but in order to illustrate the queerness of his mind, and to emphasize the gulf that was necessarily fixed in the way of an easy understanding between Blake and a person such as the Patron Saint of the Charles Lamb Society, or between Blake and the other members of Lamb's circle.

It seems improbable that Blake was known to Lamb or most others of his circle until 1809,[1] the year in which Blake held his exhibition of pictures at the house of his brother James, the hosier, 28 Broad Street, Golden Square. The exhibition was open from May until September, and Blake had high hopes that it would serve to spread his fame and obtain him the recognition that he knew he deserved. In fact it did exactly the opposite. The pictures had few visitors, and the only public notice given to it was in an article published in *The Examiner* by Robert Hunt, brother of the editor Leigh Hunt, on 17 September 1809, not long before the exhibition closed. In this article Blake is described as 'an unfortunate lunatic whose personal inoffensiveness secures him from confinement', and his now celebrated *Descriptive Catalogue* was condemned as 'a farrago of nonsense, unintelligibleness, and egregious vanity, the wild effusions of a distempered brain'.[2] Among the few visitors was Henry Crabb Robinson, a tireless hunter of interesting characters and disseminator of literary and artistic gossip. In his well-known Diary he recalled that before writing an account of Blake for a German magazine he went to see the gallery of Blake's paintings in Carnaby Market, that is in Broad Street, Golden Square. 'These paintings', he wrote, 'filled several rooms of an ordinary dwelling house. The entrance was two shillings and sixpence, catalogue included. I was

[1] In 1807 Lamb's *Tales from Shakespeare* appeared in two volumes with a number of engraved plates which have been persistently attributed to Blake by generations of booksellers. These illustrations were, however, designed by William Mulready, and the technique of the engraving does not suggest Blake's work. It may be safely assumed that Blake had no hand in them.

[2] Hunt had also been attacking the 'extravagances' of Blake's friend, Fuseli, and had indeed criticized them both in an adverse review of the edition of Blair's *Grave* illustrated by Blake. This was published in an early number of *The Examiner* (7 August 1808) and Fuseli is there characterized as 'a frantic'. It was all part of a press campaign, in Professor Edmund Blunden's view.

deeply interested by the catalogue as well as the pictures. I took four, telling the brother, I hoped he would let me come in again. He said: "Oh, as often as you please." I daresay such a thing had never happened before, or did afterwards.' Crabb Robinson added later that he took four copies of the *Catalogue* because he 'wished to send it to Germany, and to give a copy to Lamb and others'. We may be sure that he did not remain silent about his visit, and he particularly mentions that at this time 'I frequently saw Lamb, Hazlitt, indeed most of my old acquaintances as well the literary as my family connections'. It seems fairly clear, therefore, that his interest so volubly expressed, together with his gifts of the *Descriptive Catalogue*, stimulated others to visit Blake's exhibition, and these included Lamb and Robert Southey. Crabb Robinson did not meet Blake himself until many years later in 1825, and there is no evidence that Lamb ever met him at any time. Crabb Robinson recorded, however, that Lamb considered Blake's description of his 'Canterbury Pilgrims' 'the finest criticism he had ever read of Chaucer's poem', and Lamb himself, writing some years later in May 1824, to the Quaker poet, Bernard Barton, gave his own opinion as follows:

Blake is a real name, I assure you, and a most extraordinary man if he be still living. He is the Robert Blake [meaning William], whose wild designs accompany a splendid folio edition of the Night Thoughts. . . . He paints in water colours marvellous strange pictures, visions of his brain, which he asserts that he has seen. They have great merit. He has *seen* the old Welsh bards on Snowdon . . . and has painted them from memory (I have seen his paintings). . . . His Pictures—one in particular, the Canterbury Pilgrims (far above Stothard's)—have great merit, but hard, dry, yet with grace. He has written a Catalogue of them, with a most spirited criticism on Chaucer, but mystical and full of Vision. . . . There is one [song] to a tiger, which I have heard recited . . . which is glorious, but alas! I have not the book; for the man is flown, whither I know not—to Hades or a Mad House. But I must look on him as one of the most extraordinary persons of the age. . . .

In this same year, 1824, Lamb obtained a copy of Blake's poem, 'The Chimney Sweeper' from the *Songs of Innocence* for James Montgomery's *Chimney Sweeper's Friend and Climbing Boy's Annual*, and regarded it as 'the flower of the set'. Of Montgomery, Crabb Robinson wrote in 1812: 'He looks like a methodist parson, and has what Wordsworth expressed [as] the appearance of a feeble and amiable man.' This agrees with the impression given of this sentimental poet, hymn-writer, and journalist in the *Memoirs* of him published in 1854, where we read: 'When [Blair's] Grave was afterwards published, with Blake's splendid illustrations, he [Mont-

The Dog.

Pub.d June 18. 1805. by R. Phillips. N.o 6. Bridge Street Black-Friers

gomery] became the possessor of a copy; but, as several of the plates were hardly of such a nature as to render the book proper to lie on a parlour table for general inspection, he sold his copy for the subscription price; a circumstance which he often regretted, as the death of the artist soon afterwards rendered the work both scarce and proportionately more valuable. Those persons who have once seen these illustrations will readily recollect the print representing the angel of the "last trump" descending to awake the dead. . . . The solemn absurdity of this conception, and the ingenious manner in which it is executed, afforded Montgomery a very amusing topic of conversation on one occasion when we were present.' Nevertheless this feeble and amiable man, who could sneer so amusingly at Blake, was not above stealing from the object of his ridicule, for the *Climbing Boy's Annual* contains in addition to 'The Chimney Sweeper', obtained for him by Lamb, a plagiarism of Blake's 'The Dream', which is a version of the poem extended or, as Lamb called it in his letter to Barton, 'awkwardly paraphrased from Blake'. Crabb Robinson's meeting with Blake in 1825 and his subsequent cultivation of Blake's acquaintance no doubt led to many talks on the subject with his friends, so that Lamb would soon have been enlightened, learning that Blake's first name was William, not Robert, and that he was neither dead nor in a mad-house, but still very active, and indeed at the culmination of his creative career in his designs for *The Book of Job* and Dante. The final recorded incident connecting Blake with Lamb was on 8 January 1828, when Crabb Robinson called on Blake's widow and bought two prints of 'The Canterbury Pilgrims' for $2\frac{1}{2}$ guineas each, meaning one of them for Lamb, who actually received on 22 May 1828 the picture he had so much admired nearly twenty years before.

We must now go back to the year 1805, in which was published a duodecimo volume containing the juvenile ballads of the poet of Eartham, William Hayley, illustrated with five engravings by Blake. The frontispiece illustrates the ballad of 'The Dog' in which the faithful Fido leaps into the water in order to save his master, Edward, from a crocodile waiting unnoticed beneath him (Plate 22). This book was reviewed by Robert Southey in *The Annual Register*. He ridiculed the ballads, and added: 'The poet has had the singular good fortune to meet with a painter capable of doing full justice to his conceptions; and in fact when we look at the delectable frontispiece to this volume which represents Edward starting back, Fido *volant*, and the crocodile *rampant*, with a mouth open like a bootjack to receive him, we know not whether most to admire the genius of Mr. William Blake or of Mr. William Hayley.' Southey concluded his review: 'We could not help quoting O'Keefe's song—Hayley-gaily gamboraly higgledy piggledy galloping draggle-tail'd dreary dun.' It was easy to ridicule Blake's pictures, but Southey did not know the circumstances in which they were produced—Blake's genius labouring in Hayley's fetters. He would perhaps have shewn more understanding if he could have read Blake's epigrams jotted down in his notebook at a later period to relieve his feelings:

> Of H[ayley]'s birth this was the happy lot,
> His Mother on his Father him begot,

and

> Thy Friendship oft has made my heart to ake:
> Do be my enemy for Friendship's sake.

To follow Southey's further relations with Blake we must go on to the year 1811 to attend a party at Lamb's house on 24 July. Crabb Robinson is again our informant. 'Returned late to Charles Lamb's. Found a very large party there. Southey had been with Blake, and admired both his designs and his poetic talents, at the same time that he held him for a decided madman. Blake, he says, spoke of his visions with the diffidence that is usual with such people, and did not seem to expect that he should be believed. He shewed Southey a perfectly mad poem called *Jerusalem*—Oxford Street is in Jerusalem.' It is interesting to learn from this that Robert Southey was the first member of the Lamb circle whose curiosity and interest in Blake led him to seek him out in his own surroundings. Southey had in 1811 already lived for some years at Greta Hall, Coleridge's house near Keswick, but in this year he undertook a three months' journey round England, and it was in the course of this that he visited Blake in London. Blake evidently sensed that he was the object of a somewhat patronizing curiosity, and talked with what seemed to Southey the diffidence of a diseased mind. It is much more probable that Blake gave this impression because, being accustomed to contacts with minds less intelligent and more commonplace than his own, he did not attempt to impress on his visitor a view of art and poetry which he knew would not be understood. He did not want it to be understood—this was one of Blake's great failings—and though he produced for Southey some leaves of his great poem *Jerusalem*, then only partly composed, he did so more to mystify and confound than to enlighten. What could Southey know of the building of Golgonooza, the City of Art and Imagination?

> What are those golden builders doing? Where was the burying-place
> Of soft Ethinthus? near Tyburn's fatal Tree? is that
> Mild Zion's hill's most ancient promontory, near mournful

Ever weeping Paddington? is that Calvary and Golgotha
Becoming a building of pity and compassion? Lo!
The stones are pity, and the bricks, well wrought affections
Enamel'd with love & kindness, & the tiles engraven gold,
Labour of merciful hands: the beams & rafters are forgiveness:
The mortar & cement of the work, tears of honesty: the nails
And the screws & iron braces are well wrought blandishments
And well contrived words, firm fixing, never forgotten,
Always comforting the remembrance: the floors, humility:
The cielings, devotion: the hearths, thanksgiving.
Prepare the furniture, O Lambeth, in thy pitying looms,
The curtains, woven tears & sighs wrought into lovely forms
For comfort; there the secret furniture of Jerusalem's chamber
Is wrought. Lambeth! the Bride, the Lamb's Wife, loveth thee.
Thou art one with her & knowest not of self in thy supreme joy.
Go on, builders in hope, tho' Jerusalem wanders far away
Without the gate of Los, among the dark Satanic wheels.

(*Jerusalem*, plate 12)

No wonder Southey was mystified and, in spite of himself, impressed. The only
Lamb that Blake knew was the Lamb of God, and to him the Holy Name meant
the creative imagination and the divine world of art. His poetry was overlaid with
a symbolism compounded of elements from the Celtomaniacs and the Druidists,
from the Gnostics, the Cabalists, the Hindoos, from Jacob Boehme, and from
Swedenborg. Oxford Street is mentioned in a passage on plate 38 of *Jerusalem*:

There is in Albion a Gate of Precious stones and gold
Seen only by Emanations, by vegetations viewless:
Bending across the road of Oxford Street, it from Hyde Park
To Tyburn's deathful shades admits the wandering souls
Of multitudes who die from Earth: this Gate can not be found
By Satan's Watch-fiends, tho' they search numbering every grain
Of sand on Earth every night, they never find this Gate.

This would mystify Southey as much as 'mournful ever weeping Paddington',
and he could not know that the topography of London and of the Holy Land are
inextricably mixed in *Jerusalem*, both bearing a heavy burden of symbolic meaning.

Nearly twenty years after this visit to Blake, Southey described his experience
to Caroline Bowles, a minor poetess, who was afterwards to become the wife of his
declining years.

I have nothing [he wrote] of Blake's but his designs for Blair's *Grave*, which were published with the poem. His still stranger designs for his own compositions in verse were not ready for sale when I saw him, nor did I ever hear that they were so. [This evidently refers to the then unfinished *Jerusalem*, which Blake shewed him. It is significant that Blake did not apparently care to shew him any of his other earlier books, many of which could have been bought for modest sums.] Much as he is to be admired, he was at that time so evidently insane, that the predominant feeling in conversing with him, or even looking at him, could only be sorrow and compassion. His wife partook of his insanity in the same way (but more happily) as Taylor[1] the pagan's wife caught her husband's paganism. . . . I came away from the visit with so sad a feeling that I never repeated it. . . . You could not have delighted in him—his madness was too evident, too fearful. It gave his eyes an expression such as you would expect to see in one who was possessed.

A few years after writing this letter, Southey reverted to the subject of Blake in volumes six and seven of *The Doctor*, published in 1837–47, a vast, garrulous, facetious repository of curious information. He quoted from the *Descriptive Catalogue* a piece about the now lost picture of 'The Ancient Britons' and the 'Mad Song' from *Poetical Sketches*, written when Blake was a boy, introducing him as 'That painter of great, but insane, genius'. He also related John Varley's account of how Blake painted a portrait of the Ghost of a Flea, concluding with some very trite reflections of his own. It is of interest to notice that in quoting the now famous 'Mad Song' he introduced the emendation 'rustling birds of dawn' for the 'beds of dawn' in the printed text of the second stanza. It may be inferred that Southey used one of the copies of *Poetical Sketches* in which Blake had made this correction.[2]

We must depend again on Crabb Robinson's reporting for an opinion of Blake from one of the most interesting of Lamb's circle, William Hazlitt. On 10 March 1811 Robinson shewed Hazlitt Blake's designs for Young's *Night Thoughts*, published in 1797, and reported:

He saw no merit in them as designs. I read him some of the poems. He was much struck with them and expressed himself with his usual strength and singularity. 'They are beautiful,' he said, 'and only too deep for the vulgar. He has no sense of the ludicrous, and, as to a God, a worm crawling in a privy is as

[1] i.e. Thomas Taylor, the Platonist (1758–1835), with whom Blake may have been acquainted. This possibility is closely examined by Professor G. M. Harper in his book *The Neoplatonism of William Blake*, Oxford University Press, 1961.

[2] See p. 38 of the present volume.

worthy an object as any other, all being to him indifferent. So to Blake the Chimney Sweeper, etc. He is ruined by vain struggles to get rid of what presses on his brain—he attempts at impossibilities.' I added: 'He is like a man who lifts a burden too heavy for him; he bears it an instant, it then falls on him and crushes him.'

Characteristically Hazlitt's acute mind had seized quickly on some of Blake's weak points, while admiring unfeignedly the beauty of his verse. About the year 1784 Blake had attempted a satire on contemporary society in the form of a burlesque novel known as *An Island in the Moon*, and there is certainly some fun in *The Marriage of Heaven and Hell*, but otherwise we possess little evidence that he had a well-developed sense of humour.[1] This is not maintaining that a sense of humour is necessary for the flowering of poetic genius, and indeed it is impossible to imagine Blake allowing himself to be distracted by facetious trivialities. A deep seriousness pervaded all his thoughts and actions, and had he been a more ordinary person we might justly have complained that he took himself too seriously. Hazlitt was also right that Blake often attempted impossibilities. Had he known him better he might have added that *though* he attempted impossibilities, particularly in his pictures, he frequently succeeded. The engravings in Young's *Night Thoughts* which Crabb Robinson shewed to Hazlitt are some of Blake's least successful efforts, and would not be expected to impress so good a critic. But had he seen the great series of colour prints now in the Tate Gallery, the designs for *Paradise Lost*, the *Illustrations of the Book of Job*, or the water-colours for Dante, then he must have made some concession to Blake's claims.

Crabb Robinson himself was quite unable to appreciate Blake's paintings and frankly confessed to this. On one occasion after Blake's death he was offered three of his designs for £5, but rejected them as too dear. Robinson was, indeed, himself puzzled to know why he, so logical and unimaginative, was so much interested by Blake's visionary and elusive mind, and in spite of having decided, even before they had met, that Blake was mad. The explanation must surely be that he had convincingly detected the blend of intellect with true inspiration in Blake's poetry, and enjoyed the attempt to discover from his conversation the source and quality of his genius. It must be admitted that Blake's conversation as reported by Crabb Robinson was uncompromising in its assumption of the character of prophet and visionary. He made no concessions to his visitor's possible lack of sympathy and understanding, and talked of his strange doctrines and his visions of Voltaire and Shakespeare without any of the diffidence noted by Southey.

[1] Though see p. 220 for John Linnell's opinion on this point.

The subject of Blake's conversation introduces one of the most disappointing of his contacts with Lamb's circle; disappointing, that is, in the absence of any detailed account of what took place. This is Blake's meeting, or meetings, with Coleridge. In the year 1818 Charles Augustus Tulk, an eminent follower of Emmanuel Swedenborg, had lent Coleridge his copy of the *Songs of Innocence and of Experience*.[1] The exact date of this is fixed by a postscript written by Coleridge in a letter to H. F. Cary:[2]

HIGHGATE, *February 6, 1818*

. . . PS. I have this morning been reading a strange publication—*viz*. Poems with very wild and interesting pictures as swathing, etched (I suppose) but it is said printed and painted by the author, W. Blake. He is a man of Genius—and I apprehend a Swedenborgian—certainly a mystic *emphatically*. You perhaps smile at *my* calling another poet a *Mystic*; but verily I am in the very mire of common-place common-place compared with Mr. Blake, apo- or rather ana-calyptic Poet, and Painter!

When Coleridge returned the book to Tulk he wrote a letter giving an elaborate critique of the poems. He evidently thought highly of them, and marked them in order of merit. Top marks he gave to 'The Little Black Boy'. The whole letter is as follows:

To C. A. Tulk Esq[r] (or Mrs. Tulk)
    St. John's Lodge
       Regent's Park

HIGHGATE, *Thursday evening, 1818*

Blake's Poems—I begin with my Dyspathies, that I may forget them: and have uninterrupted space for Loves and Sympathies.

Title-page and the following emblem contain all the faults of the Drawings with as few beauties as could be in the composition of a man who was capable of such faults + such beauties. The faults—despotism in symbols, amounting in the title page to the $\mu\iota\sigma\eta\tau\acute{\epsilon}o\nu$[3] and occasionally regular unmodified Lines of the Inanimate, sometimes as the effect of rigidity and sometimes of exosseation—like a wet tendon. So likewise the ambiguity of the Drapery. Is it a garment—or the body incised and scored out? The Limpness (= the effect of Vinegar on an egg) in the upper one of the two prostrate figures on the Title-page, and the *eye*-likeness of the twig posteriorly on the second, and the strait line down the waist-

---

[1] Formerly in the library of Lord Rothschild, who kindly allowed me to transcribe Coleridge's letter.
[2] *Coleridge Select Poetry and Prose* (ed. Stephen Potter, London, Nonesuch Press, 1933).
[3] i.e. the thing one must hate.

coat of pinky gold beaters' skin in the next drawing, with the I-don't-know-whatness of the countenance as if the mouth had been formed by the habit of placing the tongue, not contemptuously, but stupidly, between the lower gums and the lower jaw—these are the only *repulsive* faults I have noticed. The figure, however, of the second leaf (abstracted from the *expression* of the Countenance, given it by something about the mouth and the interspace from the lower lip to the chin) is such as only a master, learned in his art, could produce.

> N.B.—1 signifies, It gave me pleasure.
> 1 still greater.
> 11 and greater still.
> θ in the highest degree.
> o in the lowest.

Shepherd 1 Spring 1 (last stanza 1)
Holy Thursday 11 Laughing Song 1
Nurses Song 1 The Divine Image θ
The Lamb 1 The Little Black Boy θ: yea, θ + θ!
Infant Joy 11 (n.b. for the 3 last lines I should wish 'When wilt thou smile', or, 'O smile, O smile! I'll sing the while'—For a Babe two days old does not, cannot, *smile*—and Innocence and the very works of nature must go together. Infancy is too holy a thing to be ornamented.
Echoing Green 1 (the figures 1, and of the second leaf 11).
The Cradle Song 1
The School Boy 11 Night θ
On another's Sorrow 1 A Dream?
The little Boy lost 1 (the drawing 1)
The little boy found 1 The Blossom o
The Chimney Sweeper o The v. of the ancient Bard o
Introduction 1 Earth's Answer 1
Infant sorrow 1 The Clod and the Pebble 1
The garden of Love 1 The fly 1 The Tyger 1
A little Boy lost 1 Holy Thursday 1
p. 13 [The Angel] o Nurse's Song o The little girl lost And found (the ornaments most exquisite! the poem 1) Chimney Sweeper in the Snow o To Tirzah and The Poison Tree 1 and yet o. A little girl lost—o (I would have had it omitted—not for the want of innocence in the poem, but by the too probable want of it in many readers).
London 1 The sick Rose 1 *The little Vagabond—*

Tho' I cannot approve altogether of this last poem and have been inclined to think that the error which is most *likely* to beset the Scholars of Em. Sw. is that of utterly *de*merging the Tremendous incompatibilities with an evil will that arise out of the essential Holiness of the abysmal Aseity, in the Love of the eternal *Person*—and thus giving temptation to weaker minds to sink this Love itself into *good nature*—yet still I disapprove the mood of mind in this wild poem so much less than I do the servile, blind-worm, wrap-rascal Scurf-coat & *fear* of the *modern Saints* (whose whole Being is a Lie, to themselves as well as to their Brethren) that I should laugh with good conscience in watching a Saint of the new stamp, one of the First stars of our eleemosynary Advertisements groaning in—wind-pipe! and with the whites of his Eyes upraised at the *audacity* of this poem!—Anything rather than *this* degradation[1] of Humanity, and there-in of the incarnate Divinity!

S. T. C.

　　　　　0 means that I am perplexed and have no opinion.
　　　　　1 with which how can we utter 'Our Father'?[1]

A few years later, in 1826, Crabb Robinson told Dorothy Wordsworth in a letter, 'Coleridge has visited Blake, and I am told talks finely about him'. Three years after this, in 1829, and about eighteen months after Blake's death, an article headed 'The Inventions of William Blake, Painter and Poet' appeared in the *London University Magazine*. It is unsigned, and no clue to its author has been discovered, though it is clearly by someone who knew and understood Blake well. Perhaps it was by Tulk himself who was a supporter of London University. The writer regarded Blake as a great genius, unjustly neglected by his own nation, and saw in him much hope for the future of English art. 'We have a confident hope,' he wrote, 'that Coleridge, Blake and Flaxman are the forerunners of a more elevated and purer system, which has even now begun to take root in the breast of the English nation; they have laid a foundation for future minds—Coleridge, for the development of a more internal philosophy—Blake and Flaxman, for a purer and

---

[1] The late J. H. Wicksteed made the following remarks on this letter quoted by his permission: 'I suggest that the full significance of this unique commentary by a unique mind does not emerge on a first reading, and that a footnote or so would be a considerable help to the average reader. I suggest, for instance, a note on the word *aseity*, which is not common enough to be in the first issue of the *Concise Oxford Dictionary*, but is adequately treated in the *Shorter Oxford Dictionary*. It is not Greek (as Atheist, Agnostic, Amoral, etc.), but Latin, *a se*, by itself, or himself, i.e. not proceeding from, or created by, something more basically real or essential than itself. The whole letter exhibits S. T. C. struggling to express his own penetrating mind in "shock" response to W. B's, and in such a way as to be intelligible and acceptable to a good, but not outstanding, contemporary intelligence. Incidentally it fails to establish its intrinsic worth with our age just because it fails to realise the profound element of Blakean humour mingled with Blake's scathing tongue. It is Swedenborg who is almost humourless, not Blake, and S. T. C. reads W. B. in the misleading light of Swedenborg.'

more ennobling sentiment in works of art.' He then discusses Blake's poetry, quoting several of the *Songs* and also parts of the exquisite *Book of Thel*. Finally, in a footnote at the end, he added: 'Blake and Coleridge, when in company, seemed like congenial beings of another sphere, breathing for a while on our earth; which may easily be perceived from the similarity of thought pervading their works.' There we are tantalizingly abandoned, for no echo of this divine conversation has come down to us. All opinions of Coleridge's contemporaries seem to agree that he was not a good listener, but it may be that Blake's conversation was arresting enough even to break the flow of Coleridge's eloquence.

It would be possible to write an essay on the similarities between Coleridge and Blake; possible, that is, for one who knows Coleridge's mind and writings more intimately than I do. There is, however, one passage in Coleridge to which Walter Pater drew attention owing to its being comparable to one of Blake's most famous designs. It is the passage in *The Ancient Mariner* describing the re-inspiriting of the dead men on the ship:

> The helmsman steered, the ship moved on;
> Yet never a breeze up-blew;
> The mariners all 'gan work the ropes,
> Where they were wont to do;
> They raised their limbs like lifeless tools—
> We were a ghastly crew.

> 'I fear thee, ancient Mariner!'
> Be calm, thou Wedding-Guest!
> 'Twas not those souls that fled in pain,
> Which to their corses came again,
> But a troop of spirits blest:

> For when it dawn'd—they dropped their arms,
> And cluster'd round the mast;
> Sweet sounds rose slowly through their mouths,
> And from their bodies pass'd.

> Around, around, flew each sweet sound,
> Then darted to the Sun;
> Slowly the sounds came back again,
> Now mix'd, now one by one.

Sometimes a-dropping from the sky
I heard the skylark sing;
Sometimes all little birds that are,
How they seem'd to fill the sea and air
With their sweet jargoning!

And now 'twas like all instruments,
Now like a lonely flute;
And now it is an angel's song,
That makes the Heavens be mute.

It is perhaps unnecessary to add that the comparison is between this passage and Blake's design, in the *Illustrations of the Book of Job*, of 'When the Morning Stars sang together'. Both the poem and the picture are at the climax of a drama of spiritual horror. Job and the Ancient Mariner have both been down into the pit to emerge at last to a scene of heavenly glory. There is both a superficial pictorial resemblance and a deeper spiritual assonance which makes it seem certain that Blake and Coleridge in their different mediums were sharing an imaginative experience (see the frontispiece, from the water-colour drawing done for Butts).

I cannot omit all mention of another very different member of Lamb's circle, the painter of historical pictures, Benjamin Robert Haydon. He was in many ways a man after Blake's heart, for he held strong views about the low state of art in England at that period and had great plans for its reform, plans which had no relation to the Royal Academy and the Old Gang established at its head. Like Blake, Haydon lived only for art, though his ambitions were more grandiose. Both Blake and Haydon were intimate friends of Fuseli the Swiss painter, and through this link alone it seems certain that they must have met. Yet all through Haydon's voluminous journals, table-talk, and letters, there is no mention of Blake whatever, so that an important potential source of information about Blake is silent. Gilchrist in his *Life of Blake* tells one anecdote which may perhaps have been retailed by Haydon, though the name is not given:[1] 'A historical painter of the class endlessly industrious yet for ever unknown, was one day pointing out to a visitor some favourite specimen of hopeless hugeness, and said, "Mr. Blake once paid me a high compliment on that picture. It was on the last occasion when the old gentleman visited me, and his words were, 'Ah! that is what I have been trying to do all my life—to paint *round* and never could!' "' This may be taken as an instance of the courteous care with which Blake would find some agreeable word

---

[1] Professor Edmund Blunden suggests the name of Solomon Hart as more likely.

for an inoffensive inferior in art.' Through Haydon Blake might have met Keats
—but conjecture of this kind will lead me from my proper theme, and the temptation must be resisted.

Two other friends of Lamb, who were also acquaintances of Blake, were Thomas
Griffiths Wainewright, painter, critic, journalist, and, later, criminal, and H. F.
Cary, translator of Dante. Little record remains of their contacts with Blake,
though Gilchrist, who knew Cary in later years and evidently gathered what
information he could from him, refers to Wainewright's 'intimacy with Blake,
whom he assisted by buying two or three of his expensive illustrated books'.
Gilchrist adds the statement that 'Blake entertained . . . a kindness for him and his
works'. Certain it is that Wainewright included in an article published in the
London Magazine for September 1820, under the pseudonym of Janus Weathercock,
a facetious reference to Blake's *Jerusalem*. 'It contains a good deal anent one *Los*, who
it appears, is now, and hath been, from the creation, the *sole* and fourfold dominator
of the celebrated city of Golgonooza! . . . the redemption of mankind hangs on the
universal diffusion of the doctrines broached in this MS.' Wainewright may not
have met Blake in person until two or three years later and there is no evidence that
he owned a copy of *Jerusalem*, though he certainly possessed a very fine copy of the
Songs of Innocence and of Experience made by Blake in 1825[1] and of *Milton*,[2] he also
subscribed for a copy of the *Illustrations of the Book of Job*.[3]

Cary's biographer[4] thinks that it was most likely Wainewright who introduced
Cary to Blake, in 1825, the year in which Crabb Robinson, calling on Blake on
17 December, found him at work on the Dante illustrations with Cary's translation
open before him. Gilchrist does not seem to have obtained much help from Cary,
though he records that, after getting to know Blake, Cary abandoned the idea that
he was mad, and simply pronounced him an 'enthusiast'. Immediately after Blake's
death Cary bought from his widow the water-colour painting of 'Oberon and
Titania' now in the Tate Gallery.

It may not be fair to include William Wordsworth as a member of Lamb's circle.
Wordsworth certainly numbered many of them among his friends, and was sometimes seen in Lamb's house with the others, but for the most part he remained aloof
in his home in Westmorland, and there is no suggestion that he and Blake ever
met one another. Crabb Robinson would have liked to see the meeting, and he did
see to it that they knew and appreciated one another's poetry. As early as 1812 he

[1] Copy X in the *Census of Illuminated Books* (Keynes and Wolf, 1953).
[2] Copy D in the *Census*. [3] See also p. 223 of the present book.
[4] R. W. King, *The Translator of Dante* (Secker, 1925), p. 170.

read Wordsworth some of Blake's poems. He reported: 'He was pleased with some of them, and considered Blake as having the elements of poetry a thousand times more than either Byron or Scott.' They must often have discussed Blake on other occasions, and in 1825 and 1826 Blake was expressing to Crabb Robinson his opinions of Wordsworth. He thought Wordsworth was no Christian, but a Platonist, and asked whether he believed in the Scriptures. He had been greatly upset by a passage in the Introduction to the *Excursion*:

> Jehovah—with his thunder and the choir
> Of shouting angels, and the empyreal thrones—
> I pass them unalarmed.

So upset was he, indeed, that he told Crabb Robinson it had given him a bowel complaint which nearly killed him. Blake finally set down Wordsworth as a pagan, but still with praise as the greatest poet of the age. In a letter to Dorothy Wordsworth written in February 1826, Crabb Robinson tells her: 'I had the pleasure of reading to Blake in my best style the Ode on Immortality (and you know I am vain on that point and think I read Wordsworth's poems peculiarly well). I never witnessed greater delight in any listener and in general Blake loves the poems. . . .' 'I doubt', he adds, 'whether what I have written [about Blake] will excite your and Mr. W.'s curiosity, but there is something so delightful about the Man—tho' in great poverty with such genuine dignity and independence, scorning presents and of such native delicacy in words, that I have not scrupled promising introducing him and Mr. W. together. He expressed his thanks strongly, saying, "You do me honour. Mr. W. is a great man. Besides he may convince me I am wrong about him. I have been wrong before now." ' The occasion for this meeting never came, and eighteen months later Blake was dead. More than twenty years later, however, Blake was again in the minds of the Wordsworth household. Edward Quillinan, Wordsworth's son-in-law, writing to Crabb Robinson from Rydal Mount in July 1848, remarks:

Among some new books that I have been looking at here this morning I observed C. Lamb's Letters and Blake's Poems—and as I was glancing over them for an hour or two, it seemed to me that both publications had the fault of *too much*. In Lamb's *too much* of childish fun, or rather that strain at fun which is the trivial imitation of child's fun; And some of Blake's verses, illustrated in the book you possess, want in this publication [evidently the Pickering edition of 1839] the poetry of the painting to support them. They seemed to sound very like nonsense-verses as we read them aloud. *Some* of them I say; for others have a real charm in their wildness and oddness. Do not suppose I undervalue the man. I have on the contrary a sort of tenderness for him that makes me disposed perhaps to overestimate the value of many of his verses. He and that good old wife of his are two very interesting persons in my mind.

In 1848 Blake was already almost completely forgotten by the world, and it is pleasant to think that he and his 'good old wife' were remembered with interest at Rydal Mount. Blake had suffered an eclipse more complete than Charles Lamb, Southey, Hazlitt, Coleridge, or Wordsworth have ever done. They all thought him mad, and I touched on the queerness of his mind at the outset of my remarks. But to say that a man like Blake is mad is but a crude way of saying that he has the kind of genius which does not easily communicate its message to the generality of mankind. An attempt has been made here to give some idea of the real impression created by Blake on Lamb and his circle. The material is incomplete and the picture, I fear, has been but imperfectly painted.

X

WILLIAM BLAKE AND SIR FRANCIS BACON[1]

W HEN William Blake was writing his annotations to the *Discourses* of Sir Joshua Reynolds about the year 1808 he remarked: 'I read Burke's Treatise [on The Sublime] when very young; at the same time I read Locke on Human Understanding & Bacon's Advancement of Learning; on Every one of these Books I wrote my Opinions, & on looking them over find that my Notes on Reynolds in this Book are exactly Similar. I felt the Same Contempt & Abhorrence then that I do now. They mock Inspiration & Vision. Inspiration & Vision was then, & now is, & I hope will always Remain, my Element, my Eternal Dwelling place; how can I then hear it Contemned without returning Scorn for Scorn?' Blake's copies of these three books, with his Opinions no doubt written, as was his habit, in the margins, are not known to have survived, but the gist of his notes may be surmised from other evidences. The names of Bacon and Locke, usually bracketed with that of Newton, remained for him the symbols of unbelief—or sometimes, perhaps, as The Three Accusers in other contexts. He was on one occasion able to quote Bacon's *Advancement of Learning* with approval when writing in 1799 to an unimaginative critic, the Reverend Dr. Trusler: 'Consider what Lord Bacon says—Sense sends over to Imagination before Reason have judged, & Reason sends over to Imagination before the Decree can be enacted', with a reference to page 47 of the first edition; but this was exceptional. Blake's usual attitude was expressed by another note on Reynolds: 'The Great Bacon—he is Call'd: I call him the Little Bacon—says that Every thing must be done by Experiment; his first principle is Unbelief, and yet here [according to Reynolds] he says that Art must be produc'd without such Method [the idea of confining proportion to rules, or of producing beauty by selection]. He is Like Sr Joshua, full of Self-Contradiction & Knavery.'

Although Blake's copy of the first edition of *The Advancement of Learning* has not been found, it has long been known that his copy of Bacon's *Essays*, an attractive small edition printed by Bensley for J. Edwards in 1798, has survived. Gilchrist had seen it, probably by the agency of Samuel Palmer, in whose hands several of Blake's books remained after the death of Mrs. Blake. In the *Life* of 1863 Gilchrist

[1] First printed in *The Times Literary Supplement* (1957), lvi. 152.

mentioned the book as 'roughly annotated in pencil in a very characteristic, if very unreasonable, fashion; marginal notes dating, I should say, during the latter years of Blake's life'. He found, however, in the notes to Bacon 'none of that leaven of real sense and acumen which tempers the violence of those on Reynolds', and accordingly gave but a few examples, even those few being none too accurately transcribed. After 1863 nothing more was heard of the volume of *Essays*, and it was only possible to include in the Nonesuch editions of Blake's writings Gilchrist's few quotations, the context of some of which it was impossible to guess. It was not until 1947, during a visit to Boston, that I learned through the courtesy of a book-seller, the late George T. Goodspeed, that Blake's Bacon had passed through his hands eighteen years before, and had reposed since then in the strong-room of a collector in Indianapolis. The history of the book from Samuel Palmer's death in 1881 until 1929, when Goodspeed handled it, is unknown, but it is likely to have been in the possession of Palmer's son, A. H. Palmer, who emigrated to British Columbia and died there about the time of the book's appearance in the American rare-book market. The owner of the book in 1947 turned out to be Mr. Josiah K. Lilly, jr., who, on inquiry, kindly suggested that I should become its owner. He preferred this to subjecting its fragile pages to the possibly rough attentions of a photographer. The transfer was accordingly effected—otherwise the book would presumably now be the property of the University of Indiana, to which Mr. Lilly later gave his collections.

The volume turned out to be in good condition with its leaves untrimmed, though somewhat shaky in its binding of worn boards with spine of patterned green cloth. It is evident that it was originally bound in grey paper boards, but that Blake, or perhaps Palmer, whose signature, dated 1833, is inside the cover, afterwards strengthened it with marbled paper sides and a cloth spine, near the top of which one or other of them laid a patch of gold leaf, as an amateur label, marked 'Bacon's Essays'. Having now been re-sewn, but not otherwise changed, the volume is in fairly sound condition, and should be able, for many years to come, to bear witness to Blake's consistent hatred of Bacon's views on almost everything, particularly on art, religion, and politics. More than ninety of its 282 pages carry Blake's pencillings, written quite legibly in the margins and other blank spaces. Gilchrist's feeling that the annotations are not of the same interest as those in Reynolds's *Discourses* is justified, but this is because Bacon's opinions were much more uniformly distasteful to Blake than were those of Reynolds, who was, after all, an artist and not, as Blake thought Bacon to be, merely a cynical time-serving politician and materialist.

Blake summed up his view of the *Essays* by writing in the middle of the title-page, 'Good Advice for Satan's Kingdom'. On the half-title he wrote two sentences: 'Is it True or is it False that the Wisdom of this World is Foolishness with God?' and, 'This is Certain: If what Bacon says Is True, what Christ says Is False. If Caesar is Right, Christ is Wrong both in Politics & Religion, since they will divide them in Two.' He followed this up, after Bacon's dedications, with: 'Every Body Knows that this is Epicurus and Lucretius [read by Gilchrist as *epicurism and libertinism*] & Yet Every Body says that it is Christian Philosophy; how is this Possible? Every Body must be a Liar & deciever. But Every Body does not do this, But The Hirelings of Kings & Courts who make themselves Every Body & Knowingly propagate Falshood. It was a Common opinion in the Court of Queen Elizabeth that Knavery Is Wisdom. Cunning Plotters were consider'd as wise Machiavels.' It was probably when he had finished his perusal of the *Essays* that Blake wrote above the beginning of the anonymous editor's Preface: 'I am astonish'd how such Contemptible Knavery & Folly as this Book contains can ever have been call'd Wisdom by Men of Sense, but perhaps this never was the Case & all Men of Sense have despised the Book as Much as I do. Per William Blake.'

Gilchrist, as already seen, assigned the annotations to 'the latter years of Blake's life'. With fuller knowledge of Blake's mental attitudes we can now assign the notes with some assurance to about 1798, the date on the title-page of the book. In that year Blake had already read and annotated Bishop Watson's *Apology for the Bible*, and prefaced his notes by saying that 'to defend the Bible in this year 1798 would cost a man his life'. He was here defending Tom Paine, whose criticism of a sermon by Bishop Watson had evoked the Bishop's *Apology*, and was attacking 'the English Crusade against France', which he attributed to 'State Religion'. Blake's opinions, both religious and political, were of a highly seditious complexion at this time, and he wrote of his notes on Watson: 'I have been commanded from Hell not to print this, as it is what our Enemies wish.' Mr. David V. Erdman in his *Blake: Prophet against Empire* (1954) has made it plain that Blake gave his poetry at this period a deliberate obscurity, since his opinions, if given clear utterance, would have consigned him to the gallows. Mr. Erdman rightly regards the notes on Bacon as contemporaneous with those on Watson and calls in evidence Blake's comment in reply to Bacon's contention that 'above all, for empire and greatness it importeth most that a nation do profess arms as their principal honour, study, and occupation'. 'Bacon', cries Blake, 'calls Intellectual Arts Unmanly. Poetry, Painting, Music are in his opinion Useless & so they are for Kings & Wars & shall in the End Annihilate them.' The notes on Bacon are, in fact, as Erdman says, to be read as 'a sort of appendage to the notes on Watson and Paine', and, indeed, Blake's anti-monarchical opinions are developed in the *Essays* to a point highly dangerous had they become known. 'This public envy seemeth to beat chiefly upon principal officers or ministers, rather than upon kings and estates themselves', wrote Bacon in the essay 'Of Envy'. 'A Lie!' Blake retorts, 'Every Body hates a King. Bacon [oddly read by Gilchrist as *David*] was afraid to say that the Envy was upon a King, but is This Envy or Indignation?' Further on he states, 'A Tyrant is the Worst disease & the Cause of all others', but the climax is reached when he comes to the essay 'Of a King'. Bacon's opening sentence, 'A king is a mortal god on earth, unto whom the living God hath lent his own name as a great honour', calls for the comment, 'O Contemptible & Abject Slave!', and on the preceding page Blake indulged his feelings with a scatological diagram (partially, though ineffectually, erased by Palmer). From the devil's buttocks descends a chain of excrement ending in a circle enclosing the words 'A King'. Gilchrist was probably affronted by this naked republicanism, and decided that no more of this unseemly book should be divulged. It is true, as he remarked, that many of Blake's notes on Bacon are mere expletives—'Fool, Liar, Villain, Atheist, Nonsense, Blasphemy, False', and so on. The explanation of a single word would often necessitate re-printing a paragraph of Bacon; but there are many more substantial opinions in the notes than Gilchrist's dismissal of the volume would imply, and their Blakeian pungency gives them all additional point. To present all the notes adequately would demand transcription together with the relevant passages from the *Essays* in full. This cannot be attempted here, but has been done for the Nonesuch edition of Blake's *Complete Writings*, 1957, reissued by the Oxford University Press, 1966.

The essay 'Of Truth' Blake prefaces with the words: 'Self Evident Truth is one Thing and Truth the result of Reasoning is another Thing. Rational Truth is not the Truth of Christ, but of Pilate. It is the Tree of the Knowledge of Good & Evil', thus answering forthwith Bacon's opening gambit: 'What is Truth? said jesting Pilate, and would not stay for an answer.' He follows this on the next page with: 'What Bacon calls Lies is Truth itself', and dismisses Bacon's remarks on the creation as, 'Pretence to Religion to destroy Religion'. Bacon's reference to 'the truth of civil business' elicits the note: 'Christianity is Civil Business Only. There is & can Be No Other to Man. What Else Can be? Civil is Christianity or Religion or whatever is Humane.' Bacon's final sentence, 'it being foretold that when Christ cometh he shall not find faith upon earth', enabled Blake to conclude: 'Bacon put an End to Faith'. The essay 'Of Death' leads Blake to remark: 'Bacon supposes all Men alike. One Man's Revenge or Love Is not the same as Another's. The tender

Mercies of some Men are Cruel.' In the essay 'Of Unity in Religion', Blake at once disagrees with the opinion that 'quarrels and divisions about religion were evils *unknown to the heathen*'; he underlined the last four words and added in the margin: 'False O Satan!' After several other brief notes, he counters Bacon's argument that 'It was great blasphemy when the devil said, I will ascend and be like the Highest; but it is greater blasphemy to personate God, and bring him in saying, I will descend, and be like the prince of darkness' with the sentence: 'Did not Jesus descend & become a Servant? The Prince of darkness is a Gentleman & not a Man: he is a Lord Chancellor.'

In the essay 'Of Envy' Bacon remarks that: 'A man that hath no virtue in himself ever envieth virtue in others . . . and whoso is out of hope to attain to another's virtue, will seek to come at even hand by depressing another's fortune.' 'What', Blake asks, 'do these Knaves mean by Virtue? Do they mean War & its horrors & its Heroic Villains?' Bacon's advice that 'the wiser sort of great persons bring in ever upon the stage somebody upon whom to derive the envy that would come upon themselves', goads Blake into saying: 'Politic Foolery & most contemptible Villainy & Murder?' The essay 'Of Great Place' naturally finds Blake at variance. 'Good thoughts (though God accept them) yet towards man are little better than good dreams except they be put in act.' 'Thought is Act', replies Blake; 'Christ's Acts were Nothing to Caesar's if this is not so.' Bacon advises that 'imitation is a globe of precepts', and Blake replies: 'Here is nothing of Thy own Original Genius, but only Imitation: what Folly!' At the beginning of the essay 'Of Nobility', Blake asks: 'Is Nobility a portion of a State, i.e. Republic?' and when Bacon says: 'Those that are first raised to nobility are commonly more virtuous, but less innocent than their descendants', Blake replies: 'Virtuous I supposed to be Innocent: was I Mistaken or is Bacon a Liar?'

In the next essay, 'Of Seditions and Troubles', Blake finds much matter for dis-agreement. 'This Section', he begins, 'contradicts the Preceding.' Bacon's opinion that 'Shepherds of all people had need know the calendars of tempests in state, which are commonly greatest when things grow to equality', makes Blake ask: 'What Shepherds does he mean? Such as Christ describes by Ravening Wolves?' Bacon: 'Also, when discords and quarrels and factions are carried openly and audaciously it is a sign the reverence of government is lost.' Blake: 'When the Reverence of Government is Lost it is better than when it is found. Reverence is all For Reverence.' To Bacon's opinion that 'The matter of seditions is of two kinds, much poverty and much discontentment' Blake replies: 'These are one Kind Only.' Bacon's advice on the regulation of trade is met with: 'You cannot regulate the price of Necessaries without destruction. All False!' and: 'The Increase of a State as of a Man is from Internal Improvement or Intellectual Acquirement. Man is not Improved by the hurt of another. States are not Improved at the Expense of Foreigners. Bacon has no notion of any thing but Mammon.'

The essay 'Of Atheism' aroused all Blake's feelings of indignation and contempt. To the observation that 'I had rather believe all the fables in the legend and the Talmud, and the Alcoran than that this universal frame is without a *mind*', Blake underlined the last word and replied: 'The devil is the Mind of the Natural Frame.' A reference to 'second causes' brings the comment: 'There is no Such Thing as a Second Cause nor as a Natural Cause for any Thing in any Way. He who says there are Second Causes has already denied a First. The Word Cause is a foolish Word.' Bacon: 'The contemplative atheist is rare, a Diagoras, a Bion, a Lucian perhaps, and some others.' Blake: 'A Lie! Few believe it is a New Birth. Bacon was a Contemplative Atheist. Evidently an Epicurean. Lucian disbeliev'd Heathen Gods; he did not perhaps disbelieve for all that. Bacon did.' Finally, after a series of expletives and exclamations, Blake concludes: 'Atheism is thus the best of all. Bacon fools us.' The essay 'Of Travel' affords Blake plenty of targets for his scorn. Bacon's list of 'things to be seen' elicits the comment: 'The Things worthy to be seen are all the Trumpery he could rake together. Nothing of Arts or Artists or Learned Men or of Agriculture or any Useful Thing. His Business & Bosom was to be Lord Chancellor' (here referring back to a passage in the Preface where the editor says the subjects of the Essays are 'such as come home to men's *business and bosoms*', Blake underlined the last three words and added: 'Erratum—to Men's Pockets'). A further list of entertainments 'not to be neglected' produces the comment: 'Bacon supposes that the dragon, Beast & Harlot are worthy of a Place in the New Jerusalem. Excellent Traveller, Go on & be dammd!'

In the essay 'Of Innovations' Bacon says: 'As the births of living creatures at first are ill shapen, so are all innovations, which are the births of time.' Blake retorts: 'What a Cursed Fool is this—Ill Shapen! are Infants or small Plants ill Shapen because they are not yet come to their maturity? What a Contemptible Fool is This Bacon!' Writing 'Of Friendship', Bacon cites examples from Roman history; Blake remarks: 'The Friendship of these Roman Villains is a strange Example to alledge for our imitation & approval.' In the essay 'Of Expense' Bacon advises: 'Certainly, if a man will keep but of even hand, his ordinary expenses ought to be but to the half of his receipts; and if he think to wax rich, but to the third part.' Blake wisely points out that: 'If this is advice to the Poor, it is mocking them. If to the Rich, it is worse still—it is The Miser. If to the Middle Class, it is the direct

Contrary to Christ's advice.' With Bacon's opinions 'Of the True Greatness of Kingdoms and Estates' Blake inevitably disagrees—'a Lord Chancellor's opinion as different from Christ as those of Caiaphas or Pilate or Herod: what such Men call Great is indeed detestable.' 'Princes' Powers! Powers of darkness!' 'The Kingdom of Heaven is the direct Negation of Earthly domination.' 'Bacon knows the Wisdom of War—if it is Wisdom.' His opinion of Bacon's glorification of 'a military disposition' has been recorded above. In the essay 'Of Regimen of Health' Bacon states that 'strength of nature in youth passeth over many excesses which are owing a man till his age', to which Blake replies: 'Excess in Youth is Necessary to Life.' Bacon advises: 'If you fly physic in health altogether, it will be too strange for your body when you shall need it', but Blake very sensibly answers: 'Very Pernicious Advice! The Work of a Fool to use Physic but for necessity!' and, 'Those that put their Bodies To endure are Fools.' It was probably a memory of this essay that brought Bacon to Blake's mind when writing to John Linnell in 1826. He believed that going to places north of London brought on the abdominal pains from which he was then suffering and so excused himself from visiting Linnell at Hampstead. 'Sir Francis Bacon would say, it is want of discipline in Mountainous Places. Sir Francis Bacon is a Liar. No discipline will turn one Man into another, even in the least particle. & such discipline I call Presumption & Folly. I have tried it too much not to know this, & am very sorry for all such who may be led to such ostentatious Exertion against their Eternal Existence itself, because it is Mental Rebellion against the Holy Spirit, & fit only for a Soldier of Satan to perform.' Blake's attitude to the Lord Chancellor had clearly not been mellowed by age. The essay 'Of Suspicion' called forth the aphorism: 'What is Suspition in one Man is Caution in Another & Truth or Discernment in Another & in Some it is Folly.' Blake will not allow that Bacon could know anything 'Of Riches'. 'Bacon was always a poor Devil if History says true: how should one so foolish know about Riches, Except Pretence to be Rich, if that is it?' On the other hand Blake prefaces the essay 'Of Usury' with: 'Bacon was a Usurer', and concludes: 'Bacon is in his Element on Usury; it is himself & his Philosophy.' The essay 'Of Youth and Age' enables Blake to repeat that 'Bacon's Business is not Intellect or Art', and the sentence, 'There be some have an over-early ripeness in their years, which fadeth betimes . . . such was Hermogenes, the rhetorician, whose books are exceeding subtile, who afterwards waxed stupid', lays the adversary open to the obvious gibe: 'Such was Bacon: Stupid Indeed!'

In the essay 'Of Faction' Bacon observes that 'the motions of factions under kings ought to be like the motions (as the astronomers speak) of the inferior orbs, which may have their proper motions, but yet are quietly carried by the higher motion of primum mobile'. Here Blake quietly notes: 'King James was Bacon's Primum Mobile.' Bacon's observations in the essay 'Of Ceremonies and Respects' that 'small matters win great commendation because they are continually in use and in note', caught Blake's attention: 'Small matters—What are They? Caesar seems to me a Very Small Matter & so he seem'd to Jesus: is the devil Great? Consider.' Blake's final remark is evoked by Bacon's writing 'Of Praise' that 'Praise is the reflection of virtue; but it is as the glass or body which giveth the reflection; if it be from the *common people*, it is commonly false and nought, and rather followeth vain persons, than virtuous.' Blake underlined the words in italics and added: 'Villain! did Christ seek the Praise of the Rulers?'

So ends what Gilchrist rightly called 'this singular dialogue at cross-purposes'; but it can scarcely be denied that Blake has found some weak places in Bacon's mental armour.

XI

WILLIAM BLAKE AND
JOHN GABRIEL STEDMAN[1]

FRESH light on the life of William Blake is not easily to be found. Almost every source seems to have been used and exhausted, and yet some unexpected flash still occasionally surprises us. One such was published in August 1962, though its significance was not at once appreciated, at any rate by me. The name of John Gabriel Stedman has often been mentioned in connexion with Blake because of Stedman's well-known book, *Narrative of a Five Years' Expedition against the Revolted Negroes of Surinam from the year 1772 to 1777*, published by Joseph Johnson in 1796. Blake engraved sixteen of the eighty plates and these have long been recognized as among the best executed and the most generally interesting of all his journeyman work, but that Blake had any close relations with Stedman has not hitherto been known.

Stedman was a picturesque, buccaneering character, son of Robert Stedman, officer in the Scots Brigade in Holland, and of a mother belonging to an aristocratic Dutch family. John Gabriel was born in 1744 as their ninth child, though the first one born alive; he had one younger brother, John Andrew, who lived to fight at Waterloo. At the age of ten John Gabriel was sent from Holland to his uncle, Dr. John Stedman, of Dunfermline, to be educated, but the boy was badly treated by his uncle and soon returned to Holland. It was suggested that he might be trained as an artist, since he had some leanings in that direction. Eventually, however, it was decided he might more easily earn a living in his father's profession, and he entered the Scots Brigade as a cadet, obtaining an ensign's commission soon afterwards. Stedman said of himself that he was 'bold, strong and quarrelsome', and he 'was certainly a wild young fellow, and of a spirit to do anything that came uppermost'.

After a few riotous years a chance very much to his taste 'came uppermost'—this was to take part in an expedition to Dutch Guiana, or Surinam, under Colonel Louis Henry Fourgeord sent to protect the European planters from their Negro

[1] First printed in *The Times Literary Supplement* (1965), lxiv. 400.

slaves, who had been so badly treated that they had risen in rebellion. Soon after arriving in Surinam Stedman fell in love with a beautiful mulatto slave girl, Joanna, the natural daughter of a wealthy Dutch planter. She nursed Stedman through a dangerous illness, and after their marriage bore him a son, John. Stedman was devoted both to Joanna and the boy, and was heartbroken when, on leaving Surinam, he was unable to take Joanna with him through not having the means to buy her liberty. When the American revolution started in 1775 the Dutch Scots Brigade was not allowed to return to Great Britain, since the Dutch Government favoured the other side. Later, when Holland became an active partner in the alliance against Great Britain, the Brigade was interned, and in 1782 was ordered either to adopt Dutch nationality or to be dismissed without compensation. Stedman chose the second alternative and returned to England with many other officers who intended to offer their services to the King. Joanna had died in the same year, supposedly from poisoning, and the boy, John, joined his father. Later he entered the British Navy, but was drowned at the age of 17. Stedman himself had married a Dutch woman in 1782, but, his health being poor, he retired from the army on full pay with the rank of major, going to live at Tiverton in Devon, a place believed to have a climate suitable for a man suffering from the effects of a riotous youth and tropical diseases. At Tiverton he raised a family of four children and farmed on a small scale, leading also an active social life with the local gentry.

★ ★ ★

Stedman's chief preoccupation during his retirement was the writing of his memoirs and the composition of the work by which his name has kept some degree of fame—his account of the five years he had spent in Surinam. Although he had started life as a quarrelsome and undisciplined youth, he had other more serious sides to his character. Through all his vicissitudes he had maintained an interest in art and in Surinam had made a large number of drawings and paintings, with which he was determined to illustrate his book on a lavish scale. He had also taken a lively interest in the plants and animals of Surinam and in its inhabitants. He was there as a soldier, whose duty it was to subdue the Negro rebels, but at the same time he was humane enough to be horrified by the brutalities suffered by the slaves and the ferocity with which they were punished for their insurrection. He was unable to do much to mitigate the horrors that he witnessed, but he was now at least able to expose to public view the abuses that existed.

Stedman had presumably kept some sort of diary through most of his life, but knowledge of his earlier years is derived from the memoir written after his retirement. From 1772 onwards we have not only his large book on Surinam, but also a day-to-day journal, not always kept scrupulously up to date, but giving many details of his life until within a few months of his death in 1797. William Blake's important share in the production of Stedman's book is seen in his engravings, and his personal relations with the author can now be to some extent reconstructed from entries in the *Journal*, edited, together with the Memoir, by Mr. Stanbury Thompson (London, The Mitre Press, 1962) from the manuscripts in his possession.

Between his frequent visits to London Stedman must have occupied much of his time in writing his book, negotiating for its publication and arranging for the illustrations. Joseph Johnson, the well-known republican sympathizer and Blake's frequent employer, had been enlisted as publisher, but the journal has no references to the early stages of the book. It is first mentioned in the laconic entry: 'Sept. 1 [1790] I ended my work.' Stedman had certainly made his arrangements with Johnson long before this, and his drawings had been distributed among several engravers—Barlow, Bartolozzi, Benedetti, Blake, Conder, Holloway, Perry, and Smith. Some of the engravings are unsigned. Many of the animal and vegetable subjects were given to Barlow. Bartolozzi, a Royal Academician and no doubt more expensive than the others, was given a few subjects, notably a drawing of Stedman himself for the frontispiece (Plate 23) and another of the beautiful Joanna (Plate 24). Blake was employed on most of the Negro subjects; he also had two of monkeys (Plate 26) and a somewhat comic one of 'The Skinning of the Aboma Snake' (an anaconda).¹ Stedman's original drawings are not known to be extant, so that it is not possible to judge how much redrawing an artist of Blake's calibre may have found to be necessary.² All Blake's prints, however, show signs of his own influence and it seems probable that they were not very exact copies. The dates on the plates probably indicate when each was finished. Thus many are dated 1791. Three of Blake's are dated 1 December 1792, twelve have 2 December 1793, and one 1 December 1794. Three are unsigned, but the subjects and style leave no doubt as to their attribution.

Although the earliest date given by Blake is 1 December 1792, he must have been working on them for some time before this. He had moved from Poland

¹ Reproduced in my *Bibliography of Blake*, 1921, plate 35.

² In June 1957 a copy of the book inscribed by Stedman to *Lieut. Colonel Ferrier* was sold in Amsterdam. According to the catalogue description this contained a drawing by Stedman of 'a horse held by a young negro groom', but this was not reproduced in the book. The recipient was probably James Ferrier, son of Major Islay Ferrier. Stedman noted in his journal 5 August 1778: 'Sup with Ferrier . . . I gave Huyzing's groom.'

PL. 23

Pl. 24

Street, Soho, to his terrace house in Hercules Buildings, Lambeth, in 1789, and the work for Stedman had been done there while the plates for *Songs of Experience*, *The Marriage of Heaven and Hell*, and other works were in progress. Stedman's first reference to Blake is under 1 December 1791: 'I wrote to the engraver, Blake, to thank him twice for his excellent work, but never received any answer.' Earlier in the year on 8 February he had sent Johnson a large parcel with manuscripts, lists of names of possible subscribers, and proposals to London, Edinburgh, York, and other cities. On the 10th he also sent Johnson 'two elegant drawings to publish or not as he shall think proper'. Perhaps these were the portraits of himself and Joanna signed by Bartolozzi and dated 1794. On 14 November he was again writing to Johnson and recording that 'in 1790—for my history of *Surinam* £500, & chance for £1,000'. On 25 December 1793 he drew on Johnson for £212. On 2 May 1794 he called on Bartolozzi. Exactly when Blake and Stedman first became personally acquainted we do not know.

The earliest mention in the *Journal* of their meeting is on 2 June 1794: 'trip to Mr. [&] Mrs. Blake'. They met again on 21 June: 'Called on Mr. Johnson and Blake.' On 30 October he was writing both to Johnson and Blake, and on 7 November he sent a fresh drawing of himself to Bartolozzi for the frontispiece. On the 21st he wrote to Bartolozzi, Johnson, and Blake. On 30 December he received prints from Bartolozzi, eighty-two in all, accounted for by the eighty illustrations and two engraved title-pages. By 9 June of the same year he was evidently becoming a familiar friend of the Blakes, for on that day he 'gave a blue sugar cruse to Mrs. Blake', and seems to have had an artists' party, dining with Palmer, Blake, Johnson, Rigaud, and Bartolozzi. Palmer was probably Sir Thomas Palmer, K.C., formerly owner of a Surinam plantation; Rigaud was a well-known portrait painter. At this time things were not always going well with the book. On 24 June he received the first volume, 'quite marr'd', and he added later, 'my book marr'd entirely. Am put to the most extreme trouble and expense.' This was no doubt the cause of another entry soon afterwards: 'A hot quarrel with Johnson', but no details of the trouble are recorded. At about this time Stedman dined once more with Blake and mentioned that he 'gave oil portrait to Blake'. Was this perhaps a portrait of himself? We cannot know. On an unspecified day Stedman dined again with Bartolozzi, but it was with the Blakes that he had become most intimate. It seems to have been in August that he wrote: 'I visit Mr. Blake for three days, who undertook to do business for me when I am not in London. I leave him all my papers.'

★   ★   ★

For a period in 1795 Stedman did not date his entries and events are recorded in continuity:

The King's coach insulted. Damn Bartolozzi. He goes away. Was at Greenwich to dinner. I was also at Lambeth Gardens. Johnson uncivil all along . . . Met 300 whores in the Strand. French prisoners come home. Abershaw &c. hang'd 8. Saw a mermaid. Meat and bread abused. Russian fleet down. Two days at Blake's. Quiberon expedition fail'd. 188 emigrants executed.

and so on, in incoherent sequence. Clearly Blake's house in Lambeth was always ready to receive Stedman as a guest.

The year 1795 was a time of social turmoil and riots were frequent. In September Stedman made the following startling entry: 'All knaves and fools, and cruel to the excess. Blake [was] mobb'd and robb'd.' No details are given, but it would have been of great interest to know where and why Blake suffered this outrage. The days were over when, in his first revolutionary ardour, Blake had, according to Gilchrist, paraded the streets of London wearing the red Cap of Liberty. Yet he remained hotly antimonarchist and there were doubtless daily events in London calculated to arouse his indignation. On the other hand the mobs often chose their victims without justification for their violence, and Blake may have only been unfortunate. Whatever the cause of his misfortune, Stedman was sympathetic and even Johnson was forgiven. Back in Tiverton on 18 December he immediately noted: 'Sent a goose to Johnson and one to Blake', though even after that: 'Johnson sends me a blurred index—the book good for nothing.' Stedman was still capable of doing some very silly things. 'In London I walk'd to Charing Cross without shirt, shoes, stockings, breeches or hat for a bett, but had on jacket, trowsers, slippers, cane and a black handkerchief.'

In January and February 1796 he wrote three letters to Johnson and the same number to Blake. In May he wrote no fewer than twelve letters to Blake; also two to Simpkins, engraver, one to Conder, and two to Johnson 'and damn him in them', but at last his great work was coming to an end. 'The whole or most of my publication, of which I send away the last cancels so late as the middle of May, 1796, having been in hand no less than 7 or 8 long years.' In July he wrote three more letters to Johnson and two to Blake, and here the record of Stedman's friendship with Blake ends. He died eight months later at the age of 52 and was buried on 7 March 1797 in Bickleigh churchyard. His *Surinam* is dated 1796 on the title-pages and the dedication to the Prince of Wales had been written on the first day of that year. Yet publication can only have been just in time for the author to see his book before his turbulent life came to an end.

Dr. David Erdman in his book, *Prophet Against Empire* (Princeton, 1954), was the first writer on Blake to emphasize the effect Stedman's *Surinam* had on Blake's mind and to correlate it with his works, particularly his *Visions of the Daughters of Albion*, completed in 1793. This poem, outwardly a kind of debate on free love, human rights, sexual frustration, and slavery, is in effect a powerful tract on the evils of slavery, against which there was a strong popular movement at the time, though the abolitionists were defeated in Parliament. Dr. Erdman remarked (p. 213) that 'Blake's knowledge of the cruelties of slavery came to him doubtless through many sources, but one was directly graphic', meaning by this his work on the plates for *Surinam*. He pointed out that the plate in Blake's *America* shewing Orc, the symbol of revolt, spread-eagled on his back and manacled to a rock, was plainly suggested by Blake's fourteenth plate in *Surinam*, depicting 'The Execution of Breaking on the Rack' (plate 25); to this plate he could not bring himself to affix his signature. We now know that Blake's knowledge was not acquired second-hand through drawings. Stedman had been a soldier, but had atoned for this in Blake's eyes by being also an artist, who could draw and paint and could even attempt engraving and versification. He was also an advocate of the abolition of slavery, the horrors of which he had seen at first-hand and could communicate to Blake in all their lurid details. He could also tell Blake of his love for Joanna and its tragic ending. In Blake's *Visions* Theotormon loved the gentle Oothoon, but was unable to set her free. So Stedman could be accepted as Blake's friend, could be welcomed into his house and be helped in his affairs. Stedman wrote Blake so many letters that many must have been posted in reply. The vanished packet of Blake's letters to Stedman, who was unlikely to destroy them all as they were received, remains for the present one of the major crimes of the 'iniquity of oblivion'.

Bibliographical note

Stedman's *Surinam* was issued in two forms in 1796. The ordinary issue, in marbled boards untrimmed, measures 26·6 × 21·5 cm., with the imprint in one line on the engraved title-pages: *London, Printed for J. Johnson, St. Paul's Church Yard, & J. Edwards, Pall Mall. 1796.* In addition an unknown number of copies were issued on large paper, measuring, trimmed, 29·5 × 23 cm., with the imprint in the first volume in two lines: *London/Printed by J. Johnson &c.*, this error being corrected for the second volume and the ordinary issue. The large paper copies have the plates admirably coloured by hand. Both issues have a List of Subscribers including: *Blake (Mr. Wm.) London.* A second edition with the plates differently placed was published in 1806, some copies having the plates coloured as before. The unsold copies of the second edition were reissued with a new title-page in 1813. The book was also published in Paris: *Voyage à Surinam, et dans l'intérieur de la Guiane, . . . Traduit de l'anglais par P. F. Henry: Suivi du Tableau de la Colonie Française de Cayenne. À Paris, Chez F. Buisson, An VII de la République* (1799). The Surinam plates, finely re-engraved by *Tardieu l'aîné*, were gathered in a separate volume.

XII

'LITTLE TOM THE SAILOR'[1]

WILLIAM BLAKE moved from Hercules Buildings, Lambeth, to his rented cottage at Felpham, Sussex, on Thursday, 18 September 1800, to be met by William Hayley 'with his usual brotherly affection'. Blake had been working on his engraving after Flaxman's medallion of Hayley's son, Thomas Alphonso, earlier in the year, and it is clear from a letter written by Hayley to John Flaxman on 16 July that Blake had just been visiting him at Felpham, presumably staying in his house, known as 'The Turret'. Blake was therefore well aware of Hayley's intentions towards himself and would have been ready to begin work on Hayley's projects as soon as he could get his tools and materials unpacked. He had travelled with sixteen heavy boxes necessitating the hiring of seven different chaises between Lambeth and Felpham, going by the Petworth road. The boxes would have contained heavy objects such as the copper-plates already etched for his Illuminated Books, spare plates for work in progress, a hand-press for printing his designs, and a stock of paper, probably heavy hand-made sheets produced by Whatman and others, these being the preferred material for his books.

On 22 September Hayley wrote his ballad entitled 'Little Tom the Sailor', having been moved to do so by a story told him by his friend, Samuel Rose, a young barrister. Blake was immediately prevailed upon to use his talents for etching the text of the ballad together with his own illustrations to form a broadside. Blake was presumably to do this without reward since the whole enterprise was charitable in favour of 'the Widow Spicer'. According to Hayley's mawkish ballad Mrs. Spicer had been called away from her home at Folkestone to see her husband lying ill in a distant hospital. She left her son, Thomas, aged 10, to care for the other children, one feeble-minded, the other an infant. Blake illustrated the mother's departure in his characteristic and delightful tailpiece to the broadside. It is easy to assume from the circumstances, as was done by Mona Wilson in her *Life of Blake*, 1927, that Tom had met his death at sea, Hayley's first stanza running:

> And does then the Ocean possess
> The promising, brave, little youth,

[1] First printed in *The Book Collector* (1968), xvii. 420–7.

> Who display'd, in a scene of distress,
> Such Tenderness, Courage, and Truth?

This, however, is misleading. It appears from a later passage that the boy was still alive aboard ship, protected, according to Hayley's fantasy, by the spirit of his father:

> And when He's aloft in the Shrouds,
> If a Storm threats aloud to destroy,
> His Father's free Soul, in the Clouds,
> Will watch o'er the venturous Boy.

Blake's crude, though spirited, headpiece for the broadside illustrates Tom 'aloft in the Shrouds', with his father parting the clouds above him. The Widow Spicer's necessities were nevertheless great, even if Tom were not already drowned, so that Hayley's charitable gesture can be understood.

The broadside, Blake's first task at Felpham, was soon completed, being dated 'October 5, 1800'. The printing was done by Catherine Blake on her husband's hand-press. In November Hayley had gone to London and on the 26th Blake, occupied in painting 'the Heads of the Poets' for a frieze in Hayley's study, wrote to him: 'Absorbed by the poets Milton, Homer, Camoens, Ercilla, Ariosto, and Spenser, whose physiognomies have been my delightful study, *Little Tom* has been of late unattended to, and my wife's illness not being quite gone off, she has not printed any more since you went to London. But we can muster a few in colours and some in black, which I hope will be no less favour'd, tho' they are rough like rough sailors.'[1] How many copies were printed and coloured by Blake and his wife cannot be guessed. Few have survived, and having been sold presumably for a few pence each it seems unlikely that the unfortunate widow can have profited very much by the venture. Yet Hayley reported in his *Memoirs* (1823, ii. 23) that 'the ballad was successfully devoted to relieve the necessities of a meritorious poor woman on the Kentish coast'.

At the present time the broadside is very uncommon indeed, and the situation has been complicated by the existence of a facsimile good enough to deceive many people. Gilchrist, writing before 1863, stated that he had 'come across but two or three'. My own interest in Blake over the last sixty years has identified only eight, seven of which I have seen.

The genuine prints are on sheets measuring about $22'' \times 7\frac{1}{2}''$ (56 × 19 cm.). The ballad, designs, and colophon were done in relief etching on four plates by the method used by Blake for his Illuminated Books, the plates being printed from the surface. The plates are as follows:

---

1 *Blake's Letters*, ed. Keynes, London, 1968, p. 49.

i. Headpiece, plate-mark $4\frac{1}{4}'' \times 6\frac{1}{4}''$ (11×16 cm.).

ii. The ballad, 12 stanzas of four lines each, plate-mark $8\frac{7}{8}'' \times 4\frac{1}{4}''$ ($22 \cdot 5 \times 11$ cm.).

iii. Tailpiece, plate-mark $4\frac{1}{4}'' \times 6\frac{1}{4}''$ (11×16 cm.).

iv. Colophon, $13\frac{1}{4}'' \times 4\frac{3}{4}''$ (35×12 cm.). 'Printed for & sold by the Widow Spicer of Folkstone | for the Benefit of her Orphans | October 5, 1800.'

The plates were printed in dark brown ink and were usually touched up with grey or sepia washes. The two designs were sometimes coloured with water-colours, body colour being added in places. The thick wove paper sometimes shews parts of a watermark dated [17]97, but the portions of the sheets used sometimes missed this. The paper cannot be Whatman's, since this firm used only the date 1794 until after 1800, but it is of equally good quality. Blake probably damped the paper before printing and the plate-marks of all four plates are conspicuous. The eight copies so far identified and conforming to these criteria are as follows:

1. Keynes copy. Heavily inked, with grey washes added on the father's face in the upper design, and in the lower one on Tom's left arm, on the mother's right arm, and on parts of the background and sky. In the lower left corner is a water-mark shewing half the date, '97; above this are letters, but these are encroached upon by the inking of the design, so that they cannot be made out. The sheet measures $22\frac{1}{4}'' \times 7''$ ($56 \cdot 5 \times 17 \cdot 8$ cm.). Sold from an anonymous source at Christie's, 10 July 1953, lot 79A (Keynes, 30 gns.).

2. British Museum, Dept. of Prints and Drawings. Fairly heavily inked, both designs lightly coloured with water-colour washes and some body colour. The sheet, measuring $22'' \times 7\frac{1}{16}''$ ($56 \times 17 \cdot 9$ cm.), is laid down so that no watermark can now be seen, though there is a note stating that one was visible with the date '97. When compared with no. 1, there are seen to be some variations; in the upper design some high lights have been cleaned out and the lines of the clouds appear thickened. Acquired from Colnaghi in 1862.

3. E. J. Shaw copy. The designs are touched with coloured washes and some body colour. The sheet measures $19\frac{3}{4}'' \times 7\frac{3}{8}''$ ($50 \cdot 2 \times 18$ cm.). Watermark not recorded. Sold at Sotheby's, 27 June 1906, lot 176 (Tregaskis, £7. 7s.); sold with the E. J. Shaw Collection at Sotheby's, 29 July 1925, lot 161. Present owner not traced.

4. Cunliffe copy. Similar to no. 2, though the ink has a greenish hue. There is some sepia or grey water-colour wash on the upper design and the sky is coloured

blue. The sheet, somewhat tattered, measures $21\frac{5}{8}'' \times 7''$ ($54\cdot5 \times 17\cdot8$ cm.). No watermark is visible, but the paper is similar to that of the others. Acquired by Henry Cunliffe in the last century. Now the property of his great-nephew, the present Lord Cunliffe.

The sheet is inscribed in pencil, probably by a child: 'Dr Johnson has given Ch & Fy each one of them Sonye[?] & me a coloured one. *Rememʳ it is a Fact, a true story*. Written by Mr Hayley & engrav'd by Blake.'

5. W. Graham Robertson copy. Similar to nos. 1 and 2, with some sepia water-colour washes on the designs. The sheet measures about $19'' \times 6\frac{1}{4}''$ (49×16 cm.). Watermark not deciphered. Acquired by Graham Robertson from Carfax & Co. in 1904. Sold at Christie's, 22 July 1949, lot 85 (Colnaghi, 60 gns.). Acquired by Philip Hofer, Cambridge, Mass., and still in his collection.

6. Macgeorge copy. Heavily inked. The sheet measures $20\frac{3}{4}'' \times 7\frac{1}{4}''$ ($52\cdot7 \times 18\cdot5$ cm.). No watermark visible, but the paper is similar to that of the others. Formerly in the collection of B. B. Macgeorge of Glasgow, but not included in the Macgeorge sale at Sotheby's, 1 July 1924. It was offered by McCleary's of Glasgow as from the Macgeorge Collection in May 1958 and then acquired for the Fine Art Department of Glasgow University.

7. George C. Smith copy. The sheet measures $19'' \times 6\frac{1}{2}''$ ($48 \times 16\cdot4$ cm.). It has been divided into two portions and mounted, so that no watermark can be seen. The paper resembles that used for other originals. Sold with the George C. Smith Collection at the Parke-Bernet Galleries, 2 November 1938, lot 47, $120.

Acquired by Henry S. Borneman and resold at the same Galleries, November 1955, lot 234, $320. Acquired by Mrs. Gerard B. Lambert and given by her to Princeton University in 1960.

8. Moss copy. Size $20\frac{1}{2}'' \times 7\frac{1}{4}''$ (52×18 cm.). Watermark not recorded. Offered at Sotheby's with the W. E. Moss Collection, 2 March 1937, lot 191, but not sold as the lot had been mislaid. Offered again at Sotheby's, 20 December 1938, lot 458 (Robinson, £48), and catalogued by Robinson, December 1939, at £84. Described as 'printed from four plates', suggesting that plate-marks were visible. I had seen this copy, but did not record any details. Not traced.

In the *Bibliography of Blake*, Grolier Club of New York, 1921, it was stated that a facsimile reproduction of 'Little Tom' was made by William Muir 'about 1887' (p. 203), or in 1886 (pp. 297, 385). This was an error due to my having assumed that Muir, who was issuing his series of facsimiles of Blake's Illuminated Books at

Printed for & Sold by the Widow Spicer of Folkstone for the Benefit of her Orphans
October 5, 1800

Printed for & Sold by the Widow Spicer of Folkstone for the Benefit of her Orphans
October 5, 1800.

this period, was responsible for the broadside also. Muir himself could have set this right, as I paid a number of visits to his house in Edmonton during his last years, but omitted to ask him. It was some years later that I learnt that the only facsimile of this date had been made for insertion in *The Century Guild Hobby Horse*, vol. i, no. 4, October 1886, by the firm of Emery Walker & Boutall. The reproduction printed for Richard C. Jackson in 1917 is not comparable, since this shewed the two designs only, the ballad being in ordinary typography. Walker's reproduction, owing to its excellence, has given rise to much confusion, having often been mistaken for the original print. For many years the facsimile was exhibited at the Pierpont Morgan Library as an original until I pointed out the error. I was enabled to do this through having been acquainted with Sir Emery Walker, whom I oftened visited in his office in Clifford's Inn, Fleet Street, now demolished. He told me that he had made the facsimile for *The Century Guild Hobby Horse* and followed this information by handing me half a dozen copies of the broadside printed at his workshop. These were particularly valuable because they were printed on several different kinds of paper and so provided much more information than could have been obtained by merely referring to the print as seen in the periodical.

It is at once obvious that the reproduction must have been made from a print much more lightly inked than are any of those known at the present time, since it is possible to see in the etched lines some detail which is obliterated in Blake's heavily inked prints. It is stated in the periodical that H. H. Gilchrist had supplied the 'unique original' from which the reproducer worked. This original I have been unable to trace. Some years ago I was shewn a print obtained by Dr. J. Schwartz from a grandson of Mrs. Gilchrist, but could not satisfy myself that it was authentic. The paper was of poor quality, quite unlike the stout material used by Blake. It had evidently been much tattered and extensively repaired. No watermark was visible and there was no trace of plate-marks. I concluded that Gilchrist's print had been sold or given away, the family retaining only one of Walker's reproductions. Unfortunately I omitted to make a note of the important evidence provided by the colophon as seen in the facsimile.

In Blake's prints the loop of the *P* of *Printed* has a double line and the tail of the letter is prolonged into a tassel with three floating strands; in addition, the top of the *S* of *Spicer* has a flourish extending forwards over the next four letters (Plate 27.i). The facsimile invariably lacks these features. It does not necessarily follow that the original print lacked them. Sometimes, as in the original no. 5, the colophon is poorly inked and the flourishes are barely visible. The craftsman preparing the block for the reproduction would be likely to regard them as accidental marks and would clean them away (Plate 27.ii).

It only remains to describe the different papers used by Sir Emery Walker for his prints, some of them having probably been experimental.

i. The published version in *The Century Guild Hobby Horse* has been divided into two portions. The laid paper is of good quality with conspicuous chain lines and a watermark, JOHN DICKINSON, without date.

ii. A rather poor quality laid paper, liable to become frayed at the edges, without watermark; this is the form most frequently met with. The size of the sheet, untrimmed, is $22'' \times 9\frac{1}{8}''$ (56×23 cm.).

iii. A fairly good quality wove paper, sometimes with the watermark, POUNCY. The size of the sheet, untrimmed, is $24'' \times 9\frac{7}{8}''$ ($61 \times 25 \cdot 3$ cm.). This was the form exhibited at the Pierpont Morgan Library.

iv. A thin, smooth paper resembling 'Japanese vellum', without watermark. The size of the sheet is $23'' \times 9\frac{1}{4}''$ ($58 \cdot 5 \times 23 \cdot 5$ cm.).

v. A French laid paper with watermarks, P Le BAS and LB & Cie. An example of this form is in the collection of Mr. M. D. E. Clayton-Stamm, having been since the 1880s in the collection formed by William Bell Scott.

Examples of nos. ii–iv were among those given to me by Sir Emery Walker. None has any trace of a plate-mark. The prints were presumably made from a single, large, process block, printed without much pressure on undamped paper. The ink is greyish-black, giving a rather flat effect very different from that of Blake's heavily inked prints, which are dark brown rather than black, with monochrome or coloured washes added.

I hoped that Mr. Clayton-Stamm's print (no. v above) might prove to be the lost original. Bell Scott was a noted Blake collector and is almost certain to have been acquainted with the Gilchrists, from whom he might have purchased the print. Furthermore the Le Bas family have been making paper since the sixteenth century and are still active. It is, however, very unlikely that the watermark, LB & Cie, would have been used by any member of the firm before 1840, so that another original, lightly inked, must still be sought. It will be noticed that the reproductions were printed on larger sheets than were used by Blake.

XIII

BLAKE'S MINIATURES[1]

WILLIAM HAYLEY, as is well known, in the course of his patronage of William Blake during the years 1800–3 tried to launch him on a career as painter of portraits in miniature. Blake made an honest attempt to fall in with this, but in the end became disgusted with a trade which he found to be a betrayal of his true artistic faculties. By the end of January 1803 he was writing to Butts: 'He [Hayley] thinks to turn me into a Portrait Painter as he did poor Romney, but this he nor all the devils in hell will never do.'[2] Being always a competent craftsman, Blake had some aptitude for miniature painting.

The results are to be seen in the six extant portraits (Plate 28). These are the three of Thomas Butts, Mrs. Butts, and their son, Thomas Butts, junior, all now in the British Museum; the portrait of the Revd. John Johnson, Cowper's second cousin, now belonging to Miss Mary Barham Johnson, and the two versions of William Cowper after the pastel drawing by Romney now in the National Portrait Gallery. One of the Cowper miniatures was done for William Hayley, who gave it to Harriet Welford, sister of his second wife, Mary Welford. Harriet Welford gave it in turn to John Johnson's son, the Revd. William Cowper Johnson, recording its origin in a letter still in the keeping of the Cowper Johnson family together with the portrait. The other version, differing from the first only in small details, is now in the Ashmolean Museum, Oxford; its earlier history is not known, though it is likely to have been done also for Hayley. There must certainly be a number of others in existence still remaining to be identified, since Hayley was assiduous in introducing Blake to his friends in order that he might execute miniatures for them; but hitherto there has been no clue to the identity of these possible clients. Recently, however, a letter from Hayley has come into my possession indicating clearly that Blake had painted for Hayley himself a miniature of his first wife.[3] The letter is addressed to *Daniel Parker Coke Esqr, The Temple, London*, and is dated 13 May [1801]. Hayley wrote:

My dear Sir,

    I hope the inclosed little portrait may prove an agreeable surprize to you. I

---

[1] First printed in *The Times Literary Supplement* (1960), lix. 72.

[2] *Letters of William Blake*, ed. Keynes, London, 1968, p. 63.

[3] Hayley had married Elizabeth Ball in 1769.

have long wished to send you such a memorial of a wonderful Being, equally entitled to our admiration & our pity—a Being to whom your Friendship was an Honour & a Delight.

My dear Tom [his son] intended to execute for you such a Resemblance of Mrs. H. His own calamitous Illness & Death precluded Him from that pleasure—I have recently formed a new artist for this purpose by teaching a worthy creature (by profession an Engraver) who lives in a little cottage very near me to paint in miniature—accept this little specimen of his Talent as a mark of kind remembrance from

yr sincere & affectionate Friend
W. Hayley

Daniel Parker Coke, the recipient of the letter and of the miniature of Mrs. Hayley, was a member of the Coke family of Trusley, near Derby. Born in 1745, he was admitted in 1762 to All Souls College and was later called to the Bar. After practising for many years on the Midland Circuit, he was elected Member of Parliament for Derby in 1776; in 1780 he was returned for the town of Nottingham, which he represented for the next thirty-three years. He lived for many years at the College, Derby, and died there in 1825. He was unmarried and much of his property passed to his sisters, Dorothy and Sarah Hatrell, but there is no possibility of tracing such bequests in detail.

His collections of books and pictures had been dispersed at auction in 1824. A copy of the sale catalogue has been examined in the Derby Public Library by Mr. Ronald Coke-Steel, of Trusley Old Hall, and he has very kindly helped me in the search by lending me his copy of *Coke of Trusley: A Family History by Major J. Talbot Coke*, 1880, but no miniatures were specified in the catalogue and it seems to be impossible to pursue the matter any further.

It may be noted that in no document hitherto known has Hayley been seen to boast so unashamedly of his exploitation of Blake's talents. Nowhere else has the 'worthy creature' been actually 'formed' by 'teaching' him 'to paint in miniature'. Blake's natural reaction did not show itself until two years later; it might have come sooner had he known exactly how Hayley was writing of him to his friends.

XIV

BLAKE'S TRIAL AT CHICHESTER[1]

Two documents connected with Blake's trial for seditious utterances in January 1804 at Chichester assizes were shewn at an exhibition of documents from the Sussex County Record Office held at the County Hall in 1957. The County Archivist, Mr. Francis W. Steer, F.S.A., kindly allowed me to make use of them. The larger document was the formal Indictment against Blake made by the two soldiers, John Scolfield and John Cock, with the signature of William Ellis, Gentleman Clerk of the Peace. This was printed in full by the late Herbert Jenkins, under the name 'Herbert Ives', in 1910 (*The Nineteenth Century*, lxvii. 849–61). The associated document had not been noticed before. It is concerned with the recognizances entered into by Scolfield and Cock to ensure their appearing as witnesses against Blake. It is a printed form with the particular details entered by pen, these being printed here in italic:

Be it remembered that the *sixteenth* day of *August* in the year of our Lord one Thousand seven [altered to *Eight*] Hundred and *Three John Scolfield and John Cock private Soldiers in the First Regiment of Dragoons* came before me one of his Majesty's Justices of the Peace for the said *County and severally* acknowledged *themselves* to be indebted to our Sovereign Lord the King in the sum of *Fifty Pounds each* Upon Condition that if the above bound *John Scolfield and John Cock do severally* [*do* del.] personally appear at the next General *Quarter* Session of the Peace to be holden for the said *County* and give Evidence on his Majesty's Behalf, upon a Bill of Indictment to be then and there exhibited by *George Hulton a Lieutenant in the said Regiment* to the Grand Jury against *William Blake* for a *misdemeanour* And in Case the said Bill be found a true Bill: Then if the said *John Scolfield and John Cock do also severally* [*do also* del.] give Evidence to the Jurors who shall pass upon the Trial of the said *William Blake* for the same *Then this Recognizance to be Void*

Taken and acknowledged the Day and
Year above written, before me
John Quantock

---

[1] First printed in *Notes and Queries* (1957), ccii. 484–5.

The signatory, John Quantock, was one of the Justices of the Peace who sat on the bench at the trial on 11 January 1804. His name appears with those of other Justices in Blake's *Jerusalem* among the Twelve Sons of Albion (plate 19, lines 18–19):

> Hand, Hyle & Coban, Guantock, Peachey, Brereton, Slayd & Hutton, Scofeld, Kox, Kotope & Bowen: his Twelve Sons, . . .

Of these John Quantock, John Peachey, and William Brereton were Justices on the bench either at the preliminary hearing at Petworth on 4 October 1803, or at the trial at Chichester in the following January, though why Blake chose these particular names from among a much larger number is not obvious. Bowen was the prosecuting counsel. Hand and Hyle have been supposed to represent the Hunt brothers (Robert and Leigh) and William Hayley. The names Coban, Kotope, Slayd, and Hutton have not hitherto been explained, but the new document given here appears to identify Hutton with Lieutenant George Hulton, the officer responsible for the appearance of the two soldiers at the trial; Blake has altered others of the names in some degree, so that the discrepancy of one letter between Hutton and Hulton is immaterial.

XV

NEW LINES FROM *JERUSALEM*[1]

BLAKE's *Jerusalem*, the last of his great epics, was begun about 1804 after he had returned to London from Felpham, where he had suffered so much from William Hayley's well-meant, though uncomprehending, patronage. The composition of the whole work and the etching of the 100 copper-plates occupied at least fourteen years, for, although the title-page is dated 1804, none of the extant copies of the book can have been printed before 1818, the earliest date which appears in the watermarks of the paper used. It is thus not possible to assign an accurate date to any of the plates, though it is probable that they were made more or less in the order in which they stand in the completed book.

The first plate of *Jerusalem* serves as a frontispiece, being without text in any of the five extant complete copies printed by Blake. This plate represents a figure in hat and cloak, with a fiery globe suspended from his right hand, entering a stone doorway, and is sometimes taken to represent 'Los entering the bosom of Albion'. More probably the plate shews 'Los exploring the recesses of the Grave', and is related to the tenth illustration to Blair's *The Grave*, 1808, entitled, 'The Soul exploring the recesses of the Grave'. Los, in Blake's mythology, is Imagination, or the Spirit of Poetry and Prophecy, and Albion is the original Man, the first inhabitant of Britain. Jerusalem, Albion's emanation or feminine counterpart, was separated from him at the Fall, and the poem *Jerusalem* recounts the story of Albion's regeneration and reunion with Jerusalem, and of his awakening, after the passage through Eternal Death, to Spiritual Freedom.

Although the first plate exhibited no text in the published examples of the book, I had noticed that traces of lettering could be seen on the archway and on the stones above it, though this had been very effectively obliterated. After Blake's death in 1827 his widow took charge of his stock of prints and drawings, his copper-plates and other effects, disposing of some with the help of Frederick Tatham, who was also active in using Blake's press for printing many of the plates. He produced at least three copies of *Jerusalem*, these being distinguishable from Blake's own prints by the Whatman watermarks dated 1831 or 1832 and by the colour of the ink in which they are printed. Blake printed four of his five copies in black and left them

[1] First printed in *The Times Literary Supplement* (1943), xlii. 336.

uncoloured. The fifth, coloured with great magnificence, is printed in orange; he also printed a set of the first twenty-five plates in red-brown and painted them lightly with water-colour washes. Tatham, on the other hand, used only ink of a rich red-brown. One of these posthumous copies was available for examination in the Fitzwilliam Museum, Cambridge, and I was able to decipher most of the seven lines above the archway and some of the words on the right; those on the left were too indistinct for anything to be made out. These incomplete lines I printed in the notes to the three-volume edition of Blake's *Writings* (Nonesuch Press, 1925, vol. iii, p. 409), and did not think it expedient to incorporate them in the text of the later editions of 1927 or 1939. In 1943 I acquired an early proof of this plate, in which almost the whole of the lettering is made plain, so that the lines could then be added with confidence to the canon of Blake's writings (Plate 29). He had printed this proof on the reverse side of a proof of the title-page of *Europe*, 1794. The *Jerusalem* plate is printed in two colours, so that the right-hand side and upper part of the archway is light brown while the figure and the left-hand side of the archway shade off into a dense black, producing a sombre and splendid effect. The lettering, which would otherwise have been very indistinct, Blake has carefully outlined in black with a fine pen, with the exception of the first three or four words of the seventh line; these he has completely erased after the printing of the plate, leaving a narrow white space. The first word, O, is visible in the posthumous printing. Blake's original intention is revealed in this unique proof, first described in 1949. The text is as follows:

Above the archway:

> There is a Void outside of Existence, which if enterd into
> Englobes itself & becomes a Womb, such was Albions Couch
> A pleasant Shadow of Repose calld Albions lovely Land

> His Sublime & Pathos become Two Rocks fixd in the Earth
> His Reason his Spectrous Power. covers them above
> Jerusalem his Emanation is a Stone laying beneath
> O . . . behold the Vision of Albion.

On the right-hand side of the archway:

> Half Friendship is the bitterest Enmity said Los
>   As he enterd the Door of Death for Albions sake Inspired
> The long sufferings of God are not for ever there is a Judgment

On the left-hand side of the archway, in reversed writing:

> Every Thing | has its | Vermin O Spectre of the Sleeping Dead!

Pl. 29

The few stops included are the only ones supplied by Blake. These lines taken in conjunction with the rest of the book make it evident that Blake first intended his frontispiece to convey the theme of the whole work. Later he decided that this was unnecessary, the theme being announced more briefly in the first two lines of the poem:

> Of the Sleep of Ulro! and of the passage through
> Eternal Death! and of the awaking to Eternal Life.

Ulro is material existence, as opposed to the life of Imagination.

Nevertheless, readers who set a value on every scrap of Blake's writing will be grateful for the additional statement of the nature of Albion's lovely Land, that is the 'England's green & pleasant Land' of the well-known poem, so confusingly and erroneously called *Jerusalem*, although it is found at the beginning of his earlier work, *Milton*.

It is satisfactory, too, to possess Blake's new aphorism, 'Half Friendship is the bitterest Enmity'. This may be set beside the much earlier aphorism, 'Opposition is True Friendship', from *The Marriage of Heaven and Hell*, 1790, and his tortured cry 'To H——', that is 'To Hayley', scribbled down in his notebook about 1809:

> Thy Friendship oft has made my heart to ake:
> Do be my Enemy for Friendship's sake.

To the description of this discovery is added an account of the few copies of *Jerusalem* at present known. This census was first attempted in my *Bibliography of Blake*, 1921; it was revised in the separate *Census* of 1953 and is now brought more fully up to date.

The watermarks in the Whatman paper used by Blake give a clear indication of how he built up the different copies. No printing was begun before 1818 or completed before 1820. No copies are known to have been printed in the years 1821–3. The last copy was completed in 1826, the year before Blake's death. In the first year, 1818, he started to make a coloured copy, but took it no further than plate 25. Two years later, in 1820, he printed a complete copy in orange, and eventually coloured the whole of it. It was no doubt this copy of which Blake wrote on 12 April 1827 to George Cumberland:

The last work I produced is a poem entitled Jerusalem, the Emanation of the Giant Albion, but find that to print it will cost my time the amount of Twenty Guineas. One I have Finish'd. It contains 100 Plates, but it is not likely I shall get a Customer for it.

Blake did not, in fact, find a customer for it, and it seems to have passed with his other effects to Frederick Tatham. It has usually been assumed, on the authority of this remark by Blake, that only one complete coloured copy of the work has ever existed, but I was informed in 1920 by the late James Tregaskis, a well-known bookseller, that another coloured copy was sold by him to John Ruskin about 1885. I then communicated with Arthur Severn, the owner of Ruskin's library, and he stated that he had a distinct recollection of there having been such a book in the collection, but that he believed Ruskin cut it up. There is, moreover, evidence mentioned in Sotheby's *Catalogue of Fourteen Illuminated Manuscripts, the property of Henry Yates Thompson*, 22 June 1921 (p. 148), that Ruskin was in the habit of cutting to pieces illuminated manuscripts, however valuable, that were in his possession. A few plates printed on both sides of the leaves and coloured are known (see the Keynes–Wolf *Census*, pp. 111–12) and these may be surviving evidence of the extraordinary act of destruction attributed to Ruskin. An example of plate 51, representing Vala, Hyle, and Scofield, was in the John Linnell Collection, sold at Christie's, 15 March 1918 (lot 158, Martin, 70 gns.). This shewed stitch-holes near the left-hand margin, and it was numbered by Blake 51, but there is no evidence that this was taken from a complete coloured example of the book; more probably Blake took this leaf from an uncoloured copy, which he had been unable to sell, and coloured it as a specimen for Linnell. Another coloured example of the same plate was formerly in the Graham Robertson Collection and is now in mine. Separate leaves of the ordinary issue in black are also sometimes seen. One such, a specially fine impression of an early state of plate 37 with a blue and grey water-colour wash over the central portion, is in my collection. Prints from plates 9 (coloured), 19 (in blue), 20 (in black), 28 (in black with touches of red), 28 (duplicate, in green), 48 (in grey), 50 (in black), 58 (in grey), 78 (in black) were sold with the collection of George C. Smith, jr., New York, on 2 November 1938 (Parke-Bernet Galleries, lot 40); and of plate 50 (in black), 51 (in sepia), 99 (in sepia) in the same sale (lot 41).

CENSUS

Copies A–F, 1818–26

A. 100 plates on 100 leaves. Watermark J WHATMAN 1818, 1819, or 1820. Printed in black. Uncoloured except for occasional grey water-colour washes. Foliated by Blake 1–100 in black ink. Arrangement (taking copies D and E, in which Blake rearranged the plates of Chapter 2, as the standard): 1–28, 33–41,

43–6, 42, 29–32, 47–100. Plate 37 is in an early state (line 10, *pale death* afterwards altered to *blue death*). Size: 32·5 × 27 cm. Bound in half morocco, gilt edges. Now in the British Museum, Department of Prints and Drawings; purchased from Messrs. Evans in 1847.

B. 25 plates on 25 leaves, Chapter 1 only. Watermark on 6 leaves J WHATMAN 1818. Consists of the first 25 plates, arranged as in copy A, foliated by Blake 1–25. Printed in red-brown and lightly painted with water-colour washes. On plate 11 some letters and words of the text are picked out in black. On plate 19 the small recumbent figure seen in copy E below the larger figure is absent. The frontispiece faces the title-page, but stitch-holes in the free edge shew that Blake placed it the other way. Size about 37·5 × 25 cm. Now disbound; formerly in a Roxburghe binding with *America*, copy G, and *Europe*, copy B (of the Keynes–Wolf *Census*). A flyleaf has a watermark dated 1821. The composite volume was formerly in the library of P. A. Hanrott, sold with the first part at Evans's, 19 July 1833 (lot 642, French, £4). Later bought by Henry Cunliffe from C. J. Toovey, with Cunliffe's book-plate and the note 'Toovey 10-10-0'. Now the property of his great-great-nephew, the present Lord Cunliffe.

C. 100 plates on 100 leaves. Watermark J WHATMAN 1818, 1819, or 1820. Printed in black. Several plates have been touched up with sepia wash and Chinese white, and on plate 16 there is some green tinting; otherwise uncoloured. Foliated by Blake 1–100 in black ink. Arranged as in copy A. Size: 32 × 25 cm. Bound in vellum.

John Linnell's copy, sold with his collection at Christie's, 15 March 1918 (lot 194, Edwards, £89). Linnell had a receipt, dated 30 December 1819, for 14 shillings 'for Jerusalem Chap. 2',[1] perhaps referring to this copy, supplied chapter by chapter as each was completed. The book was acquired by the late Frank Rinder and is now the property of his daughter, Mrs. Ramsay Harvey. This copy was used for the facsimile published by the Trianon Press of Paris for the William Blake Trust in 1952.

D. 100 plates on 100 leaves. Watermark J. WHATMAN 1820 on 21 leaves. Printed in black with a single framing line round each print. Touched up with black or grey water-colour washes, otherwise uncoloured. Foliated by Blake 1–100 in black. Arranged as in copy A. Size: 33·8 × 26·8 cm. Unbound and matted.

The early history is unknown until it came into the collection of E. W. Hooper. It passed by bequest to his daughter, Mrs. Ward Thoron, of Boston, who gave it

[1] See *Blake's Letters*, ed. Keynes, London, 1968, p. 143.

to Harvard University Library in 1941 in memory of her father. Inserted is a note by E. W. Hooper stating that this copy was used for the Pearson facsimile of 1877.

E. 100 plates on 100 leaves. Watermark J WHATMAN 1820. Printed in orange. Elaborately coloured with water-colour washes, sometimes heightened with gold. Foliated by Blake 1–100 in orange ink. The plates of Chapter 2 have the second ordering as in copy D. Size: 33·5 × 27·5 cm. Bound in green morocco with clasps, together with the manuscript of Tatham's *Life of Blake*, 12 leaves, drawings of Blake at the ages of 28 and 69 by Frederick Tatham, and a drawing of Mrs. Blake by George Richmond after Tatham.

Blake referred to this copy in his letter to George Cumberland of 12 April 1827,[1] saying that it was not likely that he would get a customer for it. In fact he did not and it passed to Tatham after Mrs. Blake's death. At some date thereafter it was acquired by George Blamire, a barrister, with whose library it was sold at Christie's on 6 November 1863 (lot 213). It was then in its present binding with the additional matter. Bids were made by Brown (3 gns.) and by F. T. Palgrave (£5), but it was bought by Daniel, a dealer, for 48 gns.[2] The book was sold again at Christie's from an anonymous source on 1 June 1887 (lot 225, Quaritch, £166), and was acquired by General Archibald Stirling of Keir. At his death it passed to his son, Lt.-Col. William Stirling, who sold it in 1954 to Mr. Paul Mellon, Washington, D.C. Lt.-Col. Stirling in 1949 allowed the volume to be disbound in order that an accurate facsimile might be made by the Trianon Press of Paris for the William Blake Trust. This was published in an edition of 500 copies in 1951, the original book then being rebound in the original covers, though the leaves were guarded and properly sewn instead of overcast, as they had previously been.

F. 100 plates on 100 leaves. Watermark J WHATMAN 1824 on four leaves and 1819 on 19 leaves. Printed in black with touches of grey wash and some Chinese white. Foliated by Blake in black in the same order as copy A, but the pages of Chapter 2 were rearranged as in copy D when the book was last bound. Included in the book are extra proofs with variations of plates 28, 45, and 56, all with the watermark EDMEADS & PINE 1802, the date merely indicating Blake's use of old paper for his proofs. Size: 37·2 × 27·2 cm. Bound in straight-grained red morocco, top edges gilt, others untrimmed, by F. Bedford.

---

[1] See *Blake's Letters*, ed. Keynes, 1968, p. 163.

[2] This part of the history of copy E was not known to me until 1968, when I discovered it from a reference in a letter written by Mrs. Gilchrist to John Linnell in November 1863; the letter is among the Linnell family papers and was shewn to me by Miss Joan Linnell Ivimy. Messrs. Christie supplied the details from their marked catalogue.

Formerly in the possession of the London bookseller, James Toovey; bought from his son, Charles J. Toovey, in 1899 by J. Pierpont Morgan. Now in the Pierpont Morgan Library, New York.

[G]. A copy was said in 1939 to be in the library of a New York collector, but it has never been located and was probably listed in error.

[*Posthumous copies*], H–J, 1831–2

H. 100 plates on 100 leaves. Watermark J WHATMAN 1831 or 1832. Printed in dark red-brown. Uncoloured. No foliation. Size: 28·5 × 23 cm. Bound in contemporary morocco, elaborately tooled, gilt edges. Probably from the library of Francis Bedford, the book-binder, sold at Sotheby's, 21 March 1884 (lot 120, Quaritch, £5. 12s. 6d.). Afterwards in the collection of Samuel Boddington, with his book-plate. Sold again at Sotheby's, November 1895. Acquired by Charles Fairfax Murray and given by him in 1912 to the Fitzwilliam Museum, Cambridge.

I. 100 plates on 100 leaves. Watermark J. WHATMAN 1831 or 1832. Printed in dark red-brown. Uncoloured. Foliated in pencil. The plate-maker's stamp is visible on one plate. Size: 28·8 × 23·5 cm. Bound in red morocco, gilt edges, by Leighton, with the Milnes crest on the front cover.

Formerly in the collection of Thomas Butts, sold at Sotheby's, 26 March 1852 (lot 57, R. Monckton Milnes, £10. 15s.). From Monckton Milnes, afterwards Lord Houghton, it passed to his son, the Earl (later Marquess) of Crewe. Sold with the Crewe Collection at Sotheby's, 30 March 1903 (lot 15, Quaritch, £83). Then acquired by W. A. White, New York, and sold to Rosenbach with other Blake items in 1929. Now in the Lessing J. Rosenwald Collection, Library of Congress, Washington, D.C.

J. 100 plates on 100 leaves. Watermark J WHATMAN 1831 on 24 leaves. Printed in dark red-brown. Uncoloured. Plate 16 is missing and plate 20 is in duplicate. Size: 30·25 × 24·25 cm., untrimmed. Bound in contemporary half-russia with lettering piece on the cover.

There is no knowledge of provenance before 1928, when it was offered for sale by C. J. Sawyer, London. Afterwards in the Cortlandt Bishop library, sold by the American Art Association, 5 April 1938 (lot 280, Sessler, $2700). Then acquired by Charles J. Rosenbloom, Pittsburgh, Pa.

XVI

BLAKE'S COPPER-PLATES

BLAKE used the metal plate for the production of a large proportion of his literary and artistic output. He had been trained as a copper-plate engraver by Basire during his boyhood, and he set up as a print-producer in the style of the period shortly after his apprenticeship ended. Business in this line could not last long, however, for he was unable to remain in the ordinary rut, and once his irrepressible tendency to 'originality' had taken charge he had said farewell to worldly success. From ordinary engraving he passed about 1788, when he was 31, to his peculiar process of 'illuminated printing', in which both the letterpress and the designs for his pages were recorded on metal plates, either copper or pewter, chiefly by etching them with an acid.

The technical details of Blake's method remained obscure until in 1947 the English artist, S. W. Hayter, working in New York with his pupils, one of whom was Ruthven Todd, worked out a probable solution of the problem.[1]

Calligraphers had believed that the character of Blake's script proved that it had not been written out backwards in a resistant medium directly on the copper. Hayter shewed that a comparable result could be achieved by writing it with 'a solution of asphaltum and resin in benzene upon a sheet of paper previously coated with a mixture of gum arabic and soap'. The sheet was laid on a heated copper-plate and passed through the press. When the plate had cooled, the paper was soaked off with water, leaving the writing in reverse on the copper.[2] The artist then added the accompanying design around and among the text, using the same medium with a brush, and the whole was then etched with nitric acid, one part with two of water. This acid was preferred to any other mordant because it did not lead to undercutting the lettering if the plate was deeply bitten. The result was a relief plate to be used for surface printing. The inking was done by offsetting the pigment by pressure from another plate or board on to the copper before passing it through the press. Blake's peculiar reticulated effect could be imitated only in this way.

[1] See S. W. Hayter, *New Ways of Gravure*, London, Oxford University Press, 1966, pp. 64, 130.

[2] Confirmation of this transference is seen where Blake occasionally failed to get the lines of text square with the plate, so that the whole of the text appears slightly tilted, as in the prints of 'Spring' in *Songs of Innocence*.

From 1788 until 1818 Blake was intermittently occupied with the etching, printing, and colouring of his Illuminated Books, and a total of at least 363 etched plates of various sizes were completed. These formed an important part of his stock-in-trade, for he was printing small numbers of all his books throughout this period. His successive removals from one part of London to another, and, in 1800, for three years to Sussex, must have been complicated by the necessity for carting several hundredweight of metal in addition to his other paraphernalia and scanty household goods. The weight of metal was not, however, quite so great as it might have been, because Blake observed a certain degree of economy by using both sides of many of the plates. A conventional engraver, if he makes a mistake, can beat up the metal in any small area from the back and then re-engrave the surface, or he can rub down larger areas and start again; Blake's etching process did not allow of his easily correcting mistakes in either way, and the first would effectually prevent him from using the back of the plate for another etching. He could erase, and this he occasionally did, but corrections of text other than very small ones had to be made by etching another plate, and this he is known to have done in a few instances.

The proof that Blake used both sides of many of his plates is to be found in the presence of a plate-maker's mark on some of the uncoloured prints, this presumably being stamped only on one side of the plate. This mark can be deciphered as *Jones and Pontifex, No 47 Shoe Lane, London*, a firm represented up to recent times by Messrs. H. Pontifex & Sons, Ltd., Engineers, 43 Shoe Lane.

In addition to the etched plates Blake made and kept a few engraved plates, such as the large one (14 × 38 inches) of *The Canterbury Pilgrims*, which has survived to the present day.[1] In the last years of his life he also engraved the twenty-one plates for his *Illustrations of the Book of Job*[2] and the seven large plates for Dante's *Inferno*. These became the property of his friend and benefactor John Linnell, and the *Job* plates were deposited by the Linnell family trustees in the British Museum in 1918. The seven Dante plates were also preserved and are now in the Lessing J. Rosenwald Collection, National Gallery, Washington, D.C.[3] The etched plates for the Illuminated Books have been less fortunate, and in fact out of the large number which Blake made only one small fragment has survived. This is a piece of a copper-plate made for *America*, 1793, but afterwards re-etched in order that

[1] For further details of this and other plates see my book, *Blake's Separate Plates*, Dublin, 1956.

[2] He was still dealing with the same firm when he bought the plates for the *Job* in 1823, for eighteen of them are stamped on the back *Pontifex & Co., 2 Lisle Street, Soho, London*. One has the stamp *G. Harris, No. 31 Shoe Lane, London*.

[3] For further history see pp. 228–9 of the present work.

alterations might be made. The rejected plate was cut up by Blake, and the unused side of this piece was used by Tommy Butts, son of Blake's most faithful patron, for his own amateur efforts at engraving a head of John the Baptist under Blake's tuition. It was found in a small engraving cabinet formerly in the Butts Collection, and at the sale of the late W. E. Moss's Blake collection at Sotheby's in 1937 was bought by Dr. Rosenbach for £50, on behalf of Mr. Lessing J. Rosenwald.

It is probable that Blake kept all the plates made for his published books up to the time of his death, and that they passed under the control of Frederick Tatham after Mrs. Blake's death in 1831. Some of them were soon afterwards taken out and printed, for copies are known of *Songs of Innocence and of Experience*, *Europe*, *America*, and *Jerusalem*, all printed on Whatman paper with watermark dated 1831 or 1832. Nothing further is known of any of the plates with the exception of those for *Songs of Innocence and of Experience*. In Gilchrist's *Life of Blake*, first published in 1863, prints were included of sixteen of the *Songs*, and it is stated concerning the plates that 'the gentleman from whom they were obtained had once the entire series in his possession; but all save these ten [six being etched on both sides] were stolen by an ungrateful black he had befriended, who sold them to a smith as old metal'. It might be supposed that these ten plates at least might have survived until the present day, but the sad tale of loss or destruction has to be continued. Inquiries made in past years of Messrs. Macmillan, the publishers of Gilchrist's *Life*, have failed to obtain any news of the whereabouts of the original plates. In 1926 the late Laurence Binyon found, however, that electrotypes of the plates, at any rate, were still in the possession of Messrs. Clay & Son, of Bungay, who had printed Gilchrist's *Life* for Macmillan. Binyon was allowed to examine some of these, and noted that a tool had been used to scoop the hollows on the plate to a greater depth.[1] In 1942 Mr. Ruthven Todd again addressed inquiries to the printers, and by the courtesy of Messrs. Macmillan I was allowed to acquire a duplicate set of the sixteen electrotypes. The interest of these blocks is very great because, being electrotypes, they are exact reproductions of Blake's plates, so that something can be learnt from them of his technique. Careful examination of the surfaces, on two of which traces of the plate-maker's stamp are visible, shews that Blake undoubtedly first carried out both the lettering and the design on the copper in the same resistant medium. The plate was then etched with acid to no very great depth, but deeply enough to allow the text to stand out in relief. Blake then gouged out some of the larger spaces more deeply to prevent unwanted ink from showing in the print, and finally added more or less detail to the designs by means of the graver. Some of

1 *The Engraved Designs of William Blake*, London, 1926, p. 10.

SONGS OF INNOCENCE

1789

The Author & Printer W Blake

The Ecchoing Green

The Sun does arise,
And make happy the skies.
The merry bells ring,
To welcome the Spring
The sky lark and thrush,
The birds of the bush,
Sing louder around,
To the bells chearful sound.
While our sports shall be seen
On the Ecchoing Green.

Old John with white hair
Does laugh away care,
Sitting under the oak,
Among the old folk,

They

The Lamb

Little Lamb who made thee
Dost thou know who made thee,
Gave thee life & bid thee feed,
By the stream & o'er the mead;
Gave thee clothing of delight,
Softest clothing wooly bright;
Gave thee such a tender voice,
Making all the vales rejoice;
  Little Lamb who made thee
  Dost thou know who made thee

  Little Lamb I'll tell thee,
  Little Lamb I'll tell thee;
He is called by thy name,
For he calls himself a Lamb;
He is meek & he is mild,
He became a little child;
I a child & thou a lamb,
We are called by his name.
  Little Lamb God bless thee,
  Little Lamb God bless thee.

Nurses Song

When the voices of children are heard on the green
And laughing is heard on the hill,
My heart is at rest within my breast
And every thing else is still

Then come home my children the sun is gone down
And the dews of night arise
Come come leave off play, and let us away
Till the morning appears in the skies

No no let us play, for it is yet day
And we cannot go to sleep
Besides in the sky, the little birds fly
And the hills are all coverd with sheep

Well well go & play till the light fades away
And then go home to bed
The little ones leaped & shouted & laugh'd
And all the hills ecchoed

HOLY THURSDAY

Is this a holy thing to see,
In a rich and fruitful land,
Babes reduced to misery,
Fed with cold and usurous hand?

Is that trembling cry a song?
Can it be a song of joy?
And so many children poor?
It is a land of poverty.

And their sun does never shine,
And their fields are bleak & bare,
And their ways are fill'd with thorns,
It is eternal winter there.

For where-e'er the sun does shine,
And where-e'er the rain does fall,
Babe can never hunger there,
Nor poverty the mind appall

LONDON

I wander thro' each charter'd street
Near where the charter'd Thames does flow
And mark in every face I meet
Marks of weakness marks of woe.

In every cry of every Man
In every Infants cry of fear
In every voice . in every ban .
The mind-forg'd manacles . I hear

How the Chimney sweepers cry
Every. blackning Church appalls'.
And the hapless Soldiers sigh
Runs in blood down Palace walls

But most thro midnight streets I hear
How the youthful Harlots curse
Blasts the new born Infants tear
And blights with plagues the Marriage hearse

INFANT SORROW

My mother groand. my father wept.
Into the dangerous world I leapt:
Helpless, naked, piping loud:
Like a fiend hid in a cloud

Struggling in my fathers hands:
Striving against my swadling bands,
Bound and weary I thought best
To sulk upon my mothers breast.

the plates were not touched by the graver at all, particularly among the *Songs of Experience*, where Blake seems to have aimed at a somewhat harsher effect than in the *Songs of Innocence*. On others many engraved lines were added which profoundly affected the appearance of the finished prints by helping to break up the larger flat surfaces, as in the tongues of flame twining round the text of 'The Divine Image' in *Songs of Innocence*.

A few sets of the sixteen prints were made for the use of Ruthven Todd and myself, and the blocks were then deposited in the Fitzwilliam Museum, Cambridge; a second set of electrotypes was made in 1947 and was afterwards given to the Victoria and Albert Museum. Eight of the blocks are reprinted here. A third set was made for the Trianon Press (Paris) and Messrs. Clay & Son then destroyed their set of electrotypes.

There is a curious discrepancy to be seen in the electrotype of the title-page to *Songs of Experience*, which shews a different state of the plate from that with the date 1794 used in authentic copies of the *Songs* and for prints made after Blake's death by Tatham or Mrs. Blake. The Gilchrist plate has no date and many other differences in detail. Perhaps, therefore, the surviving plate was an earlier version not ordinarily used by Blake.

★   ★   ★

Blake had been familiar with printing techniques from the days of his apprenticeship to Basire and would have been well accustomed to using the engraver's rolling press or 'plate press'. He had taught his wife the art of printing, and on 30 January 1803 wrote from Felpham to his brother James: 'My Wife has undertaken to Print the whole number of the Plates for Cowper's work, which She does to admiration & being under my own eye the prints are as fine as the French prints & please everyone.'[1] These were the four plates for the first two volumes of Hayley's *Life and Writings of William Cowper*, Chichester, 1803. We know also that Mrs. Blake printed the broadside, 'Little Tom the Sailor', soon after their arrival at Felpham in 1800[2] and, from references in Hayley's letters,[3] that she shared with her husband the labour of printing the plates for the quarto edition of Hayley's *Ballads*, Chichester, 1802.

The rolling press was constructed on much the same principle as the household mangle and the pressure of its rollers could be adjusted in a similar way. A long

---

[1] *Blake's Letters*, ed. Keynes, 1968, p. 65.   [2] See p. 106 of the present work.
[3] See N. J. Barker, 'Some Notes on the Bibliography of William Hayley', *Trans. Camb. Bib. Soc.* (1963), iii. 341, 345.

plank, or bed, supported the plate, the paper, and a covering of resilient woollen blanket as they travelled together through the press. Four to six long spokes attached to one of the trunnions of the upper roller provided powerful leverage for driving it, so that it could be operated by a sturdy woman such as Mrs. Blake. The very heavy pressure thus generated forced the damped paper into the recessed lines of engraved plates, so drawing out the ink they retained after the plate had been wiped clean. Moreover the machine's facility for adjustment to a lighter pressure made it possible for the Blakes to use it for printing from the surface of the relief-etched plates; there is no reason to suppose that Blake ever used, or even had room for, a common press.[1] To the eye of someone accustomed to the use of a rolling press Blake's surface prints provide telling evidence. Many shew a heavy indentation and the distinct plate-mark peculiar to blanket-and-roller printing, as well as, occasionally, that common annoyance to the plate printer—creasing of the paper spreading sideways from the corners of the hind end of the plate. This can be caused by a number of factors, among them inequality of roller pressure and too heavily, or unevenly, damped paper; it is a fault that can disclose the direction in which a plate has been passed through the press.[2]

Blake's press was certainly built of wood, since heavy iron presses did not come into general use much before 1820. Moreover it was capable of being dismantled, as when it was transported to Felpham in September 1800. Later, in December 1803, soon after his return to London, Blake wrote to Hayley: 'Mr Romney's portrait goes on with spirit. I do not send a proof because I cannot get one, the Printers having been this afternoon unable or unwilling & my Press not yet being put up.'[3] Its size is a matter for speculation, but, Gilchrist having been informed that 'it was a very good one for that day, having cost £40 when new',[4] it would certainly have been of reasonable proportions judging by the prices of contemporary common presses. The average roller width in Blake's time was about 30 inches. The large *Ezekiel* and *Job* coppers of 1793–4 measure 18 × 22 inches, so that such a size would have been adequate for all his work except for the large 14 × 38 inch plate for *The Canterbury Pilgrims*; even this, at the risk of a greater number of spoiled impressions, could have been accommodated if the short dimension of 14 inches had been placed across the press. Printers would always

---

[1] This was the normal printer's press in which the impression was achieved by screwing down a heavy plane surface on to the paper to give an impression from a forme of type.

[2] Mr. Iain Bain has helped me with the technical facts of this study; without his kindness it could not have been made either accurate or intelligible.

[3] *Blake's Letters*, ed. Keynes, 1968, p. 81.

[4] Gilchrist's *Life*, 1880, i. 176; Everyman edn., p. 153.

prefer to put the plate with its long edge to the rollers in order to minimize the impression time and the risk of paper creasing. So it is perhaps likely that, having an average-sized press, both portable and suitable for his limited space, Blake would have taken this, the largest of his plates, to a trade house for printing, a practice to which, as we have seen, he was not unaccustomed. If, however, an impression from the first printing can be found carrying a faulty crease, it would be possible to tell the direction in which it was printed. If it should prove that the short edge of the plate had been laid to the roller, this would indicate the limited width of Blake's press and that it was printed by him at home rather than by a trade house.

When Blake was engraving the plates for his *Illustrations of the Book of Job* near the end of his life he made a large number of trial proofs as the engraving proceeded, but the printing of the whole edition of the twenty-two plates would have been excessively laborious for him even if he had the time. Linnell therefore arranged for the printing to be done by James Lahee, a leading man in the trade. Lahee had served his apprenticeship with a tradesman named Ebsworth and succeeded to the management of the business when his employer retired. Already in 1807 he had printed plates for Turner's *Liber Studiorum* and later worked for other distinguished artists. He built a large workshop in Castle Street, off Oxford Street, and so was conveniently near Blake and Linnell.[1] Lahee's name occurs repeatedly in Linnell's accounts for the costs of the *Job* illustrations.[2] After her husband's death in August 1827 Mrs. Blake still had the copper-plates for the Illuminated Books and sometimes made prints, but there is evidence that their press was larger than she needed. As we know from Linnell's *Journal*,[3] it had been removed from Fountain Court to his premises in Cirencester Place on 29 August and Mrs. Blake then tried to arrange with Lahee an exchange for a smaller one, Linnell acting as intermediary. Lahee replied in an undated letter to Linnell:[4]

Sir,

In answer to your note as to Mrs Blake's press I beg to say that I am not in want of a very large press at this moment, but if it happens to be larger than Grand Eagle and is a good one in other respects I have one which would answer Mrs B's purpose, and which I would exchange with her for . . . but the fact is that wooden presses are quite gone by now & it would not answer me to give much if any Cash: notwithstanding the circumstances you mention would prevent my attempting to drive a hard bargain—I can't come out myself before

---

[1] See A. W. Tuer, *Bartolozzi and his Works*, 1885, p. 207.
[2] *Blake's Letters*, ed. Keynes, 1968, pp. 145–51.   [3] See p. 223 of the present work.
[4] Printed by permission of Miss Joan Linnell Ivimy, custodian of the Linnell family papers.

Monday morning but my man shall look in upon you about 1 Oc. who will report to me how he finds it & if likely to answer. I should wish a trial of it for a week. I remain S^r

Your ob. st. J. Lahee

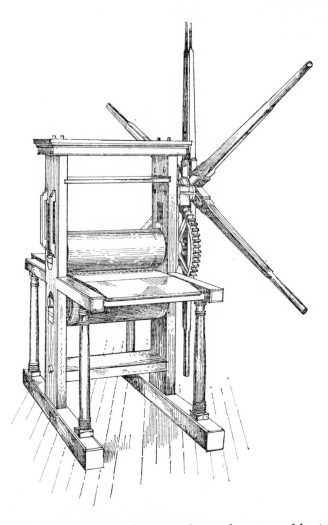

The term 'Grand Eagle' used by Lahee to indicate the acceptable size of press was in fact the name of a plate paper measuring 40 × 27 inches. To a printer the significant dimension of a press was its roller width. There was a progression in the sizes of plate papers only on their long sides and the largest 'short side' measurement was only 30½ inches, so we must assume that a 'Grand Eagle' press had a roller width of 40 inches. Small presses were made with 18-inch rollers and one of these would have served Mrs. Blake well enough, her concern being only with the relatively small plates of the Illuminated Books. It is probable, therefore, that Blake's press passed into the keeping of Lahee and that it would not have survived for many years, wooden presses being, as Lahee remarked, well out of fashion in 1827.

The only extant example of a wooden rolling press such as we may suppose Blake to have used is to be seen in the Science Museum, South Kensington. It has a roller width of 22½ inches with a plank of 53 inches and appears to be of the late eighteenth century, though it has been modified at a later date to take a single-reduced gearing, as can be seen in the drawing opposite.[1] A modification of this kind could have been made in Blake's lifetime and would certainly have helped his wife to make lighter work of the printing. The rollers are made of *lignum vitæ*, or guaiacum wood, from the West Indies, the hardest wood that is known.

[1] Made by Mr. Max Brooker from a photograph supplied by the Department of Education and Science, Science Museum, London, S.W.7.

XVII

BLAKE'S VISIONARY HEADS AND THE GHOST OF A FLEA[1]

FEW episodes in the life of William Blake have attracted more attention than his association with the water-colourist and astrologer John Varley (1779–1842). Blake had always emphasized the visionary nature of his art and claimed that the words of his poems were dictated to him by visionary figures, but it seems to have been Varley's influence that induced him, late in life, to draw the portraits of a great variety of historical personages who appeared at his command and remained while he recorded their features with his pencil. A considerable number of these 'Visionary Heads' are still in existence, and many have authenticating inscriptions by Varley or Linnell, sometimes with a date, indicating that they were done during the years 1819 to 1825. Blake's friend John Linnell had been a pupil of Varley and is believed to have brought the two artists together, and most of the drawings remained in the collections of Varley and Linnell. Many, therefore, were not dispersed until the sale of the Linnell Collection at Christie's in March 1918.

Gilchrist wrote of Varley in his *Life of Blake*: 'Superstitious and credulous, he cultivated his own credulity, cherished a passion for the marvellous, and loved to have the evidence of his senses contradicted.'[2] Many anecdotes have been related of this association between Blake and Varley, and some will be found in the pages of Gilchrist's *Life*. That these are not all apocryphal is shown by the inscriptions written on the drawings at the time of their execution. 'Rd. Coeur de Lion Drawn from his Spectre Born 1156 Died April 6 1199 [astrological characters] at Birth W Blake fecit Octr 14 1819 at ¼ past 12 Midnight'; 'Wat Tyler By Wm Blake from his spectre as in the Act of Striking the Tax Gatherer on the head Drawn Octr 30 1819 1h.A.M.'; 'Head of Achilles drawn by William Blake at my request 1825'—these are some examples of Varley's immediate statements.

Blake's capacity for drawing visionary portraits has often in the past been taken as evidence of mental instability. The late Dr. Charles Singer gave me the alternative suggestion that his 'visions' might have had a migrainous origin. But

---

[1] First printed in *Bulletin of The New York Public Library* (1960), lxiv. 567–72.
[2] Alexander Gilchrist, *Life of William Blake* (1863), i. 250.

neither explanation has seemed to me to be either probable or necessary. Blake was always proud of the vigour of his imaginative faculty, and it is more likely that, while enjoying Varley's eccentric character, he was very willing to enter fully into the spirit of the game that he and his friend had invented, regarding it not too seriously, but nevertheless allowing it to be a legitimate outlet for artistic creation. Many of the drawings are very carefully finished and are far from being rough sketches thrown off in an idle hour.

The fullest and most authentic account of the Visionary Heads is that given by Allan Cunningham in his memoir of Blake written soon after Blake's death and published in 1830 (revised 1833). The anecdotes were related to Cunningham by Varley himself (Plate 30), the 'friend' who told him:

I know much about Blake—I was his companion for nine years. I have sat beside him from ten at night till three in the morning, sometimes slumbering and sometimes waking, but Blake never slept; he sat with a pencil and paper drawing portraits of those whom I most desired to see.

Varley provided details about individual drawings:

He was requested to draw the likeness of Sir William Wallace—the eye of Blake sparkled, for he admired heroes. 'William Wallace!' he exclaimed, 'I see him now—there, there, how noble he looks—reach me my things!' Having drawn for some time, with the same care of hand and steadiness of eye, as if a living sitter had been before him, Blake stopt suddenly, and said, 'I cannot finish him— Edward the First has stept in between him and me.' 'That's lucky,' said his friend, 'for I want the portrait of Edward too.' Blake took another sheet of paper, and sketched the features of Plantagenet; upon which his majesty politely vanished, and the artist finished the head of Wallace.

Cunningham was shewn the portraits, framed, on the wall behind him, and Varley then produced a book filled with drawings, in which Cunningham saw a series of heads—Corinna the Theban, Lais the courtesan, the taskmaster slain by Moses in Egypt, Herod, and so on. The climax of the conversation was reached when Varley

closed the book, and taking out a small parcel from a private drawer, said, 'this is the last which I shall show you; but it is the greatest curiosity of all. Only look at the splendour of the colouring and the original character of the thing!' 'I see', said I, 'a naked figure with a strong body and a short neck—with burning eyes which long for moisture, and a face worthy of a murderer, holding a bloody cup in its clawed hands, out of which it seems eager to drink. I never saw any shape so strange, nor did I ever see any colouring so curiously splendid—a kind of glistening green and dusky gold, beautifully varnished. But what in the world is it?' 'It is a ghost, Sir—the ghost of a flea—a spiritualization of the thing!' 'He saw this in a vision then', I said. 'I'll tell you about it, Sir. I called on him one evening, and found Blake more than usually excited. He told me he had seen a wonderful thing—the ghost of a flea! And did you make a drawing of him? I inquired. No, indeed, said he, I wish I had, but I shall, if he appears again! He looked earnestly into a corner of the room, and then said, here he is—reach me my things—I shall keep my eye on him. There he comes! his eager tongue whisking out of his mouth, a cup in his hand to hold blood, and covered with a scaly skin of gold and green;—as he described him so he drew him.'[1]

So we have in Varley's words, as reported by Cunningham, the genesis of the famous tempera painting (Plate 30) on a panel now in the Tate Gallery. It passed out of the Varley family in 1878 and was acquired by the artist William Bell Scott (1811–90). After Scott's death it was sold at Sotheby's, 14 July 1892 (lot 235, £10. 5s.). Quaritch then offered it in August of the same year for £18, and it was bought by the late W. Graham Robertson, the first picture by Blake that he acquired. It was bequeathed by Robertson to the Tate Gallery in 1949.

Although Cunningham was shewn the tempera painting as the first revelation of this curiosity, it seems that Varley might have exhibited Blake's preliminary drawing of the figure which was contained in the book of drawings already mentioned. This book, in drab boards and inscribed *Blake Sketches* on the upper cover, passed from Varley into the possession of William Mulready (1786–1863), another friend of both Varley and Blake. It was sold at Christie's 28 April 1864 (lot 86, Rimpton, 5 gns.) and was described in the sale catalogue as: 'A volume containing 49 heads, in pencil, from visions which appeared to him and remained while he completed them; at the other end of the book are 16 landscapes by Varley.' A number of leaves were then removed and it was acquired, thus mutilated, by William Bell Scott, who contributed an article about it, entitled 'A Varley and Blake Sketch book', to *The Portfolio* (July 1871), 103–5. This was illustrated by a lithographic plate giving copies of a landscape by Varley, Blake's full-length drawing of the Ghost of a Flea (Plate 31), and other drawings by Blake, including another version of the head of the Flea taken from the engraving included among the plates in Varley's *Zodiacal Physiognomy*, 1828. This engraving was taken from a pencil drawing in Linnell's collection (Plate 32), which may also have been once

---

[1] Allan Cunningham, *The Lives of the Most Eminent British Painters, Sculptors and Architects* (1833), ii. 167–70.

J. Varley Born
august 17. 1778
18.56 ascending

Portrait of J. Varley
B. Wm Blake.

Pl. 32

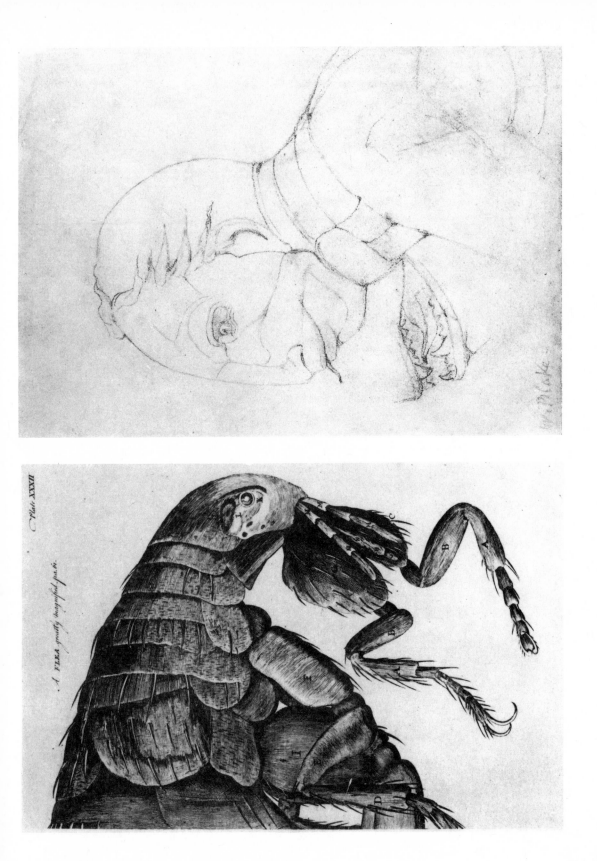

Pl. 33

in the book described above. The drawing shows the Flea's head with the mouth closed and tongue protruded, and below it an enlarged study of the open mouth with the pointed tongue lying between two rows of sharp teeth. This drawing was acquired by Miss A. G. E. Carthew at the Linnell sale at Christie's, 15 March 1918 (in lot 164, £54. 12s.), and was bequeathed by her to the Tate Gallery in 1940.[1] Varley gave on pages 54–5 of his *Zodiacal Physiognomy* another account of Blake's drawing:

With respect to the vision of the Ghost of the Flea, seen by Blake, it agrees in countenance with one class of people under Gemini, which sign is the significator of the Flea; whose brown colour is appropriate to the colour of the eyes in some full-toned Gemini persons. And the neatness, elasticity, and tenseness of the Flea, are significant of the elegant dancing and fencing sign Gemini. This spirit visited his imagination in such a figure as he never anticipated in an insect. As I was anxious to make the most correct investigation in my power, of the truth of these visions, on hearing of this spiritual apparition of a Flea, I asked him if he would draw for me the resemblance of what he saw; he instantly said, 'I see him now before me.' I therefore gave him paper and a pencil, with which he drew the portrait, of which a fac-simile is given in this number. I felt convinced by his mode of proceeding, that he had a real image before him, for he left off, and began on another part of the paper, to make a separate drawing of the mouth of the Flea, which the spirit having opened, he was prevented from proceeding with the first sketch till he had closed it. During the time occupied in completing the drawing, the Flea told him that all fleas were inhabited by the souls of such men, as were by nature bloodthirsty to excess, and were therefore providentially confined to the size and form of insects: otherwise, were he himself for instance the size of a horse, he would depopulate a great portion of the country. He added that if in attempting to leap from one island to another, he should fall into the sea, he could swim, and should not be lost. This spirit afterwards appeared to Blake, and afforded him a view of his whole figure; an engraving of which I shall give in this work.

The second engraving, however, never appeared as no further instalment of the *Zodiacal Physiognomy* was published. The mutilated sketch-book was also lost for many years, so that the *Portfolio* lithograph was for a long time the only record of the full-length drawing[2]—apart from its subsequent elaboration in the tempera

[1] A reproduction of it will be found in *Blake's Pencil Drawings*, ed. Keynes (Nonesuch Press, 1927), plate 49.

[2] The book was rediscovered in 1968 by Mr. M. D. E. Clayton-Stamm and has been published in facsimile by Messrs. Heinemann, 1969, with an Introduction by Martin Butlin.

painting. The drawing shows the Flea with a clawed index finger raised to his lips and with a high spiny ridge on his back, or perhaps an indication of short bat-like wings. In the painting the whole figure and its attributes are far more vigorous and dramatic. The bull-necked scaly monster is staring into the bleeding bowl held in its left hand, and holds a two-pronged sting in its right hand behind its back. Spines on the head and behind the ears are carried on down the line of the vertebrae. The right foot is advanced and the body is springing forward from the left foot with long clawed toes. Heavy curtains hang on either side and in the dark sky behind are three large stars with a fourth descending as a meteor, the light from which illuminates the Flea with a golden glimmer.

Varley's whole description of the episode, with the details of the Flea's conversation, seems to me to provide conclusive evidence that Blake was deliberately leading on his credulous friend with his own tongue in his cheek. He was evidently very much amused, though he used the incident by making an exceedingly effective and imaginative picture. No full explanation, however, has yet been offered as to how Blake constructed his bloodthirsty monster. His artistic imagination was given full play, but it may be guessed that he built, as often in his most original compositions, on some basis taken from an outside source. Dr. Charles Singer[1] has, I think, provided the clue by pointing out that there are certain resemblances between Blake's visionary Flea and the celebrated engraving of a flea as seen under a microscope included by Dr. Robert Hooke in his *Micrographia*, first published in 1665.[2] In the pencil drawing the overlapping plates on the flea's neck are arranged very much as in Hooke's figure (Plate 32), and the protruded tongue is suggested by the palps of the flea. The plating is less conspicuous in the painting, but the eye is more like that of the engraving and the vertebral spines could have been suggested by the bristles lying along the flea's back.[3] Even more convincing is the two-pronged sting held in the monster's left hand. This exactly reproduces the curved claws which are a very conspicuous feature of Hooke's flea at the end of each of the six legs. Other books concerned with microscopy were published in the eighteenth century, also containing figures illustrating the flea, such as Baker's *The Microscope Made Easy*, London, 1743, and Adams's

[1] Dr. Singer had briefly referred to the possibility of Blake's debt in his article, 'The First English Microscopist: Robert Hooke', *Endeavour*, xiv (1955), 12–18.

[2] Robert Hooke, *Micrographia* (1665), plate xxxiv.

[3] The Editor of the New York Public Library Bulletin has pointed out that the hair in Blake's drawing, arranged in a band of pointed twists, appears to be transitional between spines edging the vertebral plates, in Hooke, and the bristling hair and bristles in Blake's painting. The hair line and the facial lines in the drawing also suggest that Blake's flea's face and head are composed of plates.

Micrographia Illustrata, London, 1746, but the suggestions of Blake's indebtedness are less convincing than they are in Hooke's volume.

There were two eighteenth-century publications in which Hooke's plate of the flea was reprinted—*Micrographia Restaurata*, London, 1745, and *Microscopic Observations*, London, 1780—either of which might have come into Blake's hands while he was entertaining Varley with his visionary faculty. Nevertheless there is some reason to believe that Blake was acquainted with the text of the original edition of the *Micrographia*. According to Varley, Blake spoke of seeing the flea's 'eager tongue whisking out of his mouth'. Hooke on pages 210–11 says: 'between these [the feelers, or smellers] it has a small proboscis, or probe, that seems to consist of a tube, and a tongue or sucker, which I have preceiv'd him to slip in and out.'

If this indebtedness be admitted, it is impossible not to admire the skill with which Blake has adapted the facts of a flea's anatomy to the demands of his own formulas for the creation of evil monsters. Earlier examples of comparable figures are to be seen in the water-colour paintings of 'Pestilence' and 'Goliath cursing David', both in the Boston Museum of Fine Arts, but in neither is the dramatic effect as well realized as in the figure inspired by Hooke's flea.

XVIII

THORNTON'S *VIRGIL*[1]

THE splendour of Blake's *Illustrations of the Book of Job* might have set him once and for all upon a pedestal from which he would never again look down to consider a trivial or ill-paid commission; but Blake had by now learnt that humility became him and his art better than pride, so that he was able to turn from the *Book of Job* and loose the full vigour of his mind upon making a series of illustrations for Dr. Robert John Thornton's *Pastorals of Virgil*. Dr. Thornton was family physician to the Linnells. He had studied medicine at Cambridge and Guy's Hospital and began practice in London in 1797. His main interest, however, was botany, and while continuing in practice as a physician, he adventured on a lavish scale in publishing botanical works. He lost heavily in some of these ventures, but he was both industrious and versatile, and published books on several other subjects, including a school *Virgil* in 1812. This was at first unadorned, illustrations being published separately in 1814. A second edition with these woodcut illustrations was published in 1819, and its success was such that a third edition was planned for publication in 1821. Owing to Thornton's association with the Linnells, it came about that in 1820 Blake was introduced to his notice with the suggestion that he should assist in illustrating the new edition of the *Virgil*. Blake was not, however, to be employed only as designer of illustrations. He was to work also, perhaps primarily, as journey-man engraver, and in this capacity he drew and engraved on copper a set of six plates showing portrait busts of Theocritus, Virgil, Augustus Caesar, Agrippa, Julius Caesar, and Epicurus. He also made a drawing after Nicolas Poussin's painting of 'The Giant Polypheme', and from this a wood-engraving was executed by Byfield. These engravings possess no artistic merit whatever, and Dr. Thornton evidently intended them only as adjuncts to the main mass of illustration, which consisted of no less than 117 pages of small woodcuts. Most of these are puerile in quality and are unsigned, though the artists included Bewick, Byfield, Hughes, Thompson, and Thurston. Some had already appeared in the earlier editions, others were newly designed or engraved, and all of them no doubt helped to render the book more

[1] First printed as Introduction to *The Illustrations of William Blake for Thornton's Virgil*, London, Nonesuch Press, 1937.

palatable to juvenile readers than if it had been without them. The volumes were entitled:

The Pastorals of Virgil, with a Course of English Reading, Adapted for Schools: in which all The Proper Facilities are given, enabling youth to acquire The Latin Language in the Shortest Period of Time. Illustrated by 230 Engravings.

They were printed by J. M'Gowan and published by F. C. and J. Rivingtons in association with a number of other publishers, and were sold in a pink sheep-skin binding at 15s. (with a full Allowance to the Trade and Schoolmasters). An advertisement card was circulated with the following announcement by Mr. Harrison, agent for Dr. Thornton:

Dr. Thornton's Greatly admired and esteemed *Virgil* illustrated by two hundred and thirty cuts! Engraved by the first Artists of this Country is now on Sale & may be purchased of W. Harrison, Wine Merchant N°. 13 Little Tower Street, London. This work is patronized by the Master of St. Paul's.

The book has a faint attraction at the present time for connoisseurs of 'period' pieces, though this would not entitle it to any more attention than many similar productions. Its only source of value and importance is, in fact, to be found in Blake's contribution to the 230 illustrations. To him was assigned the task of illustrating an Imitation of Virgil's first Eclogue by the early eighteenth-century poet Ambrose Phillips, in which two shepherds, Colinet and Thenot, engage in a mild pastoral dialogue. Blake had never before executed any wood-engravings, and his preliminary designs gave no hint of what the final result would be. He filled a small oblong sketch-book with small drawings in sepia wash which have a delicate beauty of their own, and the contrast between these and their counterparts on wood is startling (Plate 34). Blake always contrived to let his originality play upon any medium in which he chose to work, whether water-colour, tempera, or metal plate, so that the result was distinct from the work of any other artist.

The ruggedness of Blake's prints has often been attributed to his ignorance of the technique of wood-engraving. He was however, quite accustomed to working in somewhat similar media. He had himself described the method of how to 'woodcut on pewter', and examples of this process may be seen in his designs for Hayley's ballad of 'Little Tom the Sailor', published in 1800. Many of his relief-etchings on copper also produce very much the same effect as woodcuts, so that his lack of familiarity with the wood-block as a medium has been given an exaggerated importance. This is only saying, however, that Blake probably had a very clear idea of the effect that he wished to produce with his wood-engravings, and does not in any way detract from the grandeur of his achievement. Though superlatives are dangerous, it is impossible to avoid them in writing of Blake's woodcuts. The pages of Thornton's *Virgil* are filled with everything that is trite and trivial. Suddenly, as a leaf is turned, a page of Blake's woodcuts leaps into the consciousness and for a moment the world is transformed by the breath of genius. As the first shock of astonishment passes, the wonder grows how Blake has conveyed so much in such small compass. Each block as first engraved measured only 35 to 40 × 84 mm., or about $1\frac{1}{2} \times 3\frac{1}{2}$ inches, yet in that tiny space, using the greatest economy of line, Blake has depicted with complete mastery a spacious landscape, a cataclysm of nature, or a tender pastoral scene. The wood-blocks are arranged for the most part close together, four on a page, and each one gains, if possible, by the proximity of the others. The designs do not all reach the same high level, though the least successful is a masterpiece if put beside the work of most wood-engravers of the period. They are indeed, in nearly all respects, the most completely satisfying woodcuts ever executed, and yet Blake did not ever again choose to make any engravings in the same medium. Linnell's descendants possessed a wood-block[1] on which Blake made a careful pencil and Indian ink drawing of great beauty (Plate 37), representing 'The Prophet Isaiah foretelling the Destruction of Jerusalem', but this was never actually cut. No record exists of his own feelings about the woodcuts. Did he not regard them seriously as works of art, or did he feel that he could never again attain the same level of artistic creation in that particular vein? Probably neither view is true. He was busied in the succeeding years with his engravings of the *Illustrations of the Book of Job*, and had no occasion to turn his attention to wood-engraving.

Whatever Blake's thoughts about the woodcuts may have been, there can be no doubt of the effect of their impact on the consciousness of his contemporaries. Dr. Thornton was not an imaginative man. He was enterprising and prolific where botany and medicine were concerned, and employed recognized artists to illustrate his works, sometimes on a lavish scale. Unrecognized genius, however, left him unimpressed, and Blake's woodcuts only prompted him to jeer. When they were laid before him he was horrified by such rough and amateurish work, and immediately gave directions that the designs should be recut by a professional wood-engraver. This would have been done but for the intercession of Linnell, and, it is said, of Sir Thomas Lawrence and James Ward, whom Thornton happened to meet at the house of a common friend. Though these artists warmly praised the woodcuts, Thornton remained uneasy, and felt that he had to apologize for the

[1] Now in the Print Room of the British Museum.

inclusion of such work in his book. Accordingly he caused the following note to be printed below the first woodcut:

The Illustrations of this English Pastoral are by the famous BLAKE, the illustrator of *Young's* Night Thoughts, and *Blair's* Grave; who designed and engraved them himself. This is mentioned, as they display less of art than genius, and are much admired by some eminent painters.

Three of the designs, nos. 14–16, were actually re-engraved for the book by a professional hand, and lost all character and merit in the process. Fortunately they are the least important of the series. A fourth was also recut, presumably by the same hand, and the result is an interesting example of how the originality of genius may be reduced to the conventional formula of the moment. It was not used in the book but was printed side by side with an impression from Blake's corresponding wood-block in *The Athenaeum* for 21 January 1843 and this print is reproduced here (Plate 35). The writer of this article was reviewing an edition of *The Vicar of Wakefield*, illustrated by William Mulready, who had, however, not executed the wood-engravings himself, and took the opportunity to protest vigorously against the almost universal practice of having an artist's drawings engraved by a journey-man engraver. Blake's woodcuts were the most convincing argument that he could find against the prevalent mechanization of the art—worse, indeed, in its results than the photographic process reproductions of succeeding years. Dr. Thornton, a cheerful and industrious materialist, could hardly be expected to sympathize with the 'artistic' view of his friends, and so tried to cover himself with the statement quoted above. Blake's feelings on reading Thornton's note may be imagined. He had suffered from similar patronage at the outset of his creative career, when the kind friends who helped him to print his early poems in the volume of *Poetical Sketches* in 1783 apologized in a Preface for 'the irregularities and defects to be found in almost every page'. This situation was now repeated in his old age, and again Blake, still unrepentant, knew that his 'irregularities and defects' were the product of the divine imagination that was in him, and must not be altered or revised. He so far forgave Thornton as to execute another small copper-plate engraving in 1825 for an unsuccessful 'annual' called *Remember Me!* It clearly, however, gave him much satisfaction when he penned in 1827 his pungent margin-alia in a copy of Thornton's pamphlet on The Lord's Prayer. 'I look upon this', he wrote, 'as a Most Malignant & Artful attack upon the Kingdom of Jesus By the Classical Learned, thro' the Instrumentality of Dr. Thornton. The Greek & Roman Classics is the Antichrist. I say Is & not Are as most expressive & correct too.' He further developed his attack on Thornton as the arch-materialist, and gives near the end his own parody of Thornton's new translation of The Lord's Prayer, heading it: 'Doctor Thornton's Tory Translation, Translated out of its disguise in the Classical & Scotch language into the vulgar English.' He concluded:¸ Thus we see that the Real God is the Goddess Nature, & that God Creates nothing but what can be Touch'd & Weighed & Taxed & Measured; all else is Heresy & Rebellion against Caesar, Virgil's Only God—see Eclogue i; for all this we thank Dr. Thornton.' Blake was very ill and nearing his life's end, but he had not forgotten his woodcuts for the Imitation of Virgil's First Eclogue and how the breath of imagination had ruffled Dr. Thornton's Tory mind.

In 1820 Blake's defenders had been a few eminent and sophisticated persons. Four years later he was to know the greater satisfaction of being almost worshipped by less sophisticated intelligences, when he became the centre of a group of young artists, the chief of whom were Samuel Palmer, Edward Calvert, and George Richmond. It was the Virgil woodcuts that affected them beyond everything else, so that Palmer and Calvert themselves made lovely engravings and woodcuts of pastoral subjects bearing the clear inspiration of Blake in every line, and Palmer even made sepia drawings and brilliantly coloured paintings having much of the strength and ruggedness of Blake's woodcuts. In 1824 Palmer wrote in his notebook:

I sat down with Mr. Blake's Thornton's *Virgil* woodcuts before me, thinking to give to their merits my feeble testimony. I happened first to think of their sentiment. They are visions of little dells and nooks and corners of Paradise: models of the exquisitest pitch of intense poetry. I thought of their light and shade, and looking upon them I found no word to describe it. Intense depth, solemnity, and vivid brilliancy only coldly and partially describe them. There is in all such a mystic and dreamy glimmer as penetrates and kindles the inmost soul, and gives complete and unreserved delight, unlike the gaudy daylight of this world. They are like all that wonderful artist's works, the drawing aside of the fleshly curtain, and the glimpse which all the most holy, studious saints and sages have enjoyed, of that rest which remaineth to the people of God.[1]

* * *

Blake's woodcuts number seventeen in all, together with three blocks engraved from his designs by another hand. The first woodcut is larger than the others, and was printed by itself as a frontispiece to Phillips's Eclogue. Below it is the note by

---

[1] *Life and Letters of Samuel Palmer*, by A. H. Palmer (London, 1892), p. 15.

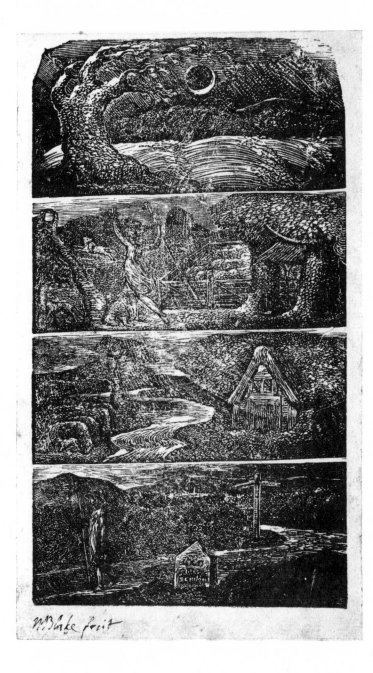

Dr. Thornton already quoted. No preliminary design for this block is extant, but the sketch-book formerly in the Linnell Collection contained drawings for the other nineteen designs with one extra drawing which was not used. The sketch-book was sold with the Linnell Collection at Christie's on 15 March 1918 (lot 205, Parsons, £113), and was afterwards traded to America. It was sold again by the American Art Association, New York, on 22 April 1924 (lot 60, $1,625), being bought by the Brick Row Bookshop Inc. The drawings were then sold separately, and are now in the possession of several collectors. Sixteen of them, by the courtesy of their owners, were photographed for reproduction by the Nonesuch Press, which first used them in *The Pencil Drawings of William Blake*, 1927, and again in *Blake's Illustrations for Thornton's Virgil*, 1937. The reproductions, which are the size of the originals, included the unused drawing, but did not include the drawings for four of the woodcuts (nos. 5, 7, 12, 18), as photographs of these could not be obtained.

The wood-blocks for all except the first as made by Blake measured 35 to 40 × 84 mm., but they were found to be somewhat too large for the pages of the *Virgil* and were ruthlessly cut down before they were printed, losing about 5 × 10 mm. Proofs taken by Blake before the blocks were mutilated shew that he intended them to be printed four together, engraved on a single block, just as they appear in the book. Very few examples of these proofs are in existence. Two sheets with nos. 2–5 and 6–9 are in the British Museum Print Room, and one of these is reproduced here (Plate 36). A sheet with the first set was in the collection of the late Frank Rinder, and comparison of this with the sheet in the British Museum shews that further work was done on the blocks after this proof was taken. A sheet with the second set is inserted in the manuscript in the Fitzwilliam Museum, Cambridge, known as *An Island in the Moon*. Another sheet of the first set, signed *W. Blake fecit*, was formerly in the possession of Samuel Palmer, and of this he wrote in 1864: 'Mr. Blake gave this page to me in Fountain Court: impressions taken there, at his own press, by his own hands, and signed by him under my eyes.'[1] It was afterwards in the possession of his son, A. H. Palmer, and was exhibited at the Victoria and Albert Museum in 1926. It is now in the collection of Mr. Philip Hofer. These are the only true proofs that are known at the present time, all having been made, probably by Blake himself, before the blocks were cut down. Other sets of so-called proofs were taken from the blocks after they had been used in the book, and were no doubt distributed to his friends by John Linnell. There exists a receipt

[1] *Catalogue of an Exhibition of Drawings, Etchings, and Woodcuts by Samuel Palmer, etc.* Victoria and Albert Museum (1926), p. 28.

written on the back of one of Harrison's advertisement cards showing that the blocks were bought by Linnell in 1825. It runs as follows:

September 16, 1825. Received of Mr. Linnell for the Wood-Blocks executed by Mr. Blake two guineas for Mr. Harrison.

R. I. Thornton, M.D.[1]

Linnell therefore obtained the blocks for about 2s. 6d. each and may have been making sets of prints for many years after Blake's death. These prints are sometimes on thin paper which gives much better impressions than the rough paper of the *Virgil*, and they are therefore sometimes erroneously described as 'early proofs'. The blocks remained in the possession of Linnell's descendants, and are in perfect condition. They were lost to sight for many years, but were eventually found among the effects of the late Herbert Linnell, one of the trustees of the Blake-Linnell collections, and were seen by me in October 1937 (Plate 38). Permission was obtained from the trustees for electrotypes to be made from the blocks for use in the Nonesuch volume of 1937, and as the quality of the prints thus obtained was the same as if the wood-blocks themselves were to be used, the designs can there again be seen as Blake saw them in 1821. The wood-blocks were sold at Christie's on 2 December 1938 and were bought for the National Art Collections Fund. They are now safely housed in the Print Room of the British Museum.

The woodcuts were first reproduced and published by Thomas B. Mosher, Portland, Maine, in 1899. They were reproduced again with an introduction by Laurence Binyon for the Unicorn Press, London, in 1902. Enlarged facsimiles in platinotype were made by Frederic H. Evans and issued privately in 1912. The two sheets of proofs were reproduced side by side with the prints as they appeared in the book in the *Burlington Magazine*, December 1920.

[1] Loc. cit.

XIX

REMEMBER ME!

In the early part of the nineteenth century the pocket Annual, published each year towards the Christmas festival, was a well-established publishers' event. *The Amulet, The Keepsake, Friendship's Offering, Forget-me-not* are the names of a few. *The Bijou* was another published by William Pickering in the years 1828–30. Some of these maintained their popularity for many years, though they are not now among the second-hand booksellers' more saleable goods, unless they happen to contain, as a few of the volumes do, pieces attributed to names such as Coleridge or Charles Lamb.

Reference has already been made to the many activities of Dr. Robert John Thornton in the publishing of books, both splendid and obscure. One of the least known of these and, it seems, one of the least successful, was a Christmas Annual entitled *Remember Me! A New Years Gift or Christmas Present*, which appeared before Christmas 1824, but then incontinently died and was no more seen. This single volume for 1825 is now a rarity, and would probably have been forgotten were it not that among its pages Blake made one of his most incongruous appearances.

The frontispiece depicts a head of the Princess Charlotte emerging from clouds below which is the legend: *A TRIBUTE OF REGARD | Presented by | Your Affectionate Friend | . . . .* The book consists of a very large number of miscellaneous items of prose and verse on 336 pages followed by eight pages of engraved music and a *Kalendar | and | Album | 1825. | Dedicated | to | Friendship | and | Superior Intellect*. The *Album* consists of twelve leaves of Whatman paper left blank for the contributions by the Superior Intellect and her friends. They have usually remained blank. The volume ends with twelve pages of print giving lists of *Bankers in London and Westminster, Terms and Returns in 1825, Bank Holidays and Transfer Days, Sovereign Princes of Europe*, and *Courts of Law*.

A few of the pieces are by well-known authors, such as Lord Byron, Sir Walter Scott, Miss Elizabeth Carter, and Christopher Smart, but the majority are unsigned. Many are informative, others are grave or gay. Gaiety is typified by the following *Anecdote of a Clergyman*: Dr. Wall, a pious minister, was never known to be out of temper. On Sunday, after praying for rain, his servant at dinner dropped some glasses on the floor, whereupon the doctor observed: 'We shall have rain now, for I see the *glass* is *low*.'

Interspersed among the gems of literature are three copper-plate engravings and eight charming coloured prints of flowers. Four of the coloured plates are apparently from drawings by Miss Thornton. The other four are of some interest, as they are miniature versions of plates from Dr. Thornton's celebrated *Temple of Flora*, 1799, one of the most magnificent botanical works ever published. These plates represent 'Snow Drop', 'Night Blowing Cereus', 'Nodding Renealmia', and 'Dragon Arum', all being *Tinted by T. Dales*. These miniatures are necessarily less splendid than the originals which were published in an elephant folio, on plates which were not merely portraits of flowers, some of them being suitably embellished. The 'Night Blowing Cereus', for example, has *The Flower by Reinagle* and *Moonlight by Pether*; but in *Remember Me!* the moonlight is left to the imagination.

Dr. Thornton spared no expense, and expended much ingenuity, in making his little Annual attractive. It is sometimes difficult to justify the acquisition by one collector of several copies of a rare book. During the last forty-five years seven copies of *Remember Me!* in original condition have come to my notice, and I am not ashamed to confess that six of them are now in my library,[1] for, owing to Dr. Thornton's ingenuity, they are all different. The book was usually bound in boards and enclosed in a slip-case of thin card, on one side of which is a pretty scene, stencilled in colours, of children gleaning. The stencilling, being done by hand, is never quite the same, and pleasing variety is introduced by changes in the colours of the binding, the endpapers, and the slip-case. Thus the seven copies are dressed as follows:

1. Cream boards, brown endpapers (no slip-case).
2. Cream boards, pink endpapers, bright green case.
3. Brown paper sides, slate-grey endpapers and case.
4. Pink boards, slate-grey endpapers, pink case, with roan strip and gilt lettering on one 'spine'.
5. Bright green boards, brown endpapers, red case.
6. Pale green boards, orange endpapers, red case.
7. Green straight-grained morocco, gilt, gilt edges, marbled endpapers.

It was in these surroundings that Blake made his last appearance as a commercial engraver, no doubt being pressed by John Linnell to oblige his friend Dr. Thornton, who may have been giving his professional services to one of Linnell's numerous

[1] No. 6 in the list is in the collection of Mr. Douglas Cleverdon.

The Hiding of Moses

W Blake, inven & sculp.

Pl. 39

family and was thus deserving some recompense. Blake had made a large water-colour drawing[1] representing the 'Hiding of the infant Moses in the bulrushes'. The mother, supported by her husband, is swooning with emotion, while her husband's sister keeps a look-out on a stone jetty in the background. The atmosphere of Egypt is sustained by a small sphinx crouching on the jetty and pyramids in the background. A palm tree overshadows the group at the river's brink. The incident is described in four pages of text (pp. 32–5), probably from the pen of Miss Thornton, in the course of which the (possibly reluctant) painter may have been appeased by the passage: 'None but an artist possessing the imagination and abilities of Mr. Blake could possibly accomplish a task so replete with difficulty that made a painter, when he was trying to represent a father sacrificing his daughter, cover his head in a mantle, feeling that the subject was beyond his power of depicting it.' The writer of the article leaves to the reader the decision whether it was the painter that covered his own head or made the father in his picture do so. Blake, at any rate, did neither, but executed a lovely engraving, 7 × 10 cm., from his painting, and signed it *Blake del. et sculpt.* This was inserted in *Remember Me!* facing page 34, and immediately invested the commonplace little book with its only real claim to distinction, and that of a high order. It seems that Blake first made his plate somewhat too large, for an apparently unique impression[2] of it, before it was cut down and the lettering altered from *W. Blake inven. & sculp.*, is now in the Lessing J. Rosenwald Collection in the National Gallery of Art at Washington D.C. (Plate 39).

It has been mentioned that no more was heard of *Remember Me!* after the first volume had appeared. In my collection, however, is evidence that a second volume may have been in preparation, Blake having again been induced to employ his genius in the service of Dr. Thornton. This evidence is in the shape of a tiny sepia drawing, a miniature version of one of his most dramatic and splendid designs, 'The Body of Abel found by Adam and Eve; Cain, who was about to bury it, fleeing from the face of his parents'. This water-colour drawing was included in Blake's Exhibition of 1809 (*Descriptive Catalogue*, no. xi) and was afterwards in the Linnell Collection.[3] A more elaborate version, painted in tempera on a panel, was in the Butts Collection and is now in the Tate Gallery. The miniature in sepia, with variations in detail, came also from the Linnell Collection, but was never seen until

---

[1] Sold with the Linnell Collection at Christie's, 15 March 1918 (lot 156, Robson, £120. 5s.). Now in the H. E. Huntington Library, California.

[2] Exhibited at the Philadelphia Museum of Art, 1939 (no. 233 in the catalogue).

[3] Sold at Christie's, 15 March 1918 (lot 157, Sabin, £105).

after the death of the last trustee, Herbert Linnell, from whose effects it came into the hands of Messrs. Robinson of Pall Mall and so into my collection. It measures only 5·5 × 6·0 cm., and is squared in pencil for engraving, though it was not actually executed so far as is known (Plate 39).

It is considerably smaller than the 'Hiding of Moses', but for this reason would go upright instead of sideways on the page of *Remember Me!* if, as seems very probable, it was intended for the second volume (for 1826) which would have been issued at the end of 1825. Blake was then completely absorbed, between bouts of illness, in his designs for Dante's *Inferno*, and cannot have regretted being released from further obligations to the egregious Dr. Thornton.

XX

BLAKE'S COPY OF DANTE'S *INFERNO*[1]

In *The Times Literary Supplement* of 8 March 1957 I described a book from Blake's library and recorded for the first time the bulk of the numerous marginal annotations with which he had enriched it. This book, the 1798 edition of *Bacon's Essays*, had been in the possession of Samuel Palmer after Blake's death and it is known that others of his books had also passed into Palmer's keeping. I conjectured that this book had been for many years in the possession of Palmer's son, A. H. Palmer, since it seemed to have turned up in the American book market at about the time when A. H. Palmer sold almost the whole of his father's collections.

This sale of Palmer's paintings and etchings, with a few Blake prints and some documents, took place at Christie's on 20 February 1928, but it had been preceded by an exhibition of the collection at the Victoria and Albert Museum from October 1926 to February 1927. The introduction to the exhibition catalogue was written by A. H. Palmer and dated August 1926, from Vancouver, B.C., whither he had emigrated together with his two sons. A correspondent, Mr. James M. Begg, of Prestwick, has told me that he had occasion to call at A. H. Palmer's house in Vancouver about the year 1925. He related that Palmer was then a recluse living in a house nearly surrounded by bush on the outskirts of Vancouver. He told Mr. Begg that he lived there because he was interested in birds—he had been in correspondence with W. H. Hudson.

When the door was unbolted, Mr. Begg had been allowed to enter the house, and found himself in a room uncarpeted and with little furniture. On the centre of the floor he saw a tin trunk and, looking around him, was astonished to see on the walls 'pictures of unusual quality for a home in such an environment'. These pictures, Palmer said, were the work of his grandfather, John Linnell, and his father, Samuel Palmer; the trunk contained the Linnell papers. Mr. Begg remembered that he picked up a document at random, which proved to be a letter from Arthur Severn with a reference to 'poor Keats'. Palmer told Mr. Begg that he lived in terror of a fire starting in the bush, which might destroy the house and its contents. It was no doubt this fear which prompted the removal of the collection of pictures and prints to London in the following year.

[1] First printed in *The Times Literary Supplement* (1957), lvi. 277.

In the same year, 1926, I wrote to Palmer asking about a book annotated by Blake which I had somehow heard might be in his possession. Two long letters came in reply saying that he had such a book, but that he was unable to reveal what it was, as it was of great importance in relation to an event in Blake's life which had been misrepresented in Story's *Life of Linnell* (1892). The letters were largely taken up with complaints about the inaccuracy of Story's *Life*, which were to be put right by his own researches into the Linnell papers. With this the correspondence ended and Palmer died not long after. I made several attempts in later years to establish contact with Palmer's sons, but was unable to get any reply to my inquiries. Thirty years later an unexpected appointment to a travelling professorship aroused fresh hopes, as my projected travels in Canada were to entail a visit to Vancouver.

Now or never was the missing volume to be found. Professor Rocke Robertson, my surgical colleague in Vancouver, was briefed and he immediately started researches through the telephone directory into the ancestry of everyone in Vancouver named Palmer, of whom there were a good many; but soon afterwards I was able to give him an address at which A. H. Palmer was living in 1927. This Mr. Geoffrey Grigson had sent me many years ago and had been mislaid. Palmer's letters had given only a box number. The use of this address had previously produced no result and the odds seemed heavily against its proving of any service now. Nevertheless, the directory proved that for once the odds were in our favour, for the late Bryan Palmer was still living in the same house and an interview was arranged.

Palmer was at first positive that he could throw no light on the matter, since he had nothing except the exercise books in which his father, A. H. Palmer, had made notes on the lives of Samuel Palmer and John Linnell. Palmer was persuaded, however, to make a search for any books that his father might have had. Successive journeys to the attic produced a number of irrelevant books, but when, on the third descent, I caught sight of a shabby volume in rough cloth with a gold label on the spine, it seemed probable that success was at hand. Blake's copy of *Bacon's Essays* already described had been bound amateurishly in quarter cloth with a gold label on the spine inscribed 'Bacon's Essays'. To my surprise the label on this occasion bore the legend 'Dante'. The binding was loose and many pages were detached, but my hopes rose still higher when under the cover was found a holograph receipt signed by Blake:

Recieved 11 Septemb^r 1818 of Mr. Linnell the Sum of Five pounds on account of Mr Upton's Plate

5–0–0   William Blake

'Mr. Upton's Plate' was an engraved portrait for which two other receipts 'on account' were already known (see my edition of the *Letters*, 1968, page 142).

The book proved to be Vol. I, Cantos I–VIII, of Henry Boyd's translation of the *Inferno*, Dublin, 1785. The leaves were untrimmed and in their original boards, which had been covered with cloth, as was the Bacon, by Blake or Samuel Palmer. A. H. Palmer's statement of the book being related to an important event in Blake's life was now explained, as he was thinking, no doubt, of the 100 designs for the *Divina Commedia* commissioned by Linnell at the end of Blake's days. Inside the front board was a pencilled note by A. H. Palmer:

Samuel Palmer's copy. The MS. notes are by William Blake. This volume as far back as I can remember stood upon one of my father's book-shelves by the side of books annotated or illustrated by Blake. Among them was the now well-known copy of Lavater's Aphorisms. . . . Bacon's Essays with Blake's notes were there, Hayley's Ballads, and a copy of Thornton's edition of Ambrose Philips' Pastorals [i.e. Thornton's *Virgil* with wood engravings by Blake and others].

Another note drew attention to the fact that in the List of Subscribers was the name of William Hayley, who took '7 sets', so that it seemed probable that it was Hayley, not Linnell, who had first interested Blake in Dante.

Blake's notes and underlinings, as set out below, are confined to the Translator's Preliminary Essays. He considered that Boyd was a traducer of poets and poetry and misunderstood the nature of Liberty, and he expressed his views with his customary vigour. There are no annotations to the poem itself, though there is evidence that Blake read this with great attention, as he has carefully corrected several misprints and mistakes. A pencilled Italian line at the beginning of Canto the First does not appear to me to be in Blake's hand, but there is no question that all the marginal annotations are in his hand, written in pencil except the last two which were inscribed with a fine pen.

There is no clear indication of the date at which the annotations were written, except that they seem to imply a wider knowledge of the *Divina Commedia* than could have been gained merely by reading the first eight Cantos of the *Inferno* in this book. Blake included in his emblem book, *The Gates of Paradise*, 1793, the subject of 'Ugolino in prison' from Canto 33 of the *Inferno*, but he might have known this from a translation of the episode included in Jonathan Richardson's *Discourse on the Dignity, Certainty, Pleasure, and Advantages of the Science of a Connoisseur*, 1719, and Sir Joshua Reynolds had contributed a painting of the subject to the Royal Academy Exhibition in 1777. Another translation of the *Inferno* by Charles Rogers had been published in 1782; Boyd did not complete the publication of his translation of the *Divine Comedy* until 1802. In addition, Blake's friend, Henry Fuseli, was deeply interested in Dante and painted a number of pictures illustrating the *Inferno*. Blake's acquaintance with Henry Cary, who had published his version of the *Inferno* in 1805-6, did not come until near the end of his life, when, according to Frederick Tatham, he learnt Italian in order to read Dante in the original, using an edition of 1564. Cary's translation of the whole poem appeared in 1814 in the three small volumes with which Keats was so familiar.

In his conversations with Henry Crabb Robinson, Blake, as recorded in Robinson's Diary, emphasized his view of Dante as a politician and therefore in error, though he still regarded him as a very great artist. The same views are indicated in these annotations (first recorded in 1957), though it is probable that they antedate the coversations by many years. It seems, on the whole, unlikely that Blake wrote them as early as 1785 when the book was first published. It is more probable, as suggested by A. H. Palmer, that Hayley gave him one of his seven copies in or soon after 1800, and that the notes are to be referred to about that date.

BLAKE'S ANNOTATIONS TO BOYD'S TRANSLATION OF DANTE'S INFERNO

Dublin 1785

In 'A Comparative View of the Inferno, With some other Poems relative to the Original Principles of Human Nature.'

P. 35. *But* the most daring flights of fancy, the most accurate delineations of character, and the most artful conduct of fable, are *not, even* when combined together, sufficient of themselves to make a poem interesting. [*The italicized words have been strongly deleted.*]

Pp. 35-6. The discord of Achilles and Agamemnon may produce the most tragical consequences; but if we, who are cool and impartial in the affair . . . cannot enter warmly into the views of either party, the story, though adorned with all the genius of an Homer, will be read by us with some degree of nonchalance. The superstitions that led the Crusaders to rescue the Holy Land from the Infidels, instead of interesting us, appear frigid, if not ridiculous. We cannot be much concerned for the fate of such a crew of fanatics, notwithstanding the magic numbers of a Tasso . . . we cannot sympathise with Achilles for the loss of his Mistress, when we feel that he gained her by the massacre of her family.

Nobody considers these things when they read Homer or Shakespear or Dante.

P. 37. When a man, where no interest is concerned, no provocation given, lays a whole nation in blood merely for his glory; we, to whom his glory is indifferent, cannot enter into his resentment.

false: All poetry gives the lie to this.

Pp. 37–8. Such may be good poetical characters, of that mixt kind that Aristotle admits; but the most beautiful mixture of light and shade has no attraction unless it warms *or freezes* the heart. [*The words italicized inserted by Blake.*] It must have something that engages the sympathy, something that appeals to the *moral sense*. [*These two words deleted and altered to*: passions & senses]; for nothing can thoroughly captivate the fancy, however artfully delineated, that does not awake the sympathy and interest the passions *that enlist on the side of Virtue* [*Words deleted*] and appeal to our native notions of right and wrong.

Pp. 38–9. It is this that sets the Odyssey, in point of sentiment, so far above the Iliad. We feel the injuries of Ulysses; . . . we seem to feel the generous indignation of the young Telemachus, and we tremble at the dangers of the fair Penelope . . . we can go along with the resentment of Ulysses, because it is just, but our feelings must tell us that Achilles carries his resentment to a savage length, a length where we cannot follow him.

If Homer's merit was only in these Historical combinations & Moral sentiments he would be no better than Clarissa.[1]

Pp. 39–40. *Iliacos extra muros peccatur; et intra.* It is a contest between barbarians, equally guilty of injustice, rapine, and bloodshed; and we are not sorry to see the vengeance of Heaven equally inflicted on both parties.

Homer meant this.

Aeneas indeed is a more amiable personage than Achilles; he seems meant for a perfect character. But compare his conduct with respect to Dido with the self-denial of Dryden's Cleomenes, or with the conduct of Titus in the Berenice of Racine, we will then see what is meant by making a character interesting.

Every body naturally hates a perfect Character because they are all greater Villains than the imperfect, as Eneas is here shewn a worse man than Achilles in leaving Dido.

Pp. 45–6. Antecedent to and independent of all laws, a man may learn to argue on the nature of moral obligation, and the duty of universal benevolence, from Cumberland, Wollaston, Shaftesbury, Hutcheson; but would he feel what vice is in itself . . . let him enter into the passions of Lear, when he feels

---

[1] The reference is to Richardson's *Clarissa Harlowe*, 1740.

the ingratitude of his children; of Hamlet, when he learns the story of his father's murder; . . . and he will know the difference of right and wrong much more clearly than from all the moralists that ever wrote.

The grandest Poetry is Immoral, the Grandest characters Wicked, Very Satan—Capanius, Othello a murderer, Prometheus, Jupiter, Jehovah, Jesus a wine bibber. Cunning & Morality are not Poetry but Philosophy; the Poet is Independent & Wicked; the Philosopher is Dependent & Good.
Poetry is to excuse Vice & shew its reason & necessary purgation.

P. 49. The industrious knave cultivates the soil; the indolent good man leaves it uncultivated. Who ought to reap the harvest? . . . The natural course of things decides in favour of the villain; the natural sentiments of men in favour of the man of virtue.

false

Pp. 56–7. As to those who think the notion of a future Life arose from the descriptions and inventions of the Poets, they may just as well suppose that eating and drinking had the same original. . . . The Poets indeed altered the genuine sentiments of nature, and tinged the Light of Reason by introducing the wild conceits of Fancy. . . . But still the root was natural, though the fruit was wild. All that *nature teaches* [*underlined by Blake*] is, that there is a future life, distinguished into different states of happiness and misery.

False

Nature Teaches nothing of Spiritual Life but only of Natural Life.

P. 74. [On a blank page at the end of 'A Comparative View'] Every Sentiment & Opinion as well as Every Principle in Dante is in these Preliminary Essays Controverted & proved Foolish by his Translator, If I have any Judgment in Such Things as Sentiments Opinions & Principles.

In 'Historical Essay of the State of Affairs in the thirteenth and fourteenth centuries: With Respect to the History of Florence.'

P. 118. [Concerning the quarrel between Guilielmo and Bertaccio, the heads of two branches of the family of Cancelieri.] Dante was at this time Prior of Florence, and it was he who gave the advice, *ruinous to himself*, and *pernicious to his native country*, of calling in the heads of the two factions to Florence. [*Italicized words underlined by Blake.*]

Dante was a Fool or his Translator was Not: That is, Dante was Hired or Tr. was Not. It appears to me that Men are hired to Run down Men of Genius under the Mask of Translators, but Dante gives too much Caesar: he is not a Republican. [*at the top of the page*] Dante was an Emperor's, a Caesar's Man; Luther also left the Priest & join'd the Soldier.

Pp. 129–30. The fervours of religion have often actuated the passions to deeds of the wildest fanaticism. The booted Apostles of Germany, and the Crusards of Florence, carried their zeal to a very guilty degree. But the passion for anything laudable will hardly carry men to a proper pitch, unless it be so strong as sometimes to push them beyond the golden mean.

How very Foolish all this Is.

P. 131. Such were the effects of intolerance even in the extreme. In a more moderate degree, every well-regulated government, both ancient and modern were so *far intolerant,* as not to admit the pollutions of every superstition and *every pernicious opinion.* It was from a regard to the morals of the people, that the Roman Magistrates expelled the Priests of Bacchus, in the first and most virtuous ages of the republic. It was on this principle that the *Persians* destroyed the *temples of Greece wherever they came.* [*Italicized words are underlined by Blake.*]

If Well regulated Governments act so who can tell so well as the hireling Writer whose praise is contrary to what he Knows to be true. Persians destroy the Temples & are praised for it.

Pp. 133–4. The Athenians and Romans kept a watchful eye, not only over the grosser superstitions, but over impiety. . . . Polybius plainly attributes the fall of freedom in Greece to the prevalence of atheism. . . . It was not till the republic was verging to its fall, that Caesar dared in open senate to laugh at the speculative opinion of a future state. These were the times of universal toleration, when every pollution, from every clime, flowed to Rome, whence they had carefully been kept out before.

What is Liberty without Universal Toleration?

Pp. 135–6. I leave it to those who are best acquainted with the spirit of antiquity, to determine whether a species of religion . . . had or had not a very principal share in raising those celebrated nations to the summit of their glory: their decline and fall, at least, may be fairly attributed to irreligion, and to the want of some general standard of morality, whose authority they all allowed and to which they all appealed. The want of this pole-star left them adrift in the boundless ocean of conjecture; the disputes of their philosophers were endless, and their opinions of the grounds of morality were as different as their conditions, their tastes and their pursuits.

Yet simple country Hinds are Moral Enthusiasts, Indignant against Knavery, without a Moral criterion other than Native Honesty untaught, while other country Hinds are as indignant against honesty & Enthusiasts for Cunning & Artifice.

P. 148. . . . but there are certain *bounds* even to *liberty*. [*Italicized words underlined by Blake.*]

If it is thus, the extreme of black is white & of sweet sower & of good Evil & of Nothing Something.

XXI

BLAKE'S LIBRARY[1]

A MANUSCRIPT volume of twenty-two octavo pages containing fair copies of eleven poems by Blake, including 'The Mental Traveller' and 'Auguries of Innocence', has long been known to Blake students as 'The Pickering MS.' The identification of the manuscript under this name has been due to the fact that it was at one time in the possession of Basil Montagu Pickering, bookseller and publisher, son of the more famous William Pickering. It is stated that Pickering purchased it in 1866, but apart from the fact that it was seen by Alexander Gilchrist and D. G. Rossetti in 1863, before the publication of Gilchrist's *Life of Blake*, its earlier history has remained unknown. The missing facts can now be filled in through the chance survival of a leaf from a bookseller's catalogue of 1864 or 1865. This has been found among miscellaneous documents recently returned from Vancouver, B.C., to representatives of the Linnell family by the late Bryan Palmer, grandson of Samuel Palmer. The bookseller, whose evidence has thus come to light, was Francis Harvey, of 30 Cockspur Street, Charing Cross, S.W. He had acquired the manuscript from Blake's friend, Frederick Tatham, and he offered it on page 5 of his catalogue for 15 guineas, adding to his description the statement:

This manuscript had been previously offered to several gentlemen for 25 guineas. F. H. has acquired it, with other objects relating to Blake, and offers it at the price affixed. It is accompanied by the following letter from Mr. Tatham. The MS was lent to Mr. Gilchrist, who has reprinted part of it in his Life of Blake.

It thus came about that the poems were first printed in Rossetti's selection included in Gilchrist's second volume of 1863, and were reprinted in the editions of *Songs of Innocence and of Experience* edited by R. H. Shepherd for Pickering in 1866 and 1868. The manuscript, written on the blank sides of leaves from Hayley's *Ballads*, 1802,[2] was rebound by Bedford and was bought probably by William Mitchell, whose book-plate is inserted. It was later in Locker-Lampson's Rowfant Library, which

---

[1] First printed in *The Times Literary Supplement* (1959), lviii. 648.

[2] See Professor G. E. Bentley jr., 'The Date of Blake's Pickering Manuscript', *Studies in Bibliography*, Bibliographical Society of the University of Virginia (1966), xix. 232–43.

was sold in 1905 to a New York dealer. The next owner was the well-known Blake collector, W. A. White, and the manuscript is now in another private collection in the United States. At some point in its vicissitudes Tatham's letter seems to have been lost, since it has not been seen, so far as I know, by any Blake student. Fortunately it was printed in full in Harvey's catalogue and it now proves to be of some interest. Before pursuing this matter further it is worth mentioning 'other objects relating to Blake' listed by Harvey on page 6 of the catalogue. These are as follows:

(1) 'The Head of Christ in Glory, habited as a Jew, with his hand raised in the act of blessing, £15 15s.' A tempera on canvas, formerly in the Butts Collection, and now in private possession.

(2) 'The Birth of Christ, £6 6s.' A tempera on copper, now known as *The Nativity*, formerly in the Butts Collection and now in a private collection in the United States.

(3) 'Christ appearing to the Apostles after the Resurrection. £15 15s.' This may have come from Tatham, having been sold at Sotheby's in 1862, and is probably the colour-print now in the Tate Gallery; two other versions are now in the United States. Harvey rightly described the figure of Christ as 'one of the best produced by Blake—majesty and graciousness deepened into pathos'.

(4) 'The Daughters of Job', unpriced. A tempera on canvas from the Butts Collection now in the Lessing J. Rosenwald Collection in the National Gallery of Washington, D.C.

(5) 'Paul before Felix and Drusilla, £3 3s.' A water-colour drawing from the Butts Collection probably now in the United States.

(6) 'Samson Bursting his Bonds, £2 10s.' A water-colour drawing from the Butts Collection now in the United States.

(7) 'The Baptism of Christ, £6 6s.' A water-colour drawing from the Butts Collection, now in the Ashmolean Museum, Oxford.

(8) 'Book of Job, proofs, uncut, £6 6s.'

(9) 'Another copy, seperate plates', unpriced.

The first two paintings in the list are described by Harvey as 'oil paintings', though they are, of course, temperas, Blake having abandoned the use of oil paints very early in his career. Since all of the pictures except no. 3 were from the Butts Collection, these cannot have been obtained from Tatham. The nature of most of the 'other objects' must therefore remain in doubt.

Tatham's letter, which follows, has suggested the heading, 'Blake's Library', given to this study.

Odessa Road, Forest Gate,
Essex, E.
June 8, 1864.

Dear Sir,

The MS you purchased of me was part of the possessions into which I came by legacy from Mrs. Blake, the widow of that extraordinary and excellent man, William Blake, Visionary, Poet and Painter, who also had a most consummate knowledge of all the great writers in all languages. To prove that, I may say that I have possessed books well thumbed and dirtied by his graving hands, in Latin, Greek, Hebrew, French, and Italian, besides a large collection of works of the mystical writers, Jacob Behmen, Swedenborg, and others. His knowledge was immense, his industry beyond parallel, and his life innocent and simple and laborious, far beyond that of most other men. Childlike, impetuous, fiery, indomitable, proud, and humble, he carried out a sort of purpose in his life which seemed only to produce what was invisible to the natural eye, to the despising of the things which are seen: he therefore became wild and his theories wanted solidity; but he was the most delightful and interesting man that ever an intellectual lover of art could spend a day with; and he died as he lived. He was much associated with many of the great men of the age in which he lived, and was meek and companionable with them. These things are to be deduced, and the great interest which the public have taken in him, by the several Biographies that have been published of him since his death—to which the reader and yourself had better be referred.

Believe me, dear Sir,
Very faithfully yours,

FREDERICK TATHAM

I once heard a guide in a public museum explaining to his audience in front of pictures by Blake that the artist was uneducated and 'of course had never read very much'. Knowledge of Blake's life rather than of his writings might lend colour to this belief, but study of his writings can only arouse wonder about how he gained access to the very extensive literature which he must not only have read but also have pored over for long periods. He must, in fact, have possessed many books which could not be absorbed as temporary loans or in visits to the houses of his friends. Frederick Tatham, in his brief *Life of Blake*, first printed in 1906, made a reference to his books:

It is a remarkable fact that among the volumes bequeathed by Mrs. Blake to the author of this sketch the most thumbed from use are his Bible and those books in other languages. He was very fond of Ovid, especially the *Fasti*. He read Dante when he was past sixty, although before he knew a word of Italian.

Now, in this rediscovered letter, the picture is amplified. Tatham wrote, perhaps, in a somewhat hyperbolic vein when he stated that Blake had 'a most consummate knowledge of all the great writers in all languages', but he went on to specify books in 'Latin, Greek, Hebrew, French, and Italian, besides a large collection of works of the mystical writers, Jacob Behmen, Swedenborg, and others'. Blake's recent commentators and interpreters would indeed be grateful for a list of his books which, if Tatham's account be not an exaggeration, must have amounted to a small library; but knowledge of the books which Blake possessed is limited, depending largely on their containing his signature or annotations. 'William Blake' is not an uncommon combination of Christian name and patronymic, and at least two contemporary individuals bearing it came fairly close to Blake's life—William, or W. S., Blake, the engraver of *'Change Alley*, and William Blake, the attorney, who numbered Flaxman among his clients. Both have been confused with the artist-poet. (See pp. 33, 48 of the present work.)

Thus various volumes carrying the suggestive signature have come into the market, but have not all seemed to me to carry conviction on close scrutiny. A volume entitled *Sonnets, and Other poems* by W. L. Bowles, sixth edition, London, 1798, with the signature 'William Blake' on the half-title was formerly in my collection, and was recorded in my *Bibliography of Blake*, 1921, but I afterwards decided that the owner had been some other Blake. More recently a work by James Severn entitled *The Wandering Knight of Dunstanborough Castle and Miscellaneous Poems*, Alnwick, 1823, inscribed on the flyleaf 'W. Blake 1823', has been offered for sale (Sotheby's, December 1957), but in my opinion the signature is not the right one. I also have William Sotheby's *Tragedies*, London, 1814, inscribed: 'W. Blake from the Author.' The ownership remained in doubt until another book, Sotheby's copy of Virgil's *Georgica Hexaglotta*, 1827, was sold at Sotheby's in 1954 with the inscription: 'For William Blake Esqre from William Sotheby with his kind regards—London June 25th 1828', the date being ten months after the artist-poet's death.

Another class of book providing possible, but uncertain, evidence of Blake's ownership includes those with the name 'William Blake' among the list of subscribers. Such evidence will be more or less probably correct according to the subject of each book. Thus Blake's name appears among the subscribers to Stedman's *Narrative of a Five Years' Expedition against the revolted Negroes of Surinam*, London, two volumes, 1796, for which he had engraved sixteen copper-plate illustrations; also in C. H. Tatham's *Three Designs for the National Monument proposed to be erected in Commemoration of the late Glorious Victories of the British*

Navy, London, 1802. Blake had himself engraved in 1799 three plates from Flax-man's designs for the same project, and Tatham—an architect and father of Frederick—had been a friend of his at least since 1799, when he gave him a copy of *America*. Both of these books Blake might well have bought for himself. On the other hand William Collier's *Poems on Various Occasions, with Translations*, two volumes, London, 1800, seems less in tune with Blake's interests and resources at that time of his life, though his subscription might have been solicited by William Hayley, whose name also appears in the list.

Again, the name 'Mr. Blake' is found in the list of subscribers to Stockdale's edition of Gay's *Fables*, 1793, for which William Blake engraved twelve plates, but here we are not even certain that the subscriber's first name was William.

In the context of these various doubts it seems to be worth while listing all the books that are *certainly* known to have been in Blake's possession, together with a few possibilities:

1. Winkelmann's *Reflections on the Painting and Sculpture of the Greeks*. Trans-lated from the German by Henry Fuseli, London, 1765. On the flyleaf is the signature: 'William Blake, Lincoln's Inn'. Blake served his seven years' apprentice-ship to the engraver Basire, in Great Queen Street, Lincoln's Inn Fields, and the signature resembles later examples so closely that there can be no doubt of its authenticity. The book is now in my collection.

2. *The Tragedies of Æschylus*, translated by R. Potter. Second edition, London, two volumes, 1779. With the signature 'William Blake' on the half-title of each volume, and inside the cover 'Samuel Palmer 1833'. Another inscription records that it was given by Herbert Palmer to F. G. Stephens, 15 July 1890. Sold at Sotheby's, 17 June 1918. Afterwards in John Drinkwater's collection. Now in the United States. The association with Samuel Palmer would dispel any doubts that might exist about Blake's signatures.

3. Chatterton's *Poems by Thomas Rowley*. Third edition, London, 1778. With the signature 'William Blake' on the title-page and inside the cover 'Samuel Palmer'. Sold at Hodgson's about 1905 and acquired in 1908 by the late Sir Sydney Cockerell who gave it to me in 1957. Another edition of *Rowley's Poems*, quarto, 1782, also carries the signature 'W. Blake' on the title-page. This was sold at Sotheby's, 3 March 1926, but the signature was unlike Blake's usual hand and I regarded it as of very dubious authenticity.

4. John Wesley's *Hymns for the Nation in 1782*. With the signature 'W. Blake 1790' on the first leaf; of undoubted authenticity. Formerly in the possession of the late Dr. James Starkie of Dublin (Seumas O'Sullivan), and now in my

collection. Bound with a later edition of the same book containing a second part.

5. *An Account of a Series of Pictures in the Great Room of the Society of Arts, Manufacture, and Commerce at the Adelphi*. By James Barry, R.A., London, 1783. Authenticated as Blake's copy by A. H. Palmer and containing a drawing by Blake of Barry in old age. Formerly in the possession of H. Buxton Forman, and seen by Gilchrist, who refers to it in his *Life of Blake*, i. 48. Now in my collection.

6. Lavater's *Aphorisms on Man*, London, 1788, with a frontispiece engraved by Blake after Fuseli. On the title-page Blake has written his name, 'Will Blake', below Lavater's, and round the two names has drawn the outline of a heart. Extensively annotated by Blake on the flyleaves and the margins, the book also carries the signature of Samuel Palmer. Formerly in the Robert Hoe Library, sold at the Anderson Galleries, New York, 25 April 1911. Now in the H. E. Huntington Library, California.

7. Swedenborg's *Wisdom of Angels, Concerning Divine Love and Divine Wisdom*, London, 1788. Extensively annotated in Blake's hand on the margins and flyleaves. Inscribed on the half-title: 'The MS. notes by Blake the Artist, accg to Mr. Tatham (an architect) a friend of Blake from whose possession the volume came. Jan. 1, 1839.' In 1876 in the possession of J. R. P. Kirby, and sold with the library of A. G. Dew-Smith, 29 January 1878. Then acquired by the British Museum.

8. Swedenborg's *Wisdom of Angels concerning the Divine Providence*, London, 1790. With signature 'William Blake' on the half-title, and annotations in his hand on eight pages. Formerly in the library of James Spiers, publisher to the Swedenborg Society, and later in that of C. H. Whittington. Sold at Sotheby's, 27 July 1938, and now in my collection.

9. Horace Walpole's *Catalogue of the Royal and Noble Authors of England*. New edition, two volumes, Edinburgh, 1792. With the signature 'William Blake' on the flyleaf of each volume, the first being dated 1795. Now in the Widener Library, bequeathed to Harvard University in 1912. These signatures are probably authentic.

10. Bishop Watson's *An Apology for the Bible, in a Series of Letters addressed to Thomas Paine*, Eighth edition, London, 1797. Extensively annotated in Blake's hand on the back of the title-page and in the margins. The signature of Samuel Palmer is on the title-page. Formerly in the library of T. G. Arthur, sold at Sotheby's, 15 July 1914. Now in the H. E. Huntington Library, California.

11. Bacon's *Essays*, London, 1798. Extensively annotated in Blake's hand and with his signature to a note on the first page of the preface. Inside the cover is the signature, 'Samuel Palmer, 1833'. Acquired by Mr. J. K. Lilly in the United

States through Goodspeed of Boston, probably from A. H. Palmer, about 1929. Now in my collection.

12. *The Works of Sir Joshua Reynolds*, second edition, London, three volumes, 1798. Volume I, containing the *Discourses*, is extensively annotated in Blake's hand, with a note signed by him on the title-page. The annotations are to be assigned to about the year 1808. Early provenance unknown. Now in the British Museum.

13. Dante's *Inferno*, translated by Henry Boyd, Dublin, 1785. Annotated in Blake's hand on fifteen pages. Inscribed inside the cover: 'Samuel Palmer's copy', and with a note by A. H. Palmer. Until 1957 in the possession of Bryan Palmer. Now in my collection. Probably annotated about 1800.

14. Berkeley's *Siris. A Chain of Philosophical Reflexions and Inquiries concerning the Virtues of Tar Water*, Dublin, 1744. Annotated in Blake's hand in the margins of eleven pages. Inside the cover is the signature: 'Samuel Palmer 1833'. Acquired from Tregaskis by the late W. E. Moss about 1909. Sold at Sotheby's, 2 March 1937. Now in the library of Lord Rothschild. The annotations are to be assigned to about the years 1810–18.

15. Percy's *Reliques of Ancient Poetry*, London, three volumes, 1765. Inscribed on the flyleaf: 'Mary Ann Linnell, the gift of Mr. W. Blake'. The book must have been given to Mrs. Linnell in or after 1818, the year in which Blake first met John Linnell. Formerly in the collection of Professor G. H. Palmer, Newton, Massachusetts.

16. *The Lord's Prayer Newly Translated from the Greek* by R. J. Thornton, M.D., London, 1827. Extensively annotated by Blake. Formerly in the Linnell Collection. Sold at Christie's, 15 March 1918. Now in the H. E. Huntington Library, California.

17. Chapman's *Homer*, London, 1616. Story, in his *Life of Linnell*, 1892, i. 78, wrote that Linnell 'was also a great lover of Homer, and took especial delight in Chapman's robust translation, of which he subsequently bought William Blake's fine folio copy'. The receipt for the 31s. 6d. paid for this volume is extant. It is dated 18 May 1829, and is signed for Mrs. Blake by Frederick Tatham. The present whereabouts of the volume is not known.

In addition to my knowledge of these seventeen works from Blake's library I have notes of three others which I have not seen:

18. *Works of Peter Pindar*, 12mo. Sold by the late Arthur Rogers of Newcastle upon Tyne in March 1926, and stated to have Blake's signature on the flyleaf.

19. *The Complaint, or Night Thoughts*. By Edward Young. London, 1796. Stated to have Blake's signature on the flyleaf. The edition of Young's *Night Thoughts* illustrated by Blake was published in 1797.

20. *The Political Testament of the Marshal Duke of Belleisle*, London, 1762. With the signature 'W. Blake' on the half-title. This book is in the United States. It would seem most improbable that the signature is the right one.

It will be noticed that eight of the books were in Samuel Palmer's possession, often with the signature dated 1833. One is stated to have come from Frederick Tatham. If Tatham's implication that Mrs. Blake bequeathed to him most of her husband's books is correct, it seems probable that he gave Palmer the books containing his name in 1833, Mrs. Blake having died in October 1831. Tatham's letter to Harvey together with Blake's statement that in his youth he read and annotated works by Bacon, Burke, and Locke, suggests that a number of other books bearing signs of Blake's ownership still remain to be discovered. Blake also occasionally annotated books lent to him by his friends, such as Crabb Robinson's copy of Wordsworth's *Poems*, 1817 (now in Cornell University Library), but these I have not included in my list, since they were not part of Blake's library.

Professor G. E. Bentley, jr., has taken the subject of Blake's library a stage further by listing a number of books which could probably or possibly have been in Blake's possession,[1] but he has not made any addition to the list of certainties.

POSTSCRIPT

As this book goes to press, Michael Hunter of Jesus College, Cambridge, has shewn me a volume belonging to a friend, which can confidently be added to Blake's library list. This is *The Poetical Works of Will. Shenstone*. London: Printed and Embellished Under the Direction of C. Cooke. 12° [1795]. On the fly-leaf is the authentic signature: *Wm Blake / 1799*. The book itself, bound in contemporary calf, has no owner's marks or annotations; it has three steel engravings by W. Hawkins, J. Neagle, and G. Warren, two designed by Courbould and one by Kirk.

---

[1] *Bulletin of the New York Public Library*, 'Additions to Blake's Library' (1960), lxiv. 595–605.

XXII

THE PILGRIM'S PROGRESS[1]

THE plain English names of John Bunyan and William Blake had not occurred in any sort of conjunction in a book before the year 1941. The name of one does not inevitably recall that of the other, in the way that those of Milton and Blake have come to be associated. Yet Bunyan and Blake, separated in time by almost the same interval that lies between Milton and Blake, have much in common. Both were artists in their different ways, both were poets singing at first in spontaneous, rude strains, with an apparent simplicity of purpose. Both arose from obscure origins by the strength of their personalities and intellects. Both became religious visionaries, who dreamed dreams and worked for the Redemption of Man by means of their writings. A striking difference lies in their methods of working. Bunyan spoke in a language that could be readily understood by his fellow men, and rose to a contemporary pre-eminence through the immediate popularity of his writing and preaching. Blake, on the other hand, chose to deliver most of his message in a deliberately cryptic language, filled with mannerisms, which baffled his contemporaries and is only now, more than a hundred years after his death, coming to be more fully understood. Bunyan again needed a 'conversion' to bring his artistry to fruition. Blake pursued the course of artistic creation coupled with religious fervour throughout his long life, and needed no conversion to open the gates of his mind to inspiration from the spiritual world. Perhaps the greatest quality possessed by Bunyan and Blake in common was the complete integrity of their minds, maintained by both in the face of material hardships and lack of worldly possessions.

The first edition of Bunyan's *Pilgrim's Progress* was printed in London, and was entered at Stationers' Hall on 22 December 1677. It was licensed on 18 February 1678. A second edition was published in the same year, and a third in 1679. The first two editions were not illustrated. The third was provided with a frontispiece representing the author lying asleep above the 'Denn' where he dreamed his dream. There can be no doubt that he meant thereby to indicate the confined space of the Bedford gaol where his allegory first came to his mind. The illustrator, however,

[1] First printed as part of an Introduction to *The Pilgrim's Progress Illustrated with 29 watercolour paintings by William Blake.* Edited by G. B. Harrison, New York, The Limited Editions Club, 1941.

interpreted the 'Denn' more literally and provided it with a lion, which has otherwise no particular significance. This was afterwards adopted as the traditional form of the frontispiece, and for more than 250 years *The Pilgrim's Progress* has seldom appeared without the embellishment of the Dreamer with his apparently tame lion lying in a cave below him. It was to the fifth edition, published in 1680, that illustrations in the ordinary sense were added. This edition was given a portrait of Bunyan, a representation of the burning of Faithful, and 'Thirteen Copper Cuts curiously Engraven for such as desire them', these being charged 1s. extra. Innumerable later editions had illustrations of one kind or another. The subject lent itself to the 'chap-book' style of illustration with many small and rough woodcuts or copper-plates. No artist of great distinction attempted the task of illustrating Bunyan in the eighteenth century until it was undertaken by Thomas Stothard in 1788. In the nineteenth century numerous book-illustrators tried their hands, among others Turner, Cruikshank, David Scott, Holman Hunt, Gordon Browne, and Strang. Some of their designs were engraved on wood by the most celebrated craftsmen of the period, often with charming effect. In no instance, however, were the refined productions of a Stothard or a pre-Raphaelite artist suited to the plain style of Bunyan's writing. The rough and homely woodcuts of a chap-book are more in tune with the tinker-preacher's spontaneous art than the polished products of the sophisticated book-illustrator.

When my grandfather, Dr. John Brown, then Minister of the Church at Bunyan Meeting in Bedford, was writing his standard *Life of Bunyan* (first published in 1885), he was uneasily aware of this deficiency in the pictorial representation of Bunyan's allegory. He was moved to suggest that 'an ideally perfect *Pilgrim's Progress* would have been the Pilgrim story by Bunyan with illustrations by Albrecht Dürer or Hans Holbein'. Dr. Brown was naturally bringing to his mind the greatest artists of the past who had a creative faculty comparable with Bunyan's, and a capacity for simple representation of allegory such as is found in Holbein's 'Dance of Death'. There was no name of Bunyan's time or later which suggested itself to him, and this is not surprising because in 1885 the one artist since Bunyan's day who had possessed all the necessary qualities was known only to a few, and even to them connoted eccentricity, or even madness, rather than a transcendent genius fit to be placed beside that of the author of *The Pilgrim's Progress*.

William Blake, born nearly seventy years after Bunyan's death, can now be seen in his true proportions, and it is evident that he can stand beside Bunyan with undiminished stature, and that many parallels can be found between their minds and art. Blake's art became much more highly intellectualized than Bunyan's, but he never became sophisticated, and although he was a painter of the highest originality he could also, when he chose, bend his mind to illustrate the work of another with almost literal attention to detail. During his earlier years Blake worked chiefly as the engraver of designs by others, among these being many by Thomas Stothard and John Flaxman. He also illustrated a few small books with his own designs, such as Mary Wollstonecraft's *Original Stories from Real Life*, 1791. His first big venture as an illustrator was the series of 537 large water-colour designs for Young's *Night Thoughts*, begun about 1795, and partly engraved in 1797. This was followed late in 1797 by 116 water-colour drawings for the *Poems* of Thomas Gray, none of which was engraved. For many years after this Blake's main output as an illustrator was concerned with the works of Milton. Nearly every one of Milton's major poems, except *Samson Agonistes*, was furnished with a set of elaborate water-colour drawings, and several of these were done more than once. Particularly notable are the magnificent sets of designs illustrating *Paradise Lost* and *Paradise Regained*, which by themselves prove Blake to have supreme qualities as the translator of poetical conceptions into the realm of vision. Finally, during the last years of his life, Blake was engaged on his most celebrated works, the *Illustrations of the Book of Job* and the unfinished series of over 100 large designs for Dante's *Inferno*, upon which he was working at the time of his death in 1827.

Knowledge of Blake's tastes and interests would at once suggest that he must have been familiar for most of his life with Bunyan's *Pilgrim's Progress*. Its allegorical and visionary qualities would have attracted him from an early age; he was a precocious reader, and, once he had given his attention to a work of outstanding merit, he did not forget it. Yet he only once referred to Bunyan in his extant writings, saying that *Pilgrim's Progress* is full of allegory.[1] The earliest sign of any awareness of *The Pilgrim's Progress* is to be found in a very beautiful design, a 'woodcut on pewter', known as 'Sweeping the Interpreter's House'. This has usually been assigned to about the year 1817, but my investigations of all Blake's separate plates have established the fact that this design was first etched on metal about the year 1794, when Blake was 37 years old.

It has long been known that, in addition to this single print, Blake made a series of water-colour drawings illustrating *The Pilgrim's Progress*. It was recorded by W. M. Rossetti in his list of Blake's works at the end of the second volume of Gilchrist's *Life of Blake*, 1863. Rossetti's entry is as follows:

211 Twenty-eight Designs from the 'Pilgrim's Progress'. (Mr. Milnes.) Watercolours often unfinished; one or two little beyond pencil-sketches.

[1] *Complete Writings*, ed. Keynes, 1968, p. 604.

These are rather small designs having quite a sufficient measure of Blake's spirit in them, but much injured by the handiwork of Mrs. Blake, the colour being untidy-looking and heavy for the most part, and crude where strength is intended. Two of the designs, at any rate, may be considered untouched by Mrs. Blake.

(Brief descriptions of the separate designs then follow.)

The entry appears unchanged in the second edition of Gilchrist's *Life*, published in 1880.

It is clear, therefore, that Rossetti saw these designs which were in 1863 in the possession of Richard Monckton Milnes, afterwards the first Lord Houghton, and father of the late Marquess of Crewe. Rossetti seems, however, to have considered that they were of small account as works of art, and is particularly damping in his remarks as to their having been 'much injured by the handiwork of Mrs. Blake'. The previous history of the paintings is unknown, though it is very probable that they came from the collection of Thomas Butts, much of which was bought by Monckton Milnes.

After his father's death Lord Crewe sold almost the whole of the Blake collection in 1903, and he was uncertain how it came about that the designs for *The Pilgrim's Progress* were not included in the sale. He thought it probable that they were over-looked, as they came to light again some years later on somewhat ragged mounts, in a forgotten drawer; it was then that they were provided with neat mounts and a protective slip-in case. Lord Crewe appreciated the great beauty of the drawings, but he did not draw much attention to them. Few visitors ever asked to see them, so that their existence was largely forgotten. When Lord Crewe first told me of them, about the year 1928, and offered to shew them to me, I was naturally eager to see them, though Rossetti's remarks warned me not to entertain too great expectations as to their merit. Perhaps for this reason, my first impression of them was not very favourable, and I formed the opinion that they did not represent Blake's best work. Ten years later I asked permission from Lord Crewe to renew my acquaintance with the drawings, and on this occasion I saw the necessity for a complete revision of my former views. I began to doubt the justice of Rossetti's strictures on the conjectural spoiling by Mrs. Blake, and I saw instead a magnificent series of designs, of uneven quality as is inevitable among so many, but including some of the loveliest water-colours that Blake had ever made. The colouring in a few was heavy where that particular effect was suited to the subject, but Rossetti's charge that it was 'untidy-looking and heavy for the most part' was, I thought, entirely untrue. I soon decided that the designs should be made known, if possible, to a greater number of Blake's admirers, and with Lord Crewe's help the arrangements were concluded by which the Limited Editions Club of New York was enabled to produce in 1941 an edition of *The Pilgrim's Progress*, illustrated with reproductions of Blake's designs in colour. It had been intended in 1939 to make these reproductions in London and to issue them both in this country and in America. The project was abandoned owing to the Second World War, and in 1940 Blake's drawings were sent to New York. They were not brought back after the reproductions had been made, but were exhibited in New York for the benefit of a refugee organization. They are now permanently housed in the Frick Collection in New York.

An examination of the drawings made it possible to determine the approximate date of their execution. The watermark in the paper, wherever it appeared, was that of J. Whatman, associated with various parts of the date 1824. The water-colours cannot, therefore, have been made before that year, and, since Blake was not in the habit of carrying large stocks of drawing paper, but tended rather to buy it as he needed it, it is probable that 1824 was the actual year of their composition. He was at this time still engaged on the engravings for the *Illustrations of the Book of Job*, and he was soon afterwards to embark on his vast series of designs for Dante's *Inferno*. It seems likely that these preoccupations may account for the fact that the *Pilgrim's Progress* series was never finished, and it may be that Thomas Butts, if he possessed it, did not acquire it until after Blake's death, as he would have been unlikely to buy works which Blake had no doubt intended to improve and finish when the opportunity offered itself. This conjecture is made the more probable by another confusion that has arisen concerning the subject of one of the designs, as will presently be described.

The number of water-colour drawings in Lord Crewe's possession was twenty-nine. The number was given by Rossetti as twenty-eight, the difference being accounted for by the fact that he has omitted to mention No. XVII, 'Christian in the Arbour'. He has applied this title instead to the frontispiece design of the Dreamer asleep in 'a certain place where there was a Denn'. It may be assumed, therefore, that there were really twenty-nine designs in 1863, when we have the first mention of their existence. A few of the drawings have a word or two scribbled in the margin by Blake. None has any full inscription in his hand, nor is there any signature. All have been numbered and inscribed with a title by a later unknown hand, but these inscriptions carry no authority and I have ignored them in making my own descriptions and arrangements.

The subjects of twenty-eight of the designs and their order is as follows:

I. John Bunyan dreams a Dream. In his first illustration Blake follows the traditional frontispiece which embellished the earlier and many later editions of the book as an engraving or a woodcut. The design is arranged in three horizontal layers. In the centre is the figure of the author in a long blue garment lying asleep beneath a row of massive trees. Below him is the 'denn', containing a mildly sleeping lion. The upper layer among the branches of the trees is sketched in with the brush, and indicates some of the incidents of the dream. It is possible to discern Christian setting out on his journey, the combat with Apollyon, and the Gate of Heaven.

The design appears to be finished, the cloudiness of the upper layer being intended to give the effect of dream-land in contrast with the more precise outlines of the sleeper and the lion.

II. Christian reading in his Book. Christian, clothed in rags and with his back turned to the City, is walking in the fields. He is bowed down by a great burden bound on to his back, and he carries an open book in his hands. Dense clouds obscure the sky, and flames arise from the buildings he is quitting. There is a background of trees.

The design is elaborately finished with strong colours (Plate 40).

III. Christian meets Evangelist. Christian, emerging from the door of his house, meets Evangelist, who carries a scroll in his left hand and with his right points towards the Wicket Gate in the distance. The door of Christian's house is in the form of a Gothic arch. The other buildings in the background have the massive form of Druid temples. These Gothic and Druidical details denote, in Blake's symbolism, the opposed forces of Art and Materialism.

The greater part of the drawing is carefully finished, but some of the details in the figure of Evangelist appear to be unfinished, particularly his right hand.

IV. Christian pursued by Obstinate and Pliable. Christian is running with outstretched arms from the City of Destruction. Two other figures, Obstinate and Pliable, are in pursuit. Heavy clouds swag over the buildings, which consist of a church with a double spire, a castle with turrets at each corner, and rounded structures without definite form.

The drawing is fully finished in strong colour.

V. Christian in the Slough of Despond. Christian is floundering across the Slough, while Pliable extricates himself on the side towards the City of Destruction. The buildings of the City show numerous spires, and on the right a huge dome surmounted by a cross. The dome is a symbol derived from St. Paul's Cathedral,

Pl. 40

which, because of its 'mathematic form', denotes mental rigidity, that is, lack of the imaginative faculty. Portentous clouds hang over the scene.

The drawing is fully finished in heavy colouring.

VI. Christian drawn out of the Slough by Help. The powerful figure of Help stoops over Christian in the Slough and grasps him by his upraised arms. From behind Help a road leads up into the hills, above which is the rising sun.

The figures, particularly that of Christian, are naïvely drawn, much violence being done to anatomical accuracy, but the colouring is fully finished with a strong effect.

VII. Christian directed by Mr. Worldly-Wiseman. Christian crouches intent upon the Book in his hand, and above him stands the massive figure of Mr. Worldly-Wiseman, whose bearded face expresses complacency in every line. With his left hand Mr. Worldly-Wiseman points towards the Hill (Mount Sinai), which flashes fire and smoke from its summit.

The drawing is fully finished.

VIII. Christian falls at the Feet of Evangelist. Christian has fallen on his knees at the feet of Evangelist, who stoops to take him by his right hand and raise him up. The fire and smoke of the Mountain rise in the background.

The drawing is finished.

IX. Christian fears the Fire from the Mountain. Christian stands in an attitude of awe while fire and thunderbolts play around him.

The drawing is fully finished in brilliant colours (Plate 41).

X. Christian knocks at the Wicket Gate. Christian steps forward to grasp the knocker on the Gate. This is represented as a door shaped like a Gothic arch in a high wall. Around the door is a faintly indicated design of human figures, and this is overpainted with a halo of rainbow colours. Beyond the Gate rise hills, and above them is the orb of the sun. To Christian's left and behind him is a wall on the edge of which is balanced a bow and arrow. This represents the castle of Beelzebub who seeks to shoot at those entering the Gate. The door itself is inscribed, *Knock And It Shall Be Opened*.

The drawing is finished.

XI. The Gate is opened by Goodwill. Christian with his foot upon the lintel is received by Goodwill, a bearded figure with a nimbus round his head. The design of figures around the door is now more clearly drawn and is of great beauty. There are faint indications of rays of light emanating from Goodwill.

The drawing is finished, though the colouring is pale.

XII. The Man in the Iron Cage. Christian and the Interpreter stand on the left, the Interpreter having a large key in his hand. The other half of the picture is occupied by a massive iron grille behind which sits a man fettered by his neck, wrists, and ankles. This figure symbolizes the fettered mind as much for the author as for the illustrator.

The figures of Christian and the Interpreter are unfinished, though the cage of Despair and its occupant are fully finished in heavy colours.

XIII. The Man who dreamed of the Day of Judgement. Christian and the Interpreter stand on the right. In this design, which is fully finished, the Interpreter has a short beard which does not appear in the two preceding designs. The Dreamer sits, with a troubled expression on his face, on the edge of his couch, and over him hang huge and heavy curtains, which imply a sense of impending doom. The colour is correspondingly dark.

XIV. Christian before the Cross. Christian stands in adoration before the Cross, represented by Blake as a vision of Christ crucified. The figure of Christ appears in a luminous cloud with rays of light shooting downwards. The shaft of the Cross becomes in its lower part the trunk of a tree, whose roots spread in all directions over the roof of a stone vault—the Sepulchre of the text. Vines are growing up the tree and on either side. Christian's burden has fallen off his back, and is poised on the edge of the vault into which it will tumble.

The drawing is fully finished.

In this lovely design Blake has used the form of an earlier engraving contained in his illuminated book, *Jerusalem*, which was finished in 1818. This plate, known as 'Christ crucified adored by Albion', represents Christ nailed to the Tree of Good and Evil, while Albion, or Man, worships from below with arms outstretched so that he is himself in a cruciform attitude. In his interpretation of Bunyan's image Blake has modified the figure of Man, but it is clear that the memory of the plate from *Jerusalem* was in his mind.

XV. Christian met by the Three Shining Ones. Christian, now represented as clothed in a long garment instead of his rags, and carrying a staff, is on the right of the picture. A vine, such as was seen on either side of the Tree in the last design, is beside him. The Three Shining Ones, in the form of female figures, each with wings

and a nimbus, stand before him. One lays her right forefinger on his forehead, and carries a Roll with dependent seal in her left hand. Christian's discarded rags hang from the hands of the second and the third—Christian's sins, which have now been forgiven him.

The drawing is finished in delicate colours, which contrast with the heavy colouring of the first part of the pilgrimage.

XVI. Christian climbs the Hill Difficulty. Christian is clambering up steep and jagged rocks, his back and limbs being marked with blood-stains, from the scratches made by the thorns which obstruct his path. At the top of the rocks is a pent-house, indicating the 'pleasant Arbour' of the text, 'made by the Lord of the Hill for the refreshment of weary Travailers'.

The drawing is fully finished.

XVII. Christian in the Arbour. Christian, still marked with scratches, is seated on a bench in the Arbour, to which he has returned in search of the Roll. In his right hand he holds the Roll, and he raises his left hand above his head in jubilation and thanks for its recovery. The Arbour is made of brightly coloured leaves and flowers, and brilliant rainbow colours arch over it. The whole design, which is carefully finished, pulsates with colour of matchless beauty, thus expressing Christian's feelings of joy and gratitude.

XVIII. Christian passes the Lions. Christian is passing between two rocks with his left arm upraised and a sword in his right hand. On either side, chained to the rock by a foreleg, is a beast, representing a lion according to Blake's convention. Standing above, at the door of the Pilgrim's House, is the Porter calling to Christian not to be afraid of the chained lions.

The drawing is finished (Plate 42).

XIX. Christian goes forth Armed. On the right of the picture is Christian, with a sword in his left hand, and a shield buckled to his left arm. In his right hand is the Roll. By his side, with an admonishing hand uplifted, is Prudence, a female figure with long hair. Behind them is the doorway of the Armory, indicated by a row of six spears shewing at the top of the doorway. A figure stands beside the door, and two others, one seated, are seen within. These are perhaps Christian's three other friends, Discretion, Pity, and Charity.

Parts of this design are roughly sketched, and its interpretation is to some extent conjectural. The earlier numbering of the drawings made this No. 12, and placed the scene in the House of the Interpreter. But the fact that Christian is not clothed in rags and carries a sword shews that this is certainly not Blake's intention.

XX. Christian beaten down by Apollyon. Apollyon, painted in lurid colours, is covered with fish scales and has dragon's wings, as described in the text: thunderbolts issue from his mouth. His legs are straddled over his opponent who has been beaten to his knees, and his uplifted arms are holding darts with which he is about to deliver the final blows. Christian defends himself with the shield on his left arm, and his right hand is about to raise his sword from the ground. The drawing is fully finished.

Apollyon in this drawing, which has a distinctly Chinese effect, is more grotesque than terrible, although he conforms in most respects with the conception of Satan which Blake had already used with better effect in many earlier paintings and engravings.

XXI. Faithful's Narrative. The figures in this drawing are lightly sketched in pencil, only the background being worked with colour. Christian and Faithful walk together in discourse. Two of the incidents of Faithful's narrative are represented by small but vigorous sketches enclosed in circles at the top of the drawing. On the left hand Faithful is twitched back by the Old Adam taking hold of his flesh. On the right hand he is smitten to the ground by Moses.

XXII. Vanity Fair. The greater part of this design is sketched in pencil, only the two central figures being washed with colour. These figures, representing two of the rabble, are dressed as mountebanks and are performing antics before a pedestal on which Christian and Faithful are standing, with indications of chains hanging from their wrists. Behind the pedestal is a large dome surmounted by a ball elevated on a stem. On each side of the accusers are two onlookers. The front figure of each pair is a woman holding a mask near her face. The hinder figures are very roughly sketched, but that on the left hand suggests an ecclesiastic wearing a mitre, that on the right a crowned man, these being Blake's usual symbols of the authority of Church and State (Plate 43).

XXIII. Faithful's Martyrdom. On the left hand the body of Faithful is seen consuming in the fire, while his living form is springing upwards to the right with the celestial horses. The dome and cross of the previous design are seen behind the flames of the martyr's pyre. Several onlookers, who are only sketched in, fall prostrate in terror at the spectacle. Christian stands awestruck in the centre with uplifted hands, and his new companion, Hopeful, kneels at his feet.

XXIV. Christian and Hopeful in Doubting Castle. The two Pilgrims crouch in misery on the dungeon floor at the foot of the huge door. Giant Despair lowers over them, his keys hanging from his right hand.

The drawing is finished.

XXV. Christian and Hopeful escape from Doubting Castle. The iron gate of the castle is open, and the two Pilgrims are running away towards the left. Giant Despair, his limbs failing him, leans against the gate-post. His huge crab-tree cudgel is held nervelessly in his left hand.

The drawing is finished.

XXVI. The Pilgrims meet the Shepherds of the Delectable Mountains. The drawing is very unfinished, and is of the simplest possible design. The two Pilgrims, one with a staff, stand on the right facing a group of four shepherds, each in a long robe and a round hat, with a crook shewing above his head. Sheep crop the grass between their feet.

XXVII. Christian and Hopeful in the River. This drawing is only indicated by pencil sketches and a few light touches of colour. On the right the Pilgrims are immersed in the river. Christian with his head just above the water is supported by Hopeful, who points with his right hand to the opposite bank, where there is a group of Shining Ones waiting to receive them.

XXVIII. Christian and Hopeful at the Gates of Heaven. The two Pilgrims with right hands upraised are stepping forward, guarded on either side by an angel with wings spread so as to meet in an arch above their heads. In the upper part of the design is seen the heavenly host welcoming them with trumpets. Heaven itself is represented by a row of pointed towers, with a single dome surmounted by a cross on the right, indicating that there is forgiveness in Heaven even for the fettered mind of the materialist.

The lovely colour and movement of this design forms a vision of extraordinary beauty and it is a fitting climax with which to end the Dream. The greater part of the design is not rendered in much detail, and it seems as if someone of inferior skill, wishing for greater precision in the central figures, had filled in their features with ink or dark paint. The faces of these four figures have thus become foolish, and indeed almost puerile, in their drawing, but this painful impression is soon lost in contemplating the general beauty of the drawing.

Four of the designs are reproduced here (Plates 40–3) by courtesy of the Director of the Frick Collection, New York.

It will be noticed that the above description of the designs does not account for one of the original twenty-nine. This one I have omitted because a careful examination of its subject has convinced me that it has been mistakenly included in the series, perhaps, as already suggested, owing to its having been bought by Thomas Butts from Mrs. Blake after her husband's death. The subject of the design which I have set aside is given by the annotator as 'Christ delivers Faithful from Moses'. Rossetti describes it as 'Christian beset by Demons in the Valley of the Shadow of Death'. The true description of the subject appears to me to be as follows:

On the left a Christ-like figure in a long robe and with a star-shaped nimbus behind his head turns his back on the naked apparition of an old man, which rushes down in flames from the sky and is about to raise a large stone from the ground in its hands. Several heads are dimly indicated in the smoke and clouds hanging about the feet of the apparition. There are jagged mountains and trees in the background. Faithful is nowhere to be seen, and the supposed figure of Christian exactly resembles Blake's representation of Christ Himself in other designs. The naked apparition raising a stone from the ground is clearly Satan, and the whole scene undoubtedly depicts The First Temptation, with the Spirits of Hunger crowding about Satan's feet. It is, in fact, a rejected design for *Paradise Regained*—rejected because another quite different version which agreed more closely with the text was eventually included in that series. The drawing also differs from all the others in the *Pilgrim's Progress* series in that the paper has been cut round close to the margin and then mounted on another piece of paper. Furthermore, its careful technique and finish approximate more nearly to those of the *Paradise Regained* series than to *The Pilgrim's Progress*. As in many of the former, the effect of the colour has been heightened with gold, which is nowhere used in *The Pilgrim's Progress*.

I have therefore seen no alternative to removing this very beautiful drawing from the series with which it has been so long associated. It was, however, reproduced in the Limited Editions Club volume and again here (Plate 44) so that readers may form their own opinion of the propriety of this decision.

Blake's characteristics as a designer are well seen in these water-colours. His use of symmetry is conspicuous, though nowhere carried to excess. His piling on of heavy colour where the subject is one of terror or gloom is a somewhat obvious trick, but he is here conforming to the idiom of the book itself. Bunyan did not seek to produce his effect by subtle gradations of mood, but tried rather to win his readers' ear by direct and unmistakable assault. Blake's lurid passages provide, too, an admirable foil for his flights of more celestial vision such as 'Christian at the

Wicket Gate', 'Christian and Hopeful at the Gates of Heaven', and, beyond all, 'Christian in the Arbour'. Colour so lovely as this has seldom been achieved by any artist, even by Blake himself, and in this design Blake has expressed, in his old age, all the joy and exuberance of youth and life and beauty. In the unfinished drawings, such as 'Vanity Fair' and 'Christian and Hopeful in the River', the bones of the designs are so beautiful that it is difficult to believe that Blake did not intentionally leave them incomplete, having seen that they were good. In many of the individual drawings of this series Blake has indeed worked with his divine inspiration in full flight, even though he may have occasionally in others come rather heavily to earth.

Appraisal of the series of designs as a whole is difficult when the separate constituents are so various. Blake has respected Bunyan in that he has illustrated his allegory with careful attention to the details of the narrative. He has not tried to be 'original' in his choice of subjects, but has chosen for the most part the same ones that had struck the fancy of the first illustrator in the seventeenth century, even venturing his own version of the traditional frontispiece. Nevertheless he has placed the stamp of his own mind and individuality on every one of the series. Some may have a little too much of his mannerisms, others have been given a touch of his own peculiar symbolism; yet it can be claimed that Blake has interpreted perfectly the spirit of *The Pilgrim's Progress*, and that he has matched Bunyan's genius with his own.

XXIII

THE HISTORY OF THE *JOB* DESIGNS

WILLIAM BLAKE in 1821 was a lonely and disappointed man. After many years of neglect and poverty he had just moved to humble apartments consisting of two rooms on the first floor of No. 3 Fountain Court, Strand, the rest of the house being occupied by his wife's brother-in-law, Baines. His circumstances at this time were at such a low ebb that he was compelled to sell to Colnaghi's the whole collection of prints which he had been forming since his boyhood, and soon afterwards, in 1822, to accept a donation of £25 from the Council of the Royal Academy. Even his oldest friend and patron, Thomas Butts, had seemed to grow cool towards him, and transactions between them, formerly so numerous, had become rare. The last purchase, in fact, that Butts is known to have made from Blake was the set of twenty-one water-colour drawings illustrating his version of *The Book of Job*, and this he is believed to have acquired in or about the year 1820, if not earlier.[1]

Blake's interest in the theme of Job and his misfortunes dated back at least to before the year 1790, and probably even to 1785, when he was 28 years old. To about this year is assigned a pen-and-wash drawing[2] representing Job seated between his wife and his friends. It is primitive in technique, but the characters of the component figures are already there, very much as they are shewn in plate 10 of the final *Job* series designed thirty-five years later, Job's wife being on his right and the friends, pointing fingers of scorn, on his left (Plate 45).

On the back of this drawing Blake made a sketch of Job's wife as she is shewn in a later variation of the design, of which there are three versions. The earliest of these three is presumably the drawing, of approximately the same size as before, in Indian ink, pen and wash, which was in the possession of Miss Brenda G. Warr in 1912.[3] This was elaborated by Blake into a very highly finished water-colour painting in sepia, and he made also a companion painting of 'The Death of Ezekiel's

---

[1] A. T. Story's *Life of Linnell*, London, 1892, i. 169.

[2] This drawing, about 12 × 18 inches, was sold at Sotheby's on 20 April 1862, lot 164, probably from the collection of Frederick Tatham. It was afterwards in the collection of F. T. Palgrave, Thomas Woolner, and Miss Alice Carthew, by whom it was bequeathed in 1940 to the Tate Gallery.

[3] Sold at Sotheby's on 17 December 1928 (lot 138, Maggs, £115).

JOB

Wife'. Both of these were in the collection of the late W. Graham Robertson. This drawing cannot be dated with exactitude, but it was probably done about 1786, which is also the approximate date of a large copper-plate engraving, about 14 × 19 inches, of the same subject. This engraving is known only in a single impression now in my collection (Plate 46). It is a faithful copy of the sepia drawing, and is executed in the smooth and quiet style of Blake's earliest plates. A few years later, in 1793, he again took up this plate and must have rubbed down the greater part of it, keeping only the main outlines as a guide to his burin. He then re-engraved the plate and completely changed its character so that it became, in fact, startlingly different with a gleam of wildness. Both by the changed style of engraving and by the introduction of new details it has become highly dramatized, though it is also stronger and more profound.[1]

In the drawings Job is seated on the left in an attitude of despair with tears streaming down his cheeks. His wife, with her hands clasped over her knees, is seated on his left, and on her left are the three friends, gazing earnestly at Job. Eliphaz is pointing under his beard. Behind the figures are the trunks of five trees. In the engraving the positions are reversed. Job's wife is now on his right, and the friends on her right, and a zigzag of lightning is added in the background. A strange alteration is also introduced in the disposition of Job's legs. In the drawings his left leg is bare and the left foot slightly in advance of the right. In the engraving both legs are covered, the toes only being shewn, but the right foot is now slightly in advance of the left. These details are of interest, since they suggest that even at this early date Blake was attaching some symbolical significance to 'right' and 'left' and therefore to the position of the hands and feet of his figures. The late Joseph Wicksteed suggested that to this is due the uncomfortable appearance of Job's feet and legs in the engraving. The reversal of the design involved reversal of the significance of the position of the feet, so that Blake has been led into giving the impression of crossed legs, with a left foot on a right leg and vice versa. However this may be, there was probably something of the kind in Blake's mind, the 'right' and 'left' symbolism beginning to be formulated in these designs. It was highly developed afterwards at the time of the final *Job* series, as was clearly demonstrated by Wicksteed in his book on *Blake's Vision of the Book of Job* published in 1910. In No. 10 of the later designs the subject of Job and his friends is further elaborated, and a profounder meaning given to the symbolism.

To a somewhat later date belongs another design of great importance in the evolution of the *Job* theme. This is a water-colour formerly in the Graham

[1] Both versions are reproduced in my book, *Blake's Separate Engravings*, Dublin, 1956.

Robertson collection shewing Job's redemption, when he is answered by God out of the whirlwind.[1] It provided the idea for No. 13 of the series, though quite different from it in detail. This picture was probably painted about 1800, though there seems to be no means of determining the exact date. It was not shewn at the exhibition of 1809 and it is possible it was done later even than this.

About the year 1807 Blake drew the only design ever done by him upon stone. The subject of this was interpreted by A. G. B. Russell in 1912 as 'Job in Prosperity',[2] and the title was accepted by other authorities. These included Wicksteed,[3] but he later discovered that the subject is really 'Enoch', the ancestor of Noah, who, with his sons Shem and Japheth, represents, according to Blake, 'Poetry, Painting, and Music, the three Powers in Man of conversing with Paradise, which the flood did not sweep away'.[4] Enoch is seated on a stone seat with an open book on his knee carrying his name in Hebrew characters. Around him are the personifications of Painting, Poetry, and Music, the last represented by a woman. Figures of inspiration float on either hand, those on the right carrying a tablet on which is inscribed in Hebrew letters part of the verse from Genesis 5: 24: 'And Enoch walked with God, and he was not: for God took him'. Fruitful vines are climbing up the sides of the design, and the steps of the seat are decorated with Gothic arches, Blake's symbol of true art. Enoch himself is an ancient bearded figure, closely resembling Job, and this design[5] almost certainly has some relation to Blake's later conception of Job and his family as seen in the lower part of the second illustration in the *Job* series, and of Job and his daughters as represented in the first water-colour for No. 20 of the series, and in No. 21, where they represent the three Arts in Job's state of restored prosperity. A water-colour drawing[6] provides a directly connecting link between the lithograph and the second *Job* illustration. This has some features in common with the lithograph, but now definitely represents Job and his family instead of Enoch, and is clearly the foundation of the *Job* illustration, though the positions of the figures are reversed.

It has been conjectured by Wicksteed that the idea of Job in spiritual difficulties between his wife and his friends was suggested to Blake by his own troubles, first in 1785 between Catherine Blake on the one hand and his brother Robert and his friends on the other, and again in 1793 when his integrity as artist and 'prophet'

---

[1] Now in the National Gallery of Scotland.   [2] *Engravings of William Blake* (1912), p. 91.

[3] *Blake's Vision of the Book of Job* (second edition, 1924), p. 205 n. 2.

[4] 'A Vision of the Last Judgment', *Complete Writings*, ed. Keynes, 1966, p. 609.

[5] Reproduced in *Blake's Separate Engravings*, Dublin, 1956.

[6] Sold at Sotheby's on 14 November 1934, lot 551.

was threatened by the false friends who tried to dissuade him from the course he had marked out for himself. It is also suggested that the later conception of Job answered by God out of the whirlwind was the result of his own spiritual rebirth after the Felpham period as expressed in a letter to William Hayley in October 1804:

> I am really drunk with intellectual vision whenever I take a pencil or graver into my hand, even as I used to be in my youth, and as I have not been for twenty dark, but very profitable years.[1]

A few years later, after the total failure of the exhibition of his pictures in 1809, he was again cast down and he seemed to have been utterly deserted by friends and fortune. Little is known of Blake's life during the years 1810–18, but with the advent of Linnell and a circle of new friends there came a second spiritual rebirth after a period of profound misery and obscurity. Blake, like Job, had passed through the pit of suffering and come at length to a new and better understanding of intellectual truths—to be symbolized as Job's state of restored prosperity. It may thus be seen how the idea of Job had been simmering in Blake's mind for over thirty years until about 1818 the story as a whole had assumed for him a profound significance in relation to his own experiences. It was natural, therefore, that he should then set about telling the story in his own way and embody it in the series of 'Inventions', which were afterwards to be recognized as the supreme achievement of his life. Although there were only two of the *Job* designs which had actually taken shape before the full series was made, Blake used details or ideas from earlier compositions. A striking example of this is seen in No. 14 of the series, 'When the Morning Stars sang together'. The frieze of angels with uplifted arms had already been used at least twice in other compositions and may have been suggested to him by a print executed in Basire's shop while he was an apprentice about 1775 (see p. 27 and Plate 12). Another example is seen in the magnificent colour print of 'God Creating Adam', 1793, which foreshadows design No. 11 in the series, 'Job's Evil Dreams'. Many other resemblances could be found by searching through the whole body of Blake's work.

The first set of water-colours for the *Job* series was, as already stated, bought by Thomas Butts. There is no remaining record of the transaction, so that we do not know to what extent Blake profited. The drawings remained in the possession of Butts's family until his son sold them, with a large part of the Blake Collection, to Richard Monckton Milnes, first Lord Houghton. They appeared for the first and

[1] *Letters of Blake*, ed. Keynes, 1968, p. 107.

last time in the sale rooms when a large portion of his father's Blake Collection was sold by the Earl of Crewe at Sotheby's on 30 March 1903. The drawings (lot 17) were sold to Sabin for £5,600, and were acquired by the late J. Pierpont Morgan, in whose library in New York they still remain (frontispiece, water-colour for No. 14 of the series).

Blake was clearly proud of his achievement and hoped that the drawings might be the source of further profit. Butts accordingly allowed him to borrow them in order that he might shew them to other people in the hope of finding other customers for replica sets. Only one order was obtained, and this was given in 1821 by John Linnell.

Linnell was a rising artist and engraver when in 1818 at the age of 26 he first met Blake, who seems to have been brought, probably by his friend George Cumberland's son, to Linnell's house in Rathbone Place.[1] Linnell and Cumberland also visited Blake in South Molton Street, and soon Blake and Linnell were collaborating over the engraving of a portrait of a Baptist minister, Mr. Upton. This plate is dated 1 June 1819, and from that time until Blake's death in 1827 Linnell remained his closest friend and supporter, sometimes supplying him with means of subsistence even when his own affairs were none too prosperous. Linnell's knowledge of Blake's necessities and his admiration for the designs having prompted him to order a duplicate set, he proceeded to trace the outlines himself on 8 and 10 September 1821,[2] Blake afterwards finishing them with water-colours. This second set remained in the possession of Linnell and his descendants until the whole of their Blake Collection was sold at Christie's on 15 March 1918. The *Job* series (lot 149) was then bought by Sabin for £3,990, and was afterwards sold in America, eighteen of the drawings being acquired by Grenville Lindall Winthrop of New York, by whom they were later presented to the Fogg Art Museum at Harvard.

After Blake had completed the drawings for Linnell, no further orders were obtained, and there the matter rested for some eighteen months. Linnell was not satisfied, however, that Blake had yet developed his conception to the full, and so followed the further suggestion of a set of engravings to be made from the water-colours. A business-like agreement was accordingly drawn up which was clearly very generous to Blake, since he was to be paid as the plates were completed in advance of any receipts from the sale of prints, so that Linnell, who was also paying for the copper-plates, was to bear the whole risk of the venture. During Blake's life no profits were realized, but Linnell in spite of this chose to give Blake an extra

[1] A. T. Story's *Life of Linnell*, London, 1892, i. 158, but see p. 245 below.   [2] Ibid., p. 169.

£50 in consideration of future sales. Blake therefore received in all £150, and while he was at work on the plates, Linnell provided for his immediate needs by a regular weekly payment of varying amounts as can be seen in the original account book in which each payment is initialled by the engraver.[1] The engravings were not ready for publication until early in 1826, though dated 8 March 1825, in the imprint of each plate.[2] This will be referred to again later. The whole sum due to Blake had been paid by the middle of the next year, and a receipt for the £150 is dated 14 July 1826. Linnell himself discounted his generosity to Blake, and in a letter to Bernard Barton, the Quaker poet, he stated that 'this [the £25 given by the Council of the Royal Academy at his instigation] was not enough to afford him permanent support, and it was in hopes of obtaining a profit sufficient to supply his future wants that the publication of *Job* was begun at my suggestion and expense; but as I had also the expectation, and have still, of remuneration (the plates being my property), I have no claim to any notice upon that account'.[3] Sufficient recompense, as will be seen, was received by Linnell's descendants to justify his faith, but there can be no question of the generosity of his motives at the time.

Of the actual process of the conversion of the water-colour designs to the engraved prints nothing has yet been said. The water-colours were of considerable size, the largest being about 30 × 23 cm., whereas the engraved designs, excluding the borders, have but half this area. Blake's first task, therefore, was to make a series of pencil sketches of the approximate size of the engravings to serve as a basis for the copper-plates. These sketches were done on sheets of a peculiar paper resembling 'rice paper' and were carefully kept by Linnell, who marked them: 'These are Mr. Blake's reduced Drawings & studies for the Engravings of the Book of Job done for me' (Plate 48, drawing for No. 14 of the series). They include sketches, some being touched with water-colour, for all the engraved plates, except the title-page, together with one design which was not used, and a few fragmentary studies. The drawings remained in the Linnell collection until this was sold in March 1918, when they were bought for £504 on behalf of the late T. H. Riches, who had married a granddaughter of John Linnell and had so acquired a special interest in the matter. Mrs. Riches afterwards bequeathed the drawings to the Fitzwilliam Museum, Cambridge. They are for the most part unfinished and some are merely indicated, so that it was to be presumed that some more finished series must have been made before the designs could be actually engraved. Yet no

---

[1] A full account of these documents will be found in Chapter XXVI of this book, pp. 205–12.
[2] Except for the second plate which is dated in error 8 March 1828.
[3] A. G. B. Russell, *Letters of William Blake* (London, 1906), p. 228.

other link in the chain was known to exist until March 1928, when the discovery of another set of designs in Auckland, New Zealand, was announced. These had belonged to an artist, Albin Martin, who had been a pupil of Linnell and had emigrated about the year 1850 to New Zealand. He was born in 1813, and therefore was but 14 years old at the time of Blake's death. No claim is made that he knew Blake, but he was afterwards acquainted with members of Blake's circle, and there can be little doubt that he received the drawings from Linnell, although there is no documentary evidence in proof of this. The drawings, which are very carefully finished in brilliant water-colours, are of approximately the same size as the engravings, and are without the decorative borders. There are a sufficient number of variations to shew that they cannot have been copied from the engravings; on the other hand they are not uniform in quality. The finest of them could not have been produced by any hand but Blake's, though it is possible that he was helped by Linnell or another in finishing those that are less good. In 1928 the drawings were the property of Martin's daughters, Miss Fanny Martin and Mrs. E. J. Hickson, who submitted them for sale at Sotheby's in December of that year. The absence of full documentary evidence of their provenance produced an atmosphere of distrust in the sale-rooms, and Gabriel Wells was allowed to secure them for £500. They were afterwards acquired by Mr. Philip Hofer for his own collection,[1] though he disposed of them a few years later to Mr. Paul Mellon.

As already related, the actual engraving of the plates occupied nearly three years, from 25 March 1823, when the agreement was signed, to early in 1826, when the plates were finally approved. They were executed wholly with the graver, and were done in the free style which Blake had recently acquired. There are but few other plates executed by Blake in this style, and yet the *Job* plates are done with a uniform mastery which would have been thought only to come from long practice. The minor differences between the engravings and the water-colours are numerous and have been described in the introduction to the Pierpont Morgan Library reproduction. The main difference, which is at once obvious, is in the absence of the decorative borders and texts everywhere but in the plates. The general effect of the engravings is so much enhanced by these borders that it is difficult to believe that they did not form part of the original conception in Blake's mind. Yet John Linnell, in a letter to C. W. (afterwards Sir Charles) Dilke written in 1844, has stated the opposite. He was sending Dilke a copy of the *Job*, and adds: 'I have sent you a couple of proofs before the Borders as a curiosity because the Borders were an

---

[1] They were well reproduced in colour and published, with a note added by Mr. Hofer, by J. M. Dent and E. P. Dutton in 1937.

PL. 48

afterthought and designed as well as engraved upon the copper without a previous drawing'.[1] The pencil sketches for the first three designs shew the tentative beginnings of the borders, but these might have been added by Blake at any stage, and none of the other drawings has any trace of them. A few of the early proofs of the central designs in the engravings also have some pencilled suggestions for the borders, but otherwise no studies for them are known to exist. It seems possible that the addition of the borders occurred to Blake as a device for making a uniform shape for each plate, since these had to embody central designs of which some were oblong and others upright. Early proofs of plates 7 and 14 are reproduced here (Plates 47 and 49).

The number of designs in the water-colour sets is twenty-one; there are twenty-four pencil sketches, but two of these are first studies and one was not used. The number of engraved plates, however, is twenty-two, a title-page with a design of seven angels being added to this series. The preliminary sketch for this title-page was sold for Mr. G. A. Rossetti at Sotheby's on 27 March 1929 and was bought by W. T. Spencer for £50. An inscription at the bottom has the initials of Blake's friend and biographer, Frederick Tatham, and there is a note by W. M. Rossetti on the back of the sheet. It is now in the United States.

Neither Blake nor Linnell possessed any special facilities for marketing a comparatively expensive work of art such as the *Illustrations of the Book of Job*, and it is not surprising that such amateur efforts as they made should not have succeeded in selling many copies. Presumably no copies were sent out to periodicals 'for review', as no contemporary notices have been discovered. Linnell succeeded in selling some copies to his acquaintances, and it seems to have been the original intention that he should be the nominal 'publisher', for proofs exist with the imprint *Published as the Act directs March 8: 1825 by J: Linnell N 6 Cirencester Place, Fitzroy Square*. The final state of the prints has, however, after the date, the words *by William Blake N° 3 Fountain Court Strand*, a form which would be more in keeping with Blake's self-esteem than the earlier state. Blake himself, as references in his letters shew, endeavoured, sometimes successfully, to sell copies to friends such as Francis Chantrey, Henry Crabb Robinson, and George Cumberland. Thomas Butts possessed a proof copy which was sold with his collection at Sotheby's in 1903. Cumberland did his best to dispose of copies among his acquaintances in Bristol, though with small success. Blake writing to Linnell on 15 March 1827 says: 'I have reciev'd a Letter from Mr. Cumberland, in which he says he will take one Copy of Job for himself, but cannot, as yet, find a Customer for one, but

[1] The original letter, as well as the two proofs, are now in my collection.

hopes to do somewhat by perseverance in his Endeavours; he tells me that it is too much Finish'd, or over Labour'd, for his Bristol Friends, as they think'.[1] In his last letter to Cumberland himself, written on 12 April 1827, Blake says:

I thank you for the Pains you have taken with Poor Job. I know too well that a great majority of Englishmen are fond of The Indefinite which they Measure by Newton's Doctrine of the Fluxions of an Atom, A Thing that does not exist. These are Politicians & think that Republican Art is inimical to their Atom. For a line or Lineament is not formed by Chance: a Line is a Line in its Minutest Sub-divisions: Strait or Crooked It is Itself & Not Intermeasurable with or by any Thing else. Such is Job, but since the French Revolution Englishmen are all Inter-measurable One by Another, Certainly a happy state of Agreement to which I for One do not Agree. God keep me from the Divinity of Yes & No too, The Yea Nay Creeping Jesus, from supposing Up & Down to be the same Thing as all Experimentalists must suppose.[2]

It was incumbent upon Linnell to try to reimburse himself for the initial outlay, and for years he was offering copies to likely buyers. In 1830 he had sent a copy 'on approval' to Bernard Barton with a letter already mentioned (p. 181), but Barton, while expressing polite interest, pleaded poverty, and, after trying un-successfully to sell a copy to someone else, added in another letter:

There is a dryness and hardness in Blake's manner of engraving which is very apt to be repulsive to print-collectors in general—to any, indeed, who have not taste enough to appreciate the force and originality of his conceptions, in spite of the manner in which he has embodied them. I candidly own I am not surprised at this; his style is little calculated to take with the admirers of modern engraving. It puts me in mind of some old prints I have seen, and seems to combine somewhat of old Albert Durer with Bolswert. I cannot but wish he could have clothed his imaginative creations in a garb more attractive to ordinary mortals, or else given simple outlines of them. The extreme beauty, elegance, and grace of several of his marginal accompaniments induce me to think that they would have pleased more generally in that state. But his was not a mind to dictate to; and what he has done is quite enough to stamp him as a genius of the highest order.[3]

Eight years later Linnell sent Barton an ordinary copy as a present, saying:

There were some reasons at the time of publication why no copies were given, but yours should have been an exception. . . . As you value the work for the invention and execution the copy sent will be to you as good as any, though I

---

[1] *Letters of Blake*, ed. Keynes, 1968, p. 161. [2] Ibid., p. 162.
[3] A. T. Story's *Life of Linnell*, London, 1892, i. 176–7.

should have sent you the proof had I any number, but I have only a few copies left for there were not many printed. The price has been lowered (as you will perceive by the mark outside the cover) to the present scale of prices and is put on the label that you may not give an incorrect answer to any inquiries upon the subject.[1]

As to the actual date of publication and the price of the prints some mis-apprehension has arisen. Many of the existing sets have on the outer cover a printed label dated March 1826. Gilchrist stated[2] that this was the actual date of publication and not 8 March 1825, which was merely the date by which Blake had expected to finish them. That they were not completed by March 1825 is evident from a reference in a letter from Blake to Linnell dated 10 November 1825: 'I have, I believe, done nearly all that we agreed on &c. If you should put on your con-sidering Cap, just as you did last time we met, I have no doubt that the Plates would be all the better for it. . . . I hope a few more days will bring us to a conclusion.'[3] Probably the plates were completed not long after this, for in February 1826 Blake asks Linnell for 'a copy of Job to shew to Mr. Chantr[e]y'[3] as if the book was already finished and on sale.

As to the price at which the prints were sold, Gilchrist states that the price of ordinary prints was 3 guineas, of proofs, 5, and of India-paper proofs, 6.[2] The late E. J. Ellis stated, apparently on the authority of John Linnell, jr., that 'the proofs were published at £10:10s. the set, and the prints at £5:5s. the set, bound in card-board covers of terra-cotta colour with white labels pasted in the middle upon which the price is written in pencil'.[4] That this is erroneous is shewn by some existing copies of the prints which are bound in limp boards of a drab colour with the price for prints and proofs marked on the cover as stated by Gilchrist. Ellis's state-ment probably refers to a later binding, Linnell or his family having continued to sell copies in small numbers almost up to the time of the final sale of the Linnell col-lection in 1918. The original price is further established by Blake's own statement with regard to Crabb Robinson's copies. On 31 March 1826 he wrote to Linnell: 'Mr. Robinson certainly did Subscribe for Prints only & not for Proofs, for I remember that he offer'd to pay me Three Guineas for each of the Copies'.[5] In 1830, when Linnell was writing the letter to Bernard Barton already quoted, he says: 'P.S. I have sent a plain copy of the Job for your inspection. The price to you will be the same as the trade price—£2:12:6d.' indicating a retail price of 3 guineas.

[1] Letter in possession of Messrs. Tregaskis, 1932.   [2] *Life*, 1880, i. 335.
[3] *Letters of Blake*, ed. Keynes, 1968, p. 153.   [4] E. J. Ellis, *The Real Blake*, London, 1907, p. 409.
[5] *Letters*, p. 155.

These statements have now been corroborated by the evidence of the account book described in Chapter XXVI.

The paper upon which the engravings were printed shews some variation, but nearly all the India-paper proofs were on Whatman's Turkey Mill dated 1825. The ordinary proofs and the print state were on Turkey Mill 1825, ordinary Whatman paper, 1825, or on paper without a watermark. One complete set of India-paper proofs seems to have been finely coloured by Blake himself,[1] and four proofs also coloured by Blake are now in the Fitzwilliam Museum, Cambridge.

According to the account book (see p. 211) the initial printing was of 150 sets of proofs on India paper, 50 sets on French paper, and 100 sets on drawing (i.e. Whatman) paper. How many more sets were printed in later years it is impossible to say, though it may be that no more were done. It was not generally known that the prints were obtainable and the demand was certainly very small. At the Linnell sale in 1918 presumably the whole remaining stock was sold, and this consisted of 6 bound sets of India-paper proofs (£226. 16s.), 12 sets of India-paper proofs unbound (£144. 18s.), and 50 sets in 'print state' unbound (£346. 10s.) Blake had now repaid his debt with interest.

The copper-plates, being regarded by the Linnell trustees as a national possession, were not sold with the remainder of the collection, but were instead deposited in the Print Room of the British Museum.

[1] This was at one time in Sir F. Burton's Collection, and was offered for sale by the bookseller, Tregaskis, in 1901. It was probably the same copy that was sold by the American Art Association, New York, 16 April 1923 (lot 118, $3,125); then acquired by George C. Smith and sold with his collection at the Parke-Bernet Galleries, New York, 2 November 1938 (lot 58, Sessler, $3,200). Another coloured copy exists, but has no provenance.

XXIV

BLAKE'S *JOB* ON THE STAGE[1]

SOME of the story of Blake's *Illustrations of the Book of Job* has been told in the preceding chapter. The present chapter seeks to give only an idea of the meaning that Blake tried to convey by his pictures, and the history of an attempt made in recent years to convey some of this meaning to a wider audience through the media of music, dance, and mime.

Blake had certainly read the Book of Job in the Bible attentively, but he chose to put a somewhat different interpretation on the story, and to make it an entirely spiritual and symbolical history of a man's mind under the blows of adversity with some important divergences from the Bible version.

The designs until comparatively recent years were taken to be illustrations of the Bible story of Job, and this was, indeed, what Blake called them—'Illustrations of the Book of Job'. It was not until 1910, when J. H. Wicksteed first published his book, *Blake's Vision of the Book of Job*, that it began to be realized that the designs embodied a personal version of the Bible story, with a wealth of private symbolism and hidden meaning. This revision of the former view of Blake's pictures does not in any way detract from the full aesthetic enjoyment of their merits as pictures. On the other hand, it adds to their interest and to the appreciation of the details of their beauty, while affording some sort of explanation of why they seem so pregnant with meaning, even when the mind is not yet instructed enough to be able to take in all that they convey. Wicksteed's work fully established the importance of these designs in the development of Blake's philosophy and art, and demonstrated that they may be interpreted as an account of his own misfortunes and spiritual rebirth.

The first important clue to the understanding of the designs is the fact that Job and Jehovah are usually represented as almost identical figures, that is to say Blake's Jehovah is really an aspect of Job himself, and that Satan too is a spiritual 'state' of the man. The story of the designs is then seen to be a primarily subjective experience, 'the account of a man's inward struggle and triumph, the conflict between his indwelling Good and Evil powers'.

[1] First printed in a slightly different form in *Sadler's Wells Ballet Books, no. 2, Job and The Rake's Progress*, London, 1949.

The argument of the spiritual drama of Job as seen by Blake may be briefly summarized as follows. The story in the Bible is that of a human being who regards himself as virtuous, who is afflicted, as he believes, unjustly, and is accused, by his friends, of sin, since there can be no reason for affliction except sin. He denies that his misfortunes are his desert, and finally, in the Bible, repents, not of disobeying God's laws, but of presumption in trying to understand his ways, so that the mystery of suffering is left unsolved. Elihu, in the Bible, is thought to be a later interpolation in the original story, and his speeches develop and emphasize the words of Job's friends.

To Blake Job himself is in the wrong, but his sin is one of ideas, not action, and, unlike the Bible, Blake makes clear what he believes Job's sin to be. In this respect he diverges entirely from the Bible, for to him Job's spiritual sin is one of materialism and complacency. Blake's God is Divine Humanity (which he sometimes identifies as the Poetic Genius) and his Satan is constituted by the false values in man's life, which may make mortal error even of his goodness, an apparent paradox typical of Blake's thought. Job, therefore, living in material prosperity, protesting his own virtue, deriving false merit from his burnt-offerings and charity, is living in darkness, symbolized by the *setting* sun which illumines the first scene in the series. Satan's attacks are spiritual, though symbolized as material, and Job's self-righteousness makes him an easy prey. Job's friends, or 'comforters', are false friends who exhibit to him his own failings in themselves, and when in his exasperation he at last appeals to his God, it is a vision of Satan that appears.

In Blake's story it is Elihu that brings about the turning-point in Job's spiritual history. Job has descended into the pit of suffering, deluded by his materialism and self-regard into believing himself an ill-used man. Elihu shews him the falsity of his ideals and that in crediting himself with loving others he really only loves himself. But he gives Job fresh hope even though he be old, pointing to the stars and providing by contrast the stimulus of his own youth and beauty. Job is thus brought to realize his own place in the larger scheme of things and the true nature of love. Immediately his Spiritual Self, now again the person of Jehovah, is revealed to him, and, in the designs, speaks to him out of the whirlwind. Blake then shews the regenerated character of Job in a series of visions, in one of which Satan is cast out. Job is finally reunited with Jehovah in a scene of symbolic worship, and he is restored to prosperity in this new humility, love, and understanding of art—which is, to Blake, religion. He is seen at the end again with his sons and daughters in the *sunrise* of a fresh spiritual existence.

Below a pencil sketch of the supreme design of 'When the Morning Stars sang together' Blake has put a 'symbolic' signature—the words *done by* followed by a series of symbols (1) a straight line, the simplest figure with natural limit, i.e. immortality; (2) a hand; (3) a B, i.e. Blake; (4) an eye; (5) a circle, i.e. symmetry. This indicates Blake's belief that this drawing, the climax of a supreme effort, was created by the Poetic Genius in his own person. It was about 1794 that Blake had written in his poem 'The Tyger' the lines:

> What immortal hand or eye
> Dare frame thy fearful symmetry?

Twenty-five years later it was his own mortal hand and eye that dared the impossible—and succeeded. The inspired symmetry of this design and of the whole *Job* series could only have been carried through by the breath of God, that is, of the Poetic Genius, or Imagination (Plates 48 and 49).

★   ★   ★

The foregoing is a brief account of the idea embodied in Blake's great spiritual drama as portrayed in his series of engravings. At first sight these designs, with their rather obscure message, impress the mind with their elaborate grandeur and suggest that it would be almost impossible to adapt them for the purposes of the stage. There are several designs, such as 'Behemoth and Leviathan', and 'God speaking out of a whirlwind', which clearly transcend the physical limitations of any such attempt. Yet long familiarity with the designs convinced me that the inner thread of Blake's drama possessed a fundamental simplicity—and that if this could be successfully extracted it would provide the theme for a ballet of a kind which would be new to the English stage. Blake had, moreover, unconsciously provided in his pictures several settings which could easily be adapted for stage scenes, and innumerable suggestions in his figures for attitudes and groupings which cried out for their conversion by a choreographer into actuality and movement.

To be fully successful a ballet must synthesize the different arts of drama, design and colour, music, and dancing. Blake had provided in his *Vision of the Book of Job*, as we may now call it, ample material to form a basis for all of these except the music. The first necessity was to fashion the 'story' as a framework which could afterwards be clothed by the contributions of the various arts, and upon this initial simplification the success of the further developments would depend. It was soon evident that, after physical impossibilities had been eliminated, a spiritual drama could be evolved which would provide enough continuity of theme and variety of incident to sustain the interest of an audience for as long as a ballet of this kind could reasonably be made to last, that is to say for thirty or forty minutes. The co-operation of an artist, the late Mrs. Gwendolen Raverat, was obtained, and, after many months of preliminary thought and conversations, we contrived a scenario which has, with only minor alterations, formed the acting version of the ballet. The synopsis printed on the programme at all performances is as follows:

Scene 1. Job is sitting in the sunset of prosperity with his wife, surrounded by his seven sons and three daughters. They all join in a pastoral dance. When they have dispersed, leaving Job and his wife alone, Satan enters unperceived. He appeals to Heaven which opens, revealing the Godhead (Job's Spiritual Self) enthroned within. On the steps are the Heavenly Hosts. Job's Spiritual Self consents that his mortal nature be tested in the furnace of temptation.

Scene 2. Satan, after a triumphal dance, usurps the throne.

Scene 3. Job's sons and daughters are feasting and dancing when Satan appears and destroys them.

Scene 4. Job's peaceful sleep is disturbed by terrifying visions of War, Pestilence and Famine.

Scene 5. Messengers come to Job with tidings of the destruction of all his possessions and the death of his sons and daughters. Satan introduces Job's comforters, three wily hypocrites. Their dance at first simulates compassion, but this gradually changes to rebuke and anger. Job rebels: 'Let the day perish wherein I was born'. He invokes his vision of the Godhead, but the opening Heaven reveals Satan upon the throne. Job and his friends shrink in terror.

Scene 6. There enters Elihu who is young and beautiful. 'Ye are old and I am very young.' Job perceives his sin. The Heavens open revealing Job's Spiritual Self again enthroned.

Scene 7. Satan again appeals to Job's Godhead, claiming the victory, but is repelled and driven down by the Sons of the Morning. Job's household build an altar and worship with musical instruments, while the heavenly dance continues.

Scene 8. Job sits a humbled man in the sunrise of restored prosperity, surrounded by his family, upon whom he bestows his blessing.

★   ★   ★

It is plain that this synopsis is too much simplified to make a fully satisfying presentment of Blake's theme. Yet it contains the essential characters and situations of Blake's vision. The symmetry, already mentioned as a feature of Blake's designs and in particular of the *Job* series, is preserved. Job sits at the beginning in the sunset of material prosperity, he is tried and tormented and descends into the pit of affliction, the truth is revealed to him, and he repents, and he is seen at the end in the sunrise of a new and different prosperity. A dramatic climax is provided in the middle of the ballet when Job summons his vision of the Godhead, and Satan, to his horror, is revealed upon the throne. An effective contrast is made between the static characters of Job and his Spiritual Self, and the volcanic exuberance of Satan, Job's material and physical counterpart; another contrast is made between the double-faced contortions of the Comforters, the purity of the young and beautiful Elihu, and a broader one between the dark horror of Satan's enthronement and the severe beauty of the scene when the Godhead is restored to his place by Job's spiritual enlightenment. A variety in the stage effects is also introduced by the use of two levels, Jehovah's throne being set on a platform with a series of steps. The earthly characters move only on the stage level, while movements can be carried out by the heavenly beings around the throne and on the steps.

It was at first feared that a difficulty might arise by introducing a representation of the Deity on the stage, even though all reference to 'God' in the scenario was carefully avoided. It was ascertained, however, that the Lord Chamberlain's licence did not have to be obtained as no words were used in the performance. The only risk was that of prosecution by the police under the Blasphemy Laws. It was decided that this was a risk that might justifiably be taken, though additional safety was invoked by providing Jehovah with a mask so as to make the presentation quite impersonal. This mask, rather more than life-size, was originally made by Hedley Briggs after a large drawing by Blake of the Head of Job, which is in my Blake collection.

One of the scenes which it was impossible to represent exactly on the stage was Blake's design of Job tormented on his couch by evil dreams. The liberty was, therefore, taken of representing Job's torment by a dance of Satan and his 'Trinity of Accusers', called, for the purposes of the programme, 'War, Pestilence and Famine'. The grouping of their exit was modelled exactly on Blake's engraving of this subject made in 1783, and they wore masks by Hedley Briggs suggesting these figures. These masks were afterwards redesigned so as to appear rather more horrific. It should be noticed that Satan during this dance reproduces the positions shewn in one of Blake's best-known designs of 'Satan smiting Job with boils'.

The first trials of these settings were arranged on a model stage, the back scenes and the figures for the various groupings being made by Mrs. Raverat. This point in the development of the ballet was reached in 1927. In that year there were few English composers at work who had much experience of ballet music, or whose range could compass any affinity with the mind and genius of Blake. It was eventually decided to approach Dr. Ralph Vaughan Williams, O.M., and he was immediately fired with an enthusiasm for the task—though he stipulated that there should be no dancing on points, which he greatly disliked, and that the performance should not be called a 'ballet'. The prospect of getting the piece performed on the stage was then felt to be less remote than before, and plans were laid for introducing the idea to Serge Diaghileff, who was then visiting London with the Ballets Russe de Monte Carlo. A French version of the scenario was prepared and was put before Diaghileff together with a book of full-sized reproductions of the engravings. But this proved abortive, the projected ballet being pronounced to be 'too English', and 'too old-fashioned'—although it was, in fact, an entirely new conception of the possibilities of representation of a spiritual theme by means of dancing. The book of engravings was, however, not returned, and it was interesting to see distinct traces of Blake's influence appearing in another Biblical ballet 'The Prodigal Son', produced by Diaghileff in his following London season.

It now seemed unlikely that the ballet would be performed, and Dr. Vaughan Williams completed his music on the assumption that it would be played rather as a concert piece, orchestrating it for some eighty instruments. It was finished early in 1930, and was performed for the first time by the Queen's Hall Orchestra at the Thirty-third Norfolk and Norwich Triennial Musical Festival on 23 October being conducted by the composer. It is interesting, in view of subsequent events, to record the impression received at this first performance by the musical critic of *The Times*, who wrote:

The work suffered from being stage music without the stage. Vaughan Williams's Pageant for Dancing is founded on Blake's illustrations of the Book of Job, and planned in nine scenes, with an epilogue. A concert version of such a work can be little more satisfactory than is the orchestral accompaniment to a song-cycle without the singer. All that can be said is that the hearing of the music makes one want to have a realization of the ballet worthy alike of Blake and Vaughan Williams. The music, in its acceptance of form and its rejection of formalism, is of a piece with Blake. It contained tunes of such simple beauty that one seems to have known them always, but their lines lead on into a realm of musical thought that one enters for the first time. The 'Saraband of the Sons of God', Job's dream, and the Pavan and Galliard of 'the ultimate vision', the last two worked together into the long epilogue, are salient instances.

The music, in fact, met with general approval, and it was played a second time when it was broadcast from the London Regional Station on Savoy Hill on 13 February 1931.

Before this date the settings on the model stage had been shewn to Dame Lilian Baylis and Miss (now Dame) Ninette de Valois, and had won their approval.

Plans were, indeed, going actively forward for a production of the ballet (to be called, in deference to the composer's wishes, a 'masque for dancing') at the fourth season of the Camargo Society, which had been formed in 1930 to foster the art of ballet in England, lest after the death of Diaghileff it should fall into decay. I made myself responsible for the initial expenses, being generously assisted by Dr. J. N. Keynes and Sir Thomas Dunhill, and I provided Miss de Valois with all the available reproductions of the whole range of Blake's designs. She made a close study of these, taking from them many suggestions of attitude and gesture, and this helped to sustain the Blakeian atmosphere throughout the ballet. The scenery and costumes were made after Mrs. Raverat's designs, and the concert music was rescored for a much smaller orchestra by Constant Lambert. The first performances of the ballet were given at the Cambridge Theatre in London on 5 and 6 July 1931. The part of Satan was created by Anton Dolin, and that of Elihu by Stanley Judson. The ballet was repeated three weeks later by the same company during the Ninth Annual Festival of the International Society for Contemporary Music at Oxford.

Blake's *Vision of the Book of Job* was fully established in its stage form by these three performances, and it was greeted by *The Times*'s critic as 'a completely satisfying synthesis of the arts'. A month after the performance at Oxford an independent version of the ballet was given at the Lewisohn Stadium in New York, and in September 1931 the original version was incorporated in the repertory of the Vic-Wells Ballet under the direction of Miss Ninette de Valois. It was revived by the Camargo Society during a four weeks' season in June and July 1932, and was given by the same company in Copenhagen on 25 September. It was for this revival that I made the addition of the drop-scene shewing Blake's celebrated design of 'God creating the Universe', which might serve to attune the audience to the power of Blake's mind before the ballet begins, though its suitability has been criticized on other grounds.

After 1932 *Job* was a regular feature of the programmes presented by the Vic-Wells, later the Sadler's Wells, Ballet, the part of Satan usually being danced by Sir Robert Helpmann, and the theme of Blake's vision has thus been revealed in material form to many thousands of his countrymen and even to other peoples.

In 1948 the whole ballet was drastically revised by the choreographer for its first production at the Royal Opera House, Covent Garden, in June of that year, with a new décor designed by John Piper. In these forms the ballet was presented on fifty-one occasions up to and including the year 1959. It was revived with great success in April and May 1970 for six performances, the orchestra being conducted by Sir Adrian Boult. The part of Satan was taken at different performances by Kerrison Cooke, Hendrik Davel, or Stephen Jefferies. Elihu was danced on each occasion by Nicholas Johnson.

[A piano version of the music by Vally Lasker was published by the Oxford University Press in 1931. The full score was published by the same Press in 1939. A rendering on gramophone records was issued by 'His Master's Voice' in 1946, and later by Decca in a long-playing record (LXT 2937).]

XXV

THE ARLINGTON COURT PICTURE[1]

AMONG the Blake collection in the Pierpont Morgan Library is a lovely pencil drawing which came to be known as 'The River of Oblivion' (Plate 50). This drawing was once in the possession of Blake's friend John Flaxman and later of Flaxman's sister-in-law, Maria Denman. About the year 1919 it was offered for sale by the bookseller James Tregaskis and soon afterwards came to its final resting-place in the Pierpont Morgan Library. The drawing was exhibited at the Fogg Art Museum in 1930, and in 1939 at the great Blake exhibition at Philadelphia (no. 205 in the catalogue). The title given to it cannot have been originated, as were so many of the titles of Blake's designs, by William Michael Rossetti, for it is not listed in the catalogue printed in the second volume of Gilchrist's *Life of Blake* (1880), and was presumably unknown to him. The suggestion of a river in the foreground of the design together with the attitude of one of the two central figures, apparently about to dive, has no doubt inspired the title inscribed by an unknown hand on the back of the drawing. The suggestion has been made that the drawing may be related to the well-known water-colour drawing called 'The River of Life', formerly in Graham Robertson's collection, and bequeathed by him to the Tate Gallery, London. The suggestion has even been crystallized into the conjecture that the pencil drawing may illustrate Revelation 22:17. 'And the Spirit and the bride say, Come, And let him that heareth, say, Come, And let him that is athirst, come. And whosoever will, let him take the water of life freely.' This interpretation does not accord with the title, 'The River of Oblivion', and it must be conceded that either idea is highly conjectural. The elucidation of Blake's preliminary sketches is often extremely difficult in the absence of any more finished form of the design—and even in the presence of such a design it is not always easy.

The drawing in the Morgan Library is large, measuring $15\frac{1}{2} \times 18\frac{1}{2}$ inches. The main group occupying most of the left half of the design consists of two figures—a woman with indications of a starry veil enveloping her, with her left arm pointing

---

[1] Revised from an article entitled 'Blake's Vision of the Circle of the Life of Man' contributed to *Studies in Art and Literature for Belle da Costa Greene*, edited by Dorothy Miner. Princeton University Press, 1954.

upwards and her right downwards, and a man crouching on her right with his arms outstretched as if about to take a dive. The direction of his dive, however, would not take him into the river which flows in the foreground, but would land him outside the picture. The river is, indeed, not very clearly indicated, but its watery nature is suggested by the nude male figure, apparently horned, which is floating out-stretched in the stream, with some heads vaguely shewn above his left arm. The right half of the drawing is occupied by a grove of trees whose branches arch over a group of figures with raised arms. Another figure, apparently carrying something, is stepping up towards the group, and another, a girl, is reclining at the root of one of the trees with her hands above her head. Blake has sketched in the details too vaguely for recognition, his interest at this stage being only in the larger parts of the design. It is impossible also to discern the meaning of the pencillings in the sky above the man and the woman. The manner of the drawing suggests that it was done in Blake's maturer years, but there is insufficient material in it for the basis of a full interpretation, and no attempt to do this has ever been published. The sketch, however, looks purposeful, as if Blake had fully intended to take it further, and eventually, by great good fortune, the lack of a finished picture was supplied by a unexpected and dramatic discovery.

The Chichester family is of ancient and honourable lineage and has owned large estates in the west of England for many centuries. One of these estates, known as the Arlington Estate, is situated near Barnstaple in Devonshire and it was here that Colonel John Palmer Chichester (1769–1823) elected to build a large house, Arlington Court. The house was begun in 1820 and was finished three years later, but its owner did not live to enjoy it. He died in 1823, and the estate passed in due course to his great-granddaughter, Rosalie, who died unmarried in 1947. Miss Rosalie Chichester was the last representative of her branch of the family, and before her death she gave the Arlington estate, with the house and its contents, to the National Trust, which, in spite of its name, is a private charity whose object is the preservation of 'places of historic interest or natural beauty'. The house, Arlington Court, though of great charm, is not of outstanding architectural merit, but the 3,478 acres of land are of much beauty and interest, and a large area in the centre is maintained as a nature reserve. Miss Chichester was herself a great collector of shells, model ships, pewter, and other objects, and the house forms a museum for the preservation of her collections. When the house was taken over by the National Trust in 1947 it was filled with a mass of family papers and other accumulations of the last 125 years. Miss Chichester's taste did not include pictures, and she was, indeed, apt to decorate her walls with nothing more significant than

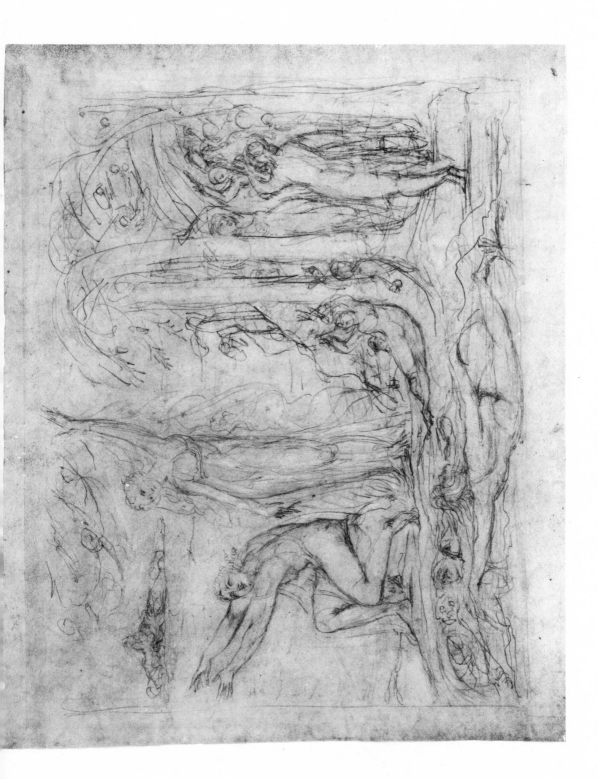

reproductions from Christmas annuals. It was reported by her domestics that she particularly disliked any picture that could be called 'religious'. The officers of the National Trust, whose duty it was to clear the house of unwanted papers and 'junk', had, therefore, to face a dreary task without hope of finding anything of value or interest—though they might have been encouraged by the notorious fecundity of the English countryside in the provision of unexpected treasures of art and letters. After days of dusty toil their task of eviction and destruction was almost at an end. There remained only what looked like a pile of broken glass and old picture frames on the top of a pantry cupboard. Their resolution almost failed in a decision to consign the remaining rubbish to destruction without close examination. Fortunately, their sense of duty was too strong and a final climb up a ladder retrieved one frame, with its glass still unbroken, from the pantry pile.

The picture which had thus been rescued at the eleventh hour from total loss was immediately brought to me for identification and was seen to be a painting by Blake which could be placed among the very finest that he had painted, and it proved to be the finished design for which he had made the preliminary sketch now in the Morgan Library (Plate 51). The painting is only a little larger than the sketch, though it contains a great deal more detail. It measures $16 \times 19\frac{1}{2}$ inches. It is signed on the left-hand side: *W. Blake inventor 1821*. It was in a plain gilt frame without a mount, and the packing at the back was partly formed by a page of *The Times* newspaper for 11 January 1820. On the board behind was written in faded ink: 'James Linnell framer / 3 Streatham Street Bloomsbury / One Door from Charlotte Street.' James Linnell (1760–1836), father of Blake's friend, John, carried on a business in Streatham Street, Bloomsbury, as gilder, framer, carver, and print-seller, and it is to be presumed that Blake's picture was framed by him in 1821, before being carried off by Colonel Chichester into the depths of the country where it remained unrecognized. The writing on the back of the frame is believed to be in Colonel Chichester's hand.

When the glass was taken out for cleaning it was found to be convex, the sides of the frame being hollowed out to accommodate this curve. The convexity is not great enough to affect the optical properties of the glass, but it has ensured that glass and picture were not in contact except along the top and bottom edges. Experts at the British Museum state that glass of this kind is known as 'Vauxhall glass', and owes its curve to the fact that glass was made, not in sheets as at the present time, but in large cylinders so that no part of it, when cut up, was quite flat. This peculiarity introduced a difficulty for the framers, but had the advantage, mentioned above, of keeping the surface away from the picture. The frame was regilded, and the original glass replaced with the picture.

Blake is not known ever to have painted in oils, but confined himself to water-colours, finding more satisfaction in the use of tempera for making what he called 'frescoes', boasting that these would outlast the oil paintings of Sir Joshua Reynolds and his other contemporaries. Blake's boast has, unfortunately, proved vain, many of his frescoes having deteriorated through cracking and flaking of the paint. Some have certainly been destroyed as worthless wrecks; others, however, have proved in recent times capable of restoration in the hands of an expert, so that the best of them are even more splendid than most of the drawings in water-colour washes. A few of Blake's latest productions have survived in perfect preservation, his technique having developed to a fine point of skill, and the Arlington Court picture is one of these. It is painted on a very thin gesso ground applied to a stiff paper, and Blake has worked up his colours on this ground with the finish of a miniature on ivory. The picture has not faded or flaked, and was unblemished except for a few nibblings by insects at the edge where they had fed on the paper lining of the frame. These small defects were painted in by Dr. Johann Hell, and the surface was gently cleaned. The picture must now be very nearly as brilliant as when it was painted.

In spite of its high finish, the picture is not over-laboured, but is a miracle of colour and design to which it is impossible to do full justice in a reduced reproduction.

To enjoy the obvious aesthetic qualities of the picture is easy. To understand the full meaning of the detailed symbolism is difficult. There are few pictures by Blake, apart from the earlier water-colours of 'The Last Judgement', at Petworth House, for which he left a full description and key, and 'The Fall of Man', now in the Victoria and Albert Museum, that can compare with this later painting in intricacy of meaning. By the year 1821, when it was painted, Blake had completed his great poem *Jerusalem* which was the final statement of his message, and had assimilated the various mystical systems of the Gnostics, the Hindoos, the Jews, the Druidists, the Neoplatonists, and others. His mind was also permeated with ideas drawn from the Bible, particularly the more symbolical books such as Revelation and Ecclesiastes, and from the poems of Milton. These had been a lifelong study, and by 1821 he was probably familiar too with Dante's *Comedia* in Cary's translation. He was never content to base his own system on any one of these, but evolved what can at first seem to be a confused mosaic with ingredients drawn from many sources. It is impossible, therefore, to offer a clear 'interpretation' of this extraordinary composition without a careful study of all the systems from which Blake may have taken his symbols, and it is only a superficial attempt that is presented here. There is, undoubtedly, much of the 'right' and 'left' symbolism of spiritual and material elements, first brought to notice by Joseph Wicksteed in his *Blake's Vision of the Book of Job*, 1910, but no attempt is made here to follow this to its conclusion.

It was suggested by Wicksteed that the picture may represent Blake's Vision of the Cabbala, a mystical system cultivated by the Jews especially in the thirteenth to sixteenth centuries. Perhaps it may be safer not to tie the interpretation down to any particular system, but to regard the picture as representing in symbols the cycle of the Life of Man, spiritual and material. The symbolic circle of Man's existence may be supposed to revolve clockwise around the two central figures. The male figure, clad in a deep crimson robe, might be the ideal Man—Adam Kadmon of the Cabbala, Blake's Albion (the personification of Britain), Blake's Christ, or all three at the same time. Beside him stands a majestic figure, who might be his female counterpart or Emanation. She is veiled and so is to be regarded as Vala rather than as Jerusalem, her pale mauve dress serving to emphasize rather than conceal the beauty of her form. According to Blake's usual right and left symbolism, she points upwards with her left hand indicating that the material body must ascend up to heaven to acquire spirituality, and downwards with her right hand, showing that the spirit must descend to earth to endure bodily existence. The Man crouches at her feet with arms outstretched, his right foot advanced, seemingly prepared to plunge into the turbulent Sea of Time and Space.

The beginning of the cycle is at the top where the Creator is seen in his chariot. In the act of creation he has fallen asleep, shewing that the act involves a corresponding retraction into his own absolute, and the four Horses of Light, suddenly stayed in their course, are being groomed by four maidens in white with curry-combs and towels. It may be that the vision is related to Milton's lines in the *Hymn on the Morning of Christ's Nativity*, vii, ll. 3–4.

> The Sun himself with-held his wonted speed,
> And hid his head for shame, . . .

The Creator as he falls asleep touches with his sceptre the heads of a number of little figures with musical instruments beside his chariot, this being his last act of outward expression.

The head of the Creator is surrounded by a yellow nimbus with another blue one outside it, and flames stream away from it in all directions. At the horses' feet, steps lead down towards a scene in Paradise where there is a grove of trees beneath which, in a kind of grotto, is a group of winged figures carrying vessels on their heads. Outside, on the edge of a cliff, recline nude figures—highest up is a woman beside a culvert from which pours a stream of water, then a bearded man and a woman (perhaps a pair of lovers), and lastly at a lower level another solitary woman, seen as a tiny figure on a separate cliff. At the foot of the cliff is seen part of a classical temple, sometimes the symbol of false religion. Beneath the feet of the dwellers in Paradise is the opening of a flame-filled cave, in the mouth of which is a group of three women with shuttles held up in their right hands. They appear to be weaving the tapestry of Fate in a frame, of which a part only can be seen. Steps with flames breaking from the eighth (counting from the bottom), lead down from the weavers, and two tall trees stand on either side, forming a sort of entrance with their roots growing over the lower steps. Beside the trees to the spectator's left stands a young woman holding in her right hand a ball of thread which she has wound from a skein held up on the hands of a young girl reclining on the roots of one of the trees. This girl gazes up at the skein as she holds it. Beside the trees on the other side is another young woman holding a cord in her right hand and the end of a net in her left. The cord appears to pass round the trunk of the tree and to descend again to be attached to the other end of the net, being held by a young girl as it does so. On the fourth step a woman is mounting upwards with a bucket full of water held in her right hand, but she is challenged by the two women standing by the trees and her left arm is raised in protest. The bucket is strangely covered with scales, the sign of evil, whether seen on Satan's loins or on the trunk of a palm tree, the symbol of suffering. The water in the bucket may, therefore, be assumed to have been taken from the River of Death which flows out of a large culvert on the extreme right below. Stretched out over the culvert, with her legs in the water, is the body of a sleeping girl with a wreath of leaves on her head. All the right-hand part of the design just described is painted in delicate shades of green shot with red.

The grey water of the River of Death below mingles with a stream of flames issuing from the mouth of another culvert on the left. Among the flames swims a nude male figure seen from behind with ram's horns on his head. His right hand grasps a huge phallic coil of rope shaped like a distaff. The rope as it unwinds passes over the heads of three stern females, and is severed as it reaches the sea by the shears in the hand of the one on the left, this signifying the end of generative life. Nevertheless, life goes on, and further coils are seen below among the roots of the left-hand tree. The lower, almost subterranean, level of the River of Death is indicated by the abrupt edge of the ground, on which the central figures are standing. This edge arches over the heads of its inhabitants.

The rough and sombre sea confronting the Man is magnificently rendered. Riding its waves on the backs of four dark sea-horses is a nude woman. The horses seem to be guided by two small figures whose upper halves emerge from the water with their arms outstretched. They appear to be standing on the bottom. The rider's left hand and right foot are stretched out over the water towards the standing woman. Her right hand is held aloft to touch a wisp of vapour which curls up to join the cloudy floor supporting the chariot of the Creator, suggesting that she will restore the souls of men to the spiritual level whence they came, so completing the circle of creation.

It may be that the conception of a single circle of Man's life is unduly simple, and probably there is much significance in the nude female riding the sea horses. Close observation detects an arrow-head of black dots pointing from her right foot, so greatly emphasized by Blake, towards the head of the other woman. This may be part of a second smaller circle—starting from the Creator's wand, through the cloud, through the Rider's right hand and right foot, through the woman's right hand, and so to the Man facing the unknown seas. Another opinion (Kerrison Preston) has regarded the whole cycle as going counter-clockwise, and it may be possible to evolve another interpretation on this basis. Yet another view (the late Archibald G. B. Russell) held that the picture is a literal illustration of a book still to be identified.

In 1954 this account of the picture was deliberately made descriptive rather than explanatory. Elucidation of its full meaning was clearly a difficult problem and any confident interpretation would have been dangerous. Three years later it turned out that Russell's guess that it was a close illustration of a book yet to be identified was nearest to the truth. In 1957 Miss Kathleen Raine published her conclusions,[1] demonstrating beyond all doubt that in this picture Blake had returned to his early interest in Neoplatonism, particularly as found in the translations of neo-classical authors made by Thomas Taylor. It has long been accepted that Blake was familiar with Taylor's writings and that he may even have been acquainted with him. Miss Raine maintained that Blake had read Taylor's translation of 'The Cave of the Nymphs', written by Porphyry in the third century A.D.[2] and had added details derived from Homer's *Odyssey* and other Platonic sources. Taylor

---

[1] In *The Journal of the Warburg and Courtauld Institutes* (1957), xx. 318–37.

[2] This appeared in Taylor's translation of the *Philosophical and Mathematical Commentaries of Proclus*, vol. ii, 1788, 4°; it was reprinted in *Select Works of Porphyry*, 1823.

first published Porphyry's elaboration of Homer in 1788, and again in 1823, two years after the painting of this picture. Miss Raine also shewed that Blake used Cowper's version of the *Odyssey* rather than Pope's, which he disliked, Pope having omitted certain details found in both Cowper's version and Blake's picture.

With Miss Raine as a guide, it is now clear that the Man is primarily Odysseus, with overtones of Blake's Albion. He had been shipwrecked, but escaped from the dangers of the turbulent Sea of Time and Space by favour of the goddess Leucothea, or Ino (Blake's Eno). Leucothea had lent him her girdle to ensure his safety in coming to the coast of Phæacia, though Blake has combined Ithaca with Phæacia by placing his landfall close to Homer's 'Cave of the Nymphs'. His attitude is not that of a diver; he has just cast away the girdle with averted face, and the fabric, caught up by Leucothea, has been transmuted into a spiral wisp of vapour rising to the upper regions, where the Sun-god is seen asleep in his chariot. The cloud of vapour is here Blake's symbol of bodily life in the material world now abandoned by Odysseus. The goddess is represented by Blake (again following Homer) as riding four dark sea-horses, attended by a lesser sea-spirit on either side. The four horses are related to Blake's basic concept of the Four Zoas, the four Living Creatures, which pervade his symbolic writings. The same idea is seen in the four white horses harnessed to the Sun-god's chariot.

Miss Raine quotes Taylor's translation of Homer's description of the 'Cave of the Nymphs', many of the details being identifiable in Blake's picture:

> High at the head a branching olive grows,
> And crowns the pointed cliffs with shady boughs.
> A cavern pleasant, though involv'd in night,
> Beneath it lies, the Naiades' delight:
> Where bowls and urns of workmanship divine
> And massy beams in native marble shine;
> On which the Nymphs amazing webs display,
> Of purple hue, and exquisite array.
> The busy bees within the urns secure
> Honey delicious, and like nectar pure.
> Perpetual waters through the grotto glide,
> A lofty gate unfolds on either side;
> That to the north is pervious to mankind;
> The sacred south t'immortals is consign'd.

As explained by Porphyry, the ever-flourishing olive trees are symbols of the

Creator's wisdom. The vessels carried by the ascending souls on their heads contain nectar or honey, the souls being like bees, sharing the watery nature of the Nymphs, or Naiades, with the sweetness of honeycombs. The purple webs indicate the flesh and blood of the mortal bodies woven on the looms of the Nymphs. The woman on the first step carrying a bucket, or tub, containing, as Porphyry wrote, the human desires, raises her hand to the celestial regions and tries to ascend through the cave; but she is a 'dry' soul, unlike the Nymphs, and her progress is opposed by one of them. The girl on the right, lying asleep with her arm over her unfilled tub (not a culvert), is an unitiated soul on her way down into the pleasant waters of generation, unaware of the celestial world above.

The majestic female figure standing behind Odysseus, though unperceived by him, is now to be understood as Athene. She points up with her left hand to the spiritual world above and down with her right to the stream of generation and materialism, the three figures forming together a clockwise circle, implying perpetual death and rebirth. In the waters below is the River-god, Phorcys, with his phallic symbol of generation, and beside him are the three Fates, not mentioned either by Homer or by Porphyry.

In his 'pictorial statement of a metaphysical theme' Blake has largely used 'traditional Neoplatonic and Hermetic symbolism', as Miss Raine has convincingly demonstrated. The conception of a single 'Circle of the Life of Man', as the picture was at first named, was an oversimplification. Human souls are passing upwards through 'the southern gate' to the realms of light, while the water from the cave, symbolizing the material world of generation, pours downwards through 'the northern gate' to join the Sea of Time and Space.

It often happens that help in understanding a design by Blake may be obtained by studying others from his hand. The series made about 1817 to illustrate Milton's *L'Allegro* and *Il Penseroso*, now in the Pierpont Morgan Library, are not very well known, having been until 1950 in private possession. The third of these for *L'Allegro* depicts 'The Sun at his Eastern Gate', that is, Los, or the Creator (Plate 52), whose refulgent figure with his sceptre is, in Blake's words, 'represented clothed in Flames, Surrounded by the Clouds in their Liveries', these floating in a zone of blue, recalling the attributes of the Creator in 'The Sea of Time and Space'. Within the yellow orb of the Sun, his attendant spirits with trumpets resemble the small figures beside the chariot.

In the next design of 'A Sunshine Holiday' 'the Clouds arise from the bosom of Mountains' and mount to heaven across the orb of the Sun in a stream of small figures symbolizing the delights of realms of the spirit, and it is noticeable that one of them carries on her head a vessel reminiscent of those carried by the souls ascending from the Cave.

Finally, the third illustration to *Il Penseroso* bears relation to the lower part of the larger design. Blake's description of this picture is as follows: 'The Spirit of Plato unfolds his World to Milton in Contemplation. The Three Destinies sit on the Circle of Plato's Heavens, weaving the Thread of Mortal Life; these Heavens are Venus, Jupiter & Mars. Hermes flies before as attending on the Heaven of Jupiter; the Great Bear is seen in the sky beneath Hermes, & the Spirits of Fire, Air, Water and Earth Surround Milton's Chair' (Plate 53). The Three Destinies with the distaff on the right, and the thread-cutting shears on the left, can be recognized as the three grim females of the River of Death, though Hermes in his winged bonnet is replaced by the River-god with his horned head. The Spirit of Fire pervades all parts of the Cave. The Spirits of Air are perhaps represented by the maidens grooming the Horses of Light. The Spirits of Water are represented by the Nymphs and perhaps by the two maidens with the net on the right of the picture, for an exactly similar net is shewn in the watery vignette behind Milton's chair. The Three Destinies and the River-god correspond at least in their subterranean position with the Spirits of Earth, though they do not throw up flowers to bloom on the surface of the earth, their mission being Death.

XXVI

THE BLAKE–LINNELL DOCUMENTS

THE story of William Blake's association with the painter John Linnell from 1818 until Blake's death in 1827 was first told in Gilchrist's *Life of Blake*, 1863, and supplemented in A. T. Story's *Life of Linnell*, 1892. To Linnell Blake owed a great change in his fortunes, so that during his last years he did not lack friends or money, while a considerable degree of recognition was accorded to his talents. In particular the world owes to Linnell's encouragement of his friend, as described in Chapter XXIII, one of the greatest works of individual genius ever produced in this country, Blake's *Illustrations of the Book of Job*, which culminated in the series of twenty-one engravings published in March 1826. In 1935 the Pierpont Morgan Library published in New York an exhaustive study of Blake's *Job*, with reproductions of all the drawings, water-colours, and engravings, and an introduction by Laurence Binyon and myself. Here was gathered all the information that was then available, though for documentation of the transaction we had to depend on the rather meagre particulars given in Story's *Life of Linnell*.

Three years later, when Blake's wood-blocks made for Thornton's *Virgil* so unexpectedly came to light,[1] some interesting documents were also discovered which threw fresh light on the genesis and publication of the *Job* engravings. These documents formed lot 62 in the sale at Christie's on 2 December 1938 when the wood-blocks were acquired for the nation. The documents were bought for 75 guineas by Messrs. Robinson on behalf of Mr. Otis T. Bradley, of New York, who presented them to Yale University Library, New Haven, Conn. Although I was the first to see these documents after their discovery in the vaults of a bank, I did not have the opportunity of fully examining them either then or at the time of the sale, but photostats of them all were sent to me by the late Chauncey Brewster Tinker, and by his courtesy and the permission of the Librarian of Yale University I was enabled to make them public in January 1943.[2]

---

[1] See p. 142.

[2] In *The Times Literary Supplement* (1943), xlii. 24. Another account of the documents with a fuller transcription was published by Mr. Edwin Wolf, 2nd, in vol. xxxvii of the papers of the Bibliographical Society of America, First Quarter, 1943.

According to Christie's sale catalogue the documents consisted of *William Blake's Account Book of the Subscribers and Purchasers of the Book of Illustrations of the History of Job . . .; A Memorandum of Agreement . . . between William Blake and John Linnell . . . three loose pages of an Account Book . . .*, and *Eleven Receipts for Money from John Linnell, signed by William Blake, of various dates.* These can now be examined in their chronological order. The earliest is a receipt from Blake dated 12 August 1818 for £2 for an unspecified object. The next three, dated from 19 September to 31 December 1818, are in Blake's hand and refer to the first commission given by Linnell to Blake—namely, the 'laying-in' of an engraving after Linnell's portrait of Mr. Upton, a Baptist minister. For this plate, published 1 June 1819, Blake received in all 15 guineas, paid in several instalments. On 27 August 1819 Blake received from Linnell £1. 19s. 6d. for a copy of the *Songs of Innocence and of Experience.* Linnell gave this book to his son William in 1863, and it was later in the possession of his granddaughter, Mrs. T. H. Riches, by whom it was deposited in the Fitzwilliam Museum, Cambridge (*Census*, copy K). On 30 December of the same year Blake received 14 shillings for some plates of *Jerusalem, chap. 2.* Probably this was part of the Linnell copy of *Jerusalem* (*Census*, copy A) which now belongs to Mrs. Ramsay Harvey. On 20 April 1821 he received 2 guineas for *Heaven and Hell*, that is *The Marriage of Heaven and Hell*, first printed in 1790, of which this is the most beautiful copy in existence (*Census*, copy I). It was sold at Christie's with Linnell's Blake collection in 1918 (lot 195, £756), and is now with the T. H. Riches Collection in the Fitzwilliam Museum, Cambridge. Another receipt, dated 1 March 1822, is for 'Three Pounds on Acco''. Mr. Edwin Wolf suggests that this was payment for the Linnell copies of *America* and *Europe* (*Census*, copies N and I) which are also now in the T. H. Riches Collection.

Next in order comes the most interesting document of the collection, the original agreement between Blake and Linnell for the *Job* engravings. A. T. Story gave an abbreviated version of the agreement, apparently quoting from memory (*Life of Linnell*, i. 169). The document is written in Linnell's hand, and is signed by both parties. It runs as follows:

Memorandum of Agreement
between William Blake and
John Linnell

March 25th, 1823.

    W. Blake agrees to Engrave the | set of Plates from his own designs of | Job's Captivity in number twenty, for | John Linnell—and John Linnell | agrees to pay William Blake five Pounds | per Plate or one hundred Pounds for | the set

Memorandum of Agreement
between William Blake and
John Linnell.
March 25th 1823 –

W. Blake agrees to Engrave The
Set of Plates from his own designs of
Job's Captivity in number twenty, for
John Linnell – and John Linnell
agrees to pay William Blake five Pounds
pr. Plate or one hundred Pounds for
The Set part before and the remainder
when the Plates are finished as Mr Blake
may require it besides which J. Linnell
agrees to give W. Blake one hundred
pounds more out of the Profits of
The work as the receipts will admit of
it. Signed J. Linnell Willm Blake

N.B. J. L. to find copper Plates.

part before and the remainder | when the Plates are finished as Mr. Blake | may require it besides which J. Linnell | agrees to give W. Blake one hundred | pounds more out of the Profits of | the work as the receipts will admit of | it.

Signed   J. Linnell   Willm Blake.

N.B.   J.L. to find copper Plates.

This agreement is written on a folded sheet of paper about 6½ × 4 inches, and on the other side is Blake's first receipt, initialled by him:

1823 March 25th
Cash on acct of Plates in the
foregoing agreement   £5–5–0   W.B.

In Christie's sale catalogue already quoted, the documents are stated to include *William Blake's Account Book . . .* and *three loose pages of an Account Book*. This statement is not accurate, all the accounts referred to having been kept by Linnell. On the *three loose pages* are recorded a long series of payments made to Blake from March 1823 to October 1825, but the entries are all in Linnell's hand, each sum being initialled by Blake as he received it. On two occasions the payment was made in the form of coals, one chaldron being reckoned at £1. 17s. Some of the payments had been received by Blake from subscribers to the work, including those from Flaxman and Calvert. The majority were made by Linnell in cash as required, the amounts varying from £1 to £10 at a time. From these accounts it appears that Blake received in all £150. 19s. 3d., and a separate document in Blake's hand gives a final receipt for the copyright as follows:

London July 14: 1826

Recievd of Mr John Linnell, the Sum of One | Hundred & fifty Pounds for the Copy-right & Plates | (Twenty-two in number) of the Book of Job, Publishd | March 1825 by Me, William Blake Author of the Work

N° 3 Fountain Court Strand

Witness: Edwd Jno Chance

The witness, Edward John Chance was a nephew of Linnell.[1]

---

[1] Linnell's nephew, Edward John Chance, was born in 1807. His father, Edward Chance, had married Linnell's elder sister, Mary Susannah, in 1806. The young man, who later became a Fellow of the Royal College of Surgeons, appears to have been lodging in his uncle's premises at 6 Cirencester Place during Mrs. Blake's time there as housekeeper, that is from September 1827 to April 1828. Among the family papers is an undated letter from Chance to Linnell, presumably in Hampstead, reporting on a copperplate wanted by Dr. Thornton. He added in a postscript: 'Mrs Blake desires me to say that every thing is

[*Footnote continued on page 210*

Recieved of Mr John Linnell. the Sum of One

Hundred & Fifty Pounds for the Copy-right & Plates

(Twenty-two in number) of the Book of Job. Published

March 1825   by Me.   William Blake Author of the Work

No 3 Fountain Court Strand)

Witness: Edwd Jno Chance

London July 14. 1826

Blake had therefore received £150 before the question of any profits had arisen, and with this he was evidently content, though he had engraved two more plates than were originally agreed upon. Linnell had undoubtedly treated him with generosity, the degree of this generosity being now made clear. The account book already referred to was wholly Linnell's record, and consists mainly of a list of the subscribers for plain and proof sets of the engravings. The list was opened in October 1823, but the entries after this are not dated for nearly nine years, the first later date being August 1832. It is therefore not possible to say exactly how much repayment Linnell had received up to the time of Blake's death in August 1827, though it could not have been more than £142. 9s. Even in 1833, when the Earl of Egremont paid 6 guineas for a proof set, the total receipts were only £167. 17s. 6d. The normal price for an ordinary set was 3 guineas, though the trade and many friends were supplied with copies at £2. 12s. 6d. The usual price for proof sets was 5 guineas, all sold to private buyers, though Mr. Butts received '1 Copy of Proofs for £3 3s. 0d. because he lent the Drawing to Copy'. Up to and including the year 1833 only twenty-three plain sets and twenty proofs had been sold. Besides these accounts there is at the end of the book an 'Account of Expenses of the Book of Job'. This details the cost of copper-plates, paper, printing and binding, and is here set out in full:

			£	s	d
1823					
	6 copper plates for Job		1		
	6 D°	D°	1	2	
	6 D°	D°	1	3	7
1825	2 D°	D°		6	
	proofs		1		
	D° at Dixons & paper		1		
	D° at Lahee & —			10	
Sep	Proofs & —			2	
Oct	D° & —			2	
Nov	Binding 3 sets			7	6
			9	19	1 [10 9 1]

right at home. The Bricklayer has not been. Col¹. Moore called to see the miniature of his Friend [perhaps Linnell's miniature of Blake painted in 1827] & was very sorry he could not see it as he feared he should not be able to call again. Mr Pye & Mr [Barron] Field called but left no message. Mr G. Cumberland called.' Fuseli had given Harriet Jane Moore a copy of *The Gates of Paradise* in November 1806. Barron Field, a barrister and friend of Lamb and his circle, is known to have called on Mrs. Blake with Crabb Robinson and to have bought a print of 'The Canterbury Pilgrims'.

	£	s	d
March 1826 Paid to Mr Lahee for 150 sets of Proofs on India paper	56	5	
to Freeman the workman	1		
to Mr White for Boarding	2	4	6
1 ream of paper for D°	1	6	
To Mr Leighton for Bind^s & paper &c	13	17	
[May *del*.] To Lahee for 65 setts 1826 of Job on french paper	16	3	
March To D° for 50 sets on Drawing paper	10	10	
To D° for D°	10	10	
	£111	15	6

Linnell's total outlay, therefore, during Blake's lifetime was about £272, and he remained at least £120 out of pocket at Blake's death, without any certainty of ever receiving reimbursement. In the event, Blake's repayment was more than adequate, but it was Linnell's descendants who received it (after the sale at Christie's in 1918), not the generous benefactor himself. It may be noted that Linnell paid for only twenty copper-plates, though twenty-two were engraved. This is explained by the fact that two of them (they may all be examined in the British Museum) had already been used for engravings of maps on the reverse sides and evidently were scrap metal obtained cheaply by Blake himself.

Linnell's account book need not be set out in full,[1] many of the names appearing in it not being of special interest. Some, however, may be mentioned. The first subscriber in 1823 was Edward Hodges Baily, R.A., the sculptor, who had been a pupil of Flaxman and may have known Blake. In 1822 he had been the mover of a proposal to give Blake a grant of £25 from the Council of the Royal Academy. Among those who followed were Flaxman, Butts, Henry Crabb Robinson (three copies), C. H. Tatham, Calvert, Sir Henry Torrens, Charles Aders, T. G. Wainewright, Sir Thomas Lawrence, and Bishop Jebb. Next to Sir T. Lawrence's name is the following entry: 'The King—1 copy of Proofs sent by the order of Sir W^m. Knighton & Dr. Gooch, & for which 10 gns. was ordered to be paid—& was p^d by Messrs Budd & Calkin, Pall Mall.'

---

[1] It is printed in *Blake's Letters*, ed. Keynes, 1956 and 1968. See also *Blake Records*, pp. 598 ff.

Immediately after this is the less august entry: 'Josiah Taylor Esq 1 copy of Proofs sent to the House of Correction by F. Tatham, Taylor being s^d H. of C. for swindling.' The King's copy is not now to be found in the Royal Library at Windsor, though the date and occasion of its loss are not recorded.

The 'Account of Expenses' provides the elucidation of a name which has hitherto puzzled Blake's biographers, that of James Lahee, the copper-plate printer. In an undated letter, now to be referred to 1825, Blake makes an appointment to meet Linnell at Lahee's house, but the name had not before been properly deciphered. It is also of interest to know that the original printing consisted of 150 sets of proofs on India paper, and 165 sets of ordinary prints—65 on French paper, and 100 on drawing paper. Examination of existing sets shews that the 'French paper' is unwatermarked, and that the 'drawing paper' is Whatman's, dated 1825. These prints remained on sale to friends of the Linnell family for almost a century after Blake's death.

Further items recorded in the account book are as follows:

1. Four payments made from 18 August 1824 to 28 January 1825, totalling £20, for 'the Portrait of Mr. Lowery', an engraving of Wilson Lowry, F.R.S., engraver and inventor, with which Blake had helped Linnell.

2. A payment of £5 in 1825 'for sketches of subjects from Dante', the beginning of another great enterprise, which is not further documented here.

3. Two payments of £5 each made in October and November 1825, 'on acc^t of Drawings of Paradise regained', that is, the exquisite set of twelve water-colour drawings sold in 1918 for £2,205, and now in T. H. Riches Collection in the Fitzwilliam Museum, Cambridge.

Another document is a receipt for 5 guineas received from Mrs. Aders through Linnell for a copy of *Songs of Innocence and of Experience* (*Census*, copy R), which Linnell afterwards bought back for himself and gave to his son James in 1863. It was sold at Christie's in 1918 (lot 215, £735), and is now with the T. H. Riches Collection in the Fitzwilliam Museum, Cambridge. The final document is a receipt for £1. 11s. 6d., dated 16 May 1829, and signed by Frederick Tatham on behalf of Mrs. Blake for *Homers Illiad & Oddisey*. Probably this was Blake's copy of Chapman's *Homer*, folio, 1606, which A. T. Story (*Life of Linnell*, i. 78) states was bought by Linnell after Blake's death.

It is obvious that these documents form only an incomplete record, not accounting for a great number of Blake's productions which were in the Linnell Collection. They provide, however, interesting sidelights on Blake's relations with Linnell, these being further developed in the next chapter.

XXVII

WILLIAM BLAKE AND JOHN LINNELL[1]

MOST of our knowledge of Blake's relations with John Linnell has hitherto been derived from two sources—Gilchrist's *Life of Blake*, 1863 and 1880, and A. T. Story's *Life of Linnell*, 1892. Gilchrist had the advantage of being able to talk to Linnell, and Story was given access to Linnell's papers after his death in 1882. Both writers naturally chose such details as they judged would be interesting to contemporary readers. With the passage of time the emphasis has changed, and almost any details of Blake's life and works are now welcome. Linnell's papers would clearly be productive from this point of view, but for many years they were inaccessible. As already related on p. 147, A. H. Palmer, son of Blake's friend Samuel Palmer and grandson of John Linnell, emigrated in 1910 to British Columbia and during his latter years interested himself in the history of his family, more particularly in the lives of his father and grandfather.

He had published the standard life of Samuel Palmer in 1892, but wished to revise this. He had also for some reason conceived a great dislike of his grandfather and wished to correct what he regarded as mis-statements in Story's *Life of Linnell*, where Linnell's character had, as he thought, been drawn in too favourable a light. He therefore asked for the loan of Linnell's papers and the Linnell trustees sent them out to him in Vancouver. I have already described (p. 147) how the papers were seen in Palmer's house by Mr. James M. Begg in 1925, and how, when I was in Vancouver in 1956, the late Bryan Palmer shewed me the pile of exercise books in which his father had copied everything he thought of interest from Linnell's papers. These books I was allowed to bring back to London, and they are now in the keeping of Miss Joan Linnell Ivimy, Linnell's great-grand-daughter.

With Miss Ivimy's permission I extracted from Palmer's notebooks everything relating to Blake which seemed to shed new light and published this material in *The Times Literary Supplement* in June 1958. It would, of course, have been preferable to work from the original documents, but when I asked Bryan Palmer about these, he denied all knowledge of them. As I left his house in Vancouver I asked him to do all he could to recover them, feeling sure that they still existed, and he

[1] First printed in *The Times Literary Supplement* (1958), lvii. 332.

promised to do so. No more was heard for over eighteen months until Miss Ivimy was informed by a letter from her cousin, Bryan Palmer, that a large trunk of papers was on its way by freighter to London. When this arrived a preliminary examination of the contents shewed that it contained a mass of Linnell and Palmer family papers and letters, including John Linnell's account books and Samuel Palmer's sketch-book of 1824.[1] I have thus been able to verify A. H. Palmer's transcription of much of the material, though it was disappointing to find that John Linnell's *Journal* was not included, and it has only come to light in 1970. I noticed also the absence of a brief letter from Blake to Linnell, dated 14 July 1826, but Bryan Palmer wrote in 1959 to say that he had found it under the floorboards of his attic and had disposed of it to the Pierpont Morgan Library, New York. Samuel Palmer's letters did not concern me at the time, and we put them aside for later consideration. Nevertheless *The Times* of 9 July 1966 announced under sensational headlines the discovery by a 'correspondent' of the papers we had in fact already examined, some of which I had published in 1958.

LINNELL'S JOURNAL

One of the most interesting documents transcribed by A. H. Palmer was Linnell's *Journal*, a brief day-to-day record of his movements. From this source Palmer copied nearly every entry concerning Blake. Linnell had been taken to see Blake in South Molton Street by George Cumberland, jr., son of Blake's old friend, in 1818, and Linnell recorded that 'we soon became intimate and I employed him to help me with an engraving of my portrait of Mr. Upton, a Baptist preacher'. The entries concerning Blake cover the years 1818 to 1827, when Blake died, with a few further entries relating to his affairs up to 1833. Blake's pencil drawing of Linnell made in 1825 is reproduced here (Plate 54).

1818

June 24. To Mr. Blake evening. Delivered to Mr. Blake the picture of Mr. Upton & the copperplate to begin the engraving.
July 10. Went with Mr. Blake to Lord Suffolk's to see pictures.
August 21. To Colnaghi with Mr. Blake. [The purpose of this visit is not disclosed. It was not until 1821 that Blake sold his collection of prints to Colnaghi.]
August 24. Mr. & Mrs. Blake to tea, &c.
Sept. 9. To W. Blake evening.

[1] Reproduced for the William Blake Trust by the Trianon Press in 1962 and subsequently acquired for the British Museum, Department of Prints and Drawings.

at Hampstead
Drawn by Mr Blake
from the Life 1825.
intended as the Portrait
of J. Linnell

Sept. 11. To Mr. Blake evening. Paid him 5£.

Sept. 12. Mr. Blake brought a proof of Mr. Upton's plate, left the Plate & named 15£ as the Price of what was already done by him. Mr. Varley and Mr. Constable stayed with Blake. [Blake gave Linnell receipts for the payments for work done on the Upton plate on 11 and 19 Sept., 9 Nov., and 31 Dec., 1818 (see *Letters*, 1968, p. 142, and *The Times Literary Supplement*, 3 May 1957). Linnell had been a pupil of Varley as a boy and they had remained friends. This date may be the first occasion on which Blake encountered Varley. One of the earliest of the famous Visionary Heads is dated 30 Oct. 1819. The extent of Blake's acquaintance with John Constable has not hitherto been known beyond a tradition that they met somewhere and that Blake, seeing a drawing by Constable of fir trees on Hampstead Health exclaimed, 'Why, this is not drawing but inspiration'. To this Constable replied, 'But I meant it for drawing' (see M. Sturge Henderson, *Constable*, 1905, p. 9). It is now established that they were on visiting terms, and, as will appear later, Constable was much concerned at Blake's death.]

Sept. 18. To Mr. Blake with Mr. Varley, Ev^g.

Sept. 19. Dr. Thornton called & Mr. Blake. Went with Mr. Blake to Mr. Varley's Ev^g. [Dr. Thornton, Linnell's medical adviser, is well known in connexion with Blake's wood engravings for the third edition of the *Pastorals of Virgil*, published in 1821. This is the first record of their having met.]

1819

June 17. To Mr. Denny, Mr. Blake, Mr. Stewart. [Linnell made portraits of members of the family of Sir Edward Denny Bt. in 1821–2 (Story, *Life*, ii. p. 248).]

August 20. With Mr. Blake to see Harlowe's copy of Transfiguration. [George Henry Harlowe, the painter, had died on 4 Feb. 1819. In the previous year he had visited Italy to study the old masters and had made a copy of Raphael's 'Transfiguration' in eighteen days. Blake's admiration of Raphael is well known.]

August 21. With Mr. Blake to Mr. Carpenter's. With Mr. Holmes to Mr. Blake Ev^g. [Mr. Carpenter was perhaps William Hookham Carpenter, 1792–1866, bookseller and connoisseur of prints, who afterwards became Keeper of Prints in the British Museum. James Holmes, 1777–1860, was a celebrated miniature painter; he made portraits of Lord Byron and enjoyed the patronage of King George IV.]

October Sat. 23^d.—Began a painting in oil colours of two Heads size of Life from Drawings by W. Blake of Wallace & Edward 1st for Mr. Varley. [By this date Blake was drawing many Visionary Heads at Varley's instigation. The drawings of Wallace and Edward I are now in the United States (collection of F. Bailey Vanderhoef, jr.). Linnell's paintings are not known to have survived.]

1820

April 24. Spring Gardens with Mr. Blake; met the Duke of Argyll [& dunned him for money due on portrait]. To Duke of Argyll appointed tomorrow. [In 1813 Linnell had become a member of the Old Water-Colour Society, which held annual exhibitions in the 'Large Room', Spring Gardens (from 1814 to 1820 under the style of the 'Society of Painters in Oil and Water-Colours'). Linnell was a regular exhibitor. He had painted small portraits of the Duke and Duchess of Argyll and of Lord John Campbell, the Duke's brother, in 1817 (Story, *Life*, ii. p. 247), and presumably had not yet been paid.]

May 8. To Mr. Wyatt with Mr. Blake. [Mr. Wyatt is probably the painter, Henry Wyatt, 1794–1840. Story records that they went also on this day to 'Lady Ford—saw her pictures', but this does not appear in Palmer's transcript.]

May 11. To Mr. Denny's & to tea with Mr. Blake & Mr. Varley.

Oct. 2. With Dr. Thornton, Dartmouth St., Westminster, to the Lythography Press to prove a Head of Virgil. [The head of Virgil was a copper-plate engraving drawn and executed by Blake for *Pastorals of Virgil*, 1821.]

Oct. 9. To Dr. Thornton, Mr. Blake, &c.

1821

Feb. 3. Dr. Thornton Dined with me—we went to Mr. Blake's.

Feb. 9. Began a small picture of my Mother. Mr. Blake came in the Evening.

March 8. To British Gallery &c. with Mr. Blake. Dined with me.

March 27. To the Theatre Drury Lane with Mr. Blake. [Mr. Edwin Kersley has ascertained by reference to the files of *The Times* that the Drury Lane performance advertised for this date was R. B. Sheridan's *Pizarro*, followed by *Thérèse, the Orphan of Geneva. Pizarro* was taken from Kotzebue's *Spaniard of Peru* and was first produced at Drury Lane in 1799 with the Kembles, Mrs. Jordan, and Mrs. Siddons in the cast. It was a popular piece and was several times revived in various forms. *Thérèse* was a new 'Drama in three acts' by J. H. Payne with music by Horn, the principals being the celebrated Jewish tenor, John Braham (1774?–1856), and Miss Wilson.]

April 30. With Mr. Blake to Water colour Exhib. &c. [The exhibition was held in Spring Gardens as in the previous year.]

May 7. With Mr. Blake to Somerset House Exh. [The Royal Academy exhibitions were held at Somerset House from 1780.]

May 27. To Hampstead with Mr. Blake. [Story states that in the summer of 1822 Linnell took lodgings for his wife and family at Hope Cottage, North End, Hampstead. He was perhaps looking for a suitable place when he first visited Hampstead with Blake. He moved his home to Collins' Farm, North End, in 1824.]

June 1. Mr. Tatham, Alpha Road, Even^g. del^d. Dr. Thornton's Virgil & rec^d· 18s. [Mr. Tatham was the architect, C. H. Tatham, known to Blake at any rate since 1799, when he gave him a copy of *America*.]

June 8. To Drury Lane Theatre with Mr. Blake. [Mr. Edwin Kersley has found the play-bill of this performance in the Enthoven Collection at South Kensington. The opera on this occasion was *Dirce, or the Fatal Urn*, a 'New Grand Serious Opera' based on Metastasio's *Demofoonte*, with music by Horn and songs set by Mozart, Rossini, and others. The principal singers were Charles Edward Horn (1786–1849), Mr. Sheriff, Lucia Elizabeth Mathews, known as Madame Vestris (1797–1856), and John Braham. The opera was followed by *The Midnight Hour, a Farce*, translated from *La Ruse contre Ruse, ou Guerre Ouverte*.]

August 26. To Hendon to Mr. Woodburn's with Mr. Blake. [Mr. Woodburn was one of three brothers who, according to Story, were well-known picture collectors. They are not known to have acquired anything by Blake.]

Sept. 8. Traced outlines from Mr. Blake's designs for Job all day. [The first set of Blake's designs for *Job* were bought by Thomas Butts. Blake and Linnell collaborated over the second set, which is now in the Fogg Museum of Art, Cambridge, Mass.]

Mr. Blake & Mr. Read with me all day. [D. C. Read was a professional engraver who afterwards became a painter. Linnell had stayed with him in Southampton in 1817.]

Sept. 10. Traced outlines &c. from Mr. Blake's drawings of Job all Day. Mr. Blake finishing the outlines all day Monday 10th. Mr. Blake took home the Drawings of Job.

Sept. 11. Mr. Blake brought a drawing of Cain & Abel. [A water-colour drawing of 'The Body of Abel found by Adam and Eve' was included in Blake's exhibition of 1809; it was presumably this drawing that was brought by Blake and not the later tempera painting now in the Tate Gallery; or possibly it was the miniature drawing described in Chapter XIX, p. 145.]

Sept. 12. Began a copy of Cain & Abel. Finished 14th. [The Linnell Collection, sold at Christie's 15 March 1918, included a water-colour drawing of this subject (lot 157), which is now in the Fogg Museum of Art, Cambridge, Mass.]

Oct. 27. Mr. Blake came to see me Ev^g.

Nov. 11. Mr. Blake dined with us.

Dec. 9. Mr. Blake dined here.

1822

May 8. To Mr. Vine's with Mr. Blake. [James Vine, a Russian merchant residing in the Isle of Wight, is said to have owned a copy of Blake's *Milton*. He did, in fact, buy a copy of the *Job* engravings.]

May 9. Mr. Blake began copies of his Drawings from Milton's P[aradise] L[ost]. [The Linnell Collection contained three magnificent replicas (lots 152–4 in the sale) of designs from the *Paradise Lost* series done for Thomas Butts in 1808.]

July 13. To Sir Thos. Lawrence's with Mr. Blake. [Lawrence is known to have been an admirer of Blake's work, and is said to have kept one of the water-colour drawings of 'The Wise and Foolish Virgins' on his desk.]

1823

April 17. With Mr. Blake to the British Museum.

April 24. To British Museum with Mr. Blake to see Prints.

May 5. To Royal Academy Exhibition with Mr. Blake.

June 25. With Mr. Blake to British Gall., &c.

1824

March 6. Moved family to Hampstead. [Linnell lived for a few years from this date at Collins' Farm, North End, Hampstead, where Blake paid many visits.]

May 18. Mr. Vine, Mr. Tanner, Blake.

August 4. Wed. Mr. Varley, Mr. Tatham, son & Mr. Blake dined with me at Hampstead. [C. H. Tatham's son, Frederick, aged about twenty, who became a close friend of Blake, is first mentioned here, but he must have known Blake all his life.]

Oct. [A. H. Palmer notes that the entries in this month were careless and that some events were omitted. There is no mention, for instance, of the visit paid to Blake by Linnell and Samuel Palmer on 9 Oct. when they found him in bed with a scalded foot at work on the Dante designs (Palmer, *Life of Samuel Palmer*, 1892, p. 9).]

1825

Jan. 28. Fri. To Cap. Buller, Rennie, Blake, Bank, Neale, &c.

March 5. With Mr. Blake to Lahee's proving Job. [Lahee was the copper-plate printer who printed all the 315 sets of the *Illustrations of the Book of Job* in this year.]

March 9. To Mr. Blake. Read.

April 8. To City. Blake &c.

May 3. To Mr. Blake. To Exh.

August 6. Sat. To Mrs. Aders, 11, Euston Square, with Mr. Blake. [According to Story, Mrs. Aders, the wife of a wealthy German merchant, kept open house for artists and literary people. Linnell met there Coleridge, Lamb, Flaxman, and Henry Crabb Robinson. It may have been here that Blake was seen in company with Coleridge (see Chapter IX, p. 82).]

Nov. 7. To Mr. Blake.

Dec. 10. Dined at Mr. Aders's with Mr. Blake & H. C. Robinson. [Robinson, according to his Diary, had known of Blake since 1811, but this was the first occasion on which they met.]

[Story in the *Life*, i, p. 173, stated that there were one or two entries in 1825, after which they cease, but this was incorrect.]

1826

Feb. 10. Sent to Mr. Denny a copy of Book of Job proofs 5g. also a copy of Blair's Grave 2. 12. 6.

May 17. Wed. To Father's; to Mr. Blake &c. [Linnell's father was James Linnell, a printseller and picture framer, who had framed Blake's picture of 'The Cave of the Nymphs' now at Arlington Court, N. Devon, in 1821. See p. 197.]

July 12. To Mr. Blake.

July 13. To Mr. Blake, Dr. Young, &c.

1827

Jan. 9. To Mr. Blake £5.

Feb. 7. To Mr. Blake to speak to him about living at C[irencester] P[lace]. [After moving to Hampstead Linnell still used his studio in his former large house in Cirencester Place. He no doubt thought Blake, who was ill, might be more comfortable there; but Blake did not care to move.]

Feb. 8. Left with Sr Thomas Lawrence Blake's drawings of Paradise Regained pr £50. [These drawings remained in Linnell's collection and were ultimately sold at Christie's in 1918 (lot 151) for £2,205. They are now in the Fitzwilliam Museum, Cambridge.]

Feb. 23. Sent a copy of Job (proofs) to Dr. Gooch. Prom^d to take them for the King's Library. [The copy of Job ordered for the King's Library is not now to be found in the Royal Library at Windsor (see p. 211).]

April 17. To Mr. Ottley with Mr. Blake. [William Young Ottley, 1771–1836, became Keeper of the Prints in the British Museum in 1833. He was himself an artist, and his work seems to have influenced Blake. He thanked Linnell 'for the prospect of Mr. Ottley's advantageous acquaintance' in a letter dated 25 April 1827 (*Letters*, 1968, p. 163).]

May 15. To Bank, Mr. Blake, &c.

July 11. To Somerset House, Mr. Blake, &c. Mr. Ottley dined with me at Hampstead.

July 17. To Bank, Mr. Blake, Cochran, &c.

Aug. 3. Friday. To Mr. Blake.

Aug. 10. Friday. To Mr. Blake. Not expected to live. [A. H. Palmer noted that the entry is accompanied by a tiny sketch, less than $1 \times \frac{1}{2}$ in., of Blake lying in bed on a big pillow in a night-cap with hollow eyes and thin, drawn face. Elsewhere he described Blake in this drawing as 'in a black skull-cap, his head lying on a great pillow', and again as with 'his head only shewing in a night cap and very thin, great dark eyes dominant'. The drawing in fact corresponds with Palmer's first description. It is so tiny that details are hard to distinguish.]

Aug. 12. Mr. Blake died.

It is evident that Linnell's *Journal*[1] does not provide a complete record of his dealings with Blake. There are long gaps in which no meetings are recorded, although some must certainly have taken place. But enough is there to give a good idea of how much Linnell cultivated the company of the ageing artist and of how carefully he tended his welfare. Constantly they visited picture exhibitions together, and continually Linnell introduced Blake to new friends. It would perhaps have been more exciting to know that Blake had been to Drury Lane to see Kean in Shakespearian tragedy than to know that he heard second-rate opera and farce. Yet it is evident that he wanted to hear the best singers of his day and Linnell has recorded that he was 'a great laugher at absurdities'. Blake's taste was also in tune with the popularity of the Italian writers among the Romantics of the 1820s (as detailed in a leading article in *The Times Literary Supplement* for 3 January 1958) and with his own interest in Dante.

[1] Now first verified from the original by courtesy of Miss Ivimy's solicitors.

XXVIII

JOHN LINNELL AND MRS. BLAKE[1]

THE last entry taken from Linnell's *Journal* near the end of the preceding chapter was the laconic statement: 'Aug. 12 Mr Blake died.' A. H. Palmer noted at this point: 'Linnell was always ready with practical help and he himself was absolutely immune from grief in any of life's bereavements, as is shewn in a striking way by his journal of work.'

This judgement seems hard, especially as Palmer continued: 'In spite of his own serious illness he at once went to the widow and made all the arrangements for the funeral with Mr Palmer of 175 Piccadilly—a friend he could trust to do what was necessary decently and without undue expense.' The friendly undertaker was Benjamin Palmer, working as Palmer & Son, Upholsterers & Cabinet Manufacturers at No. 175 Piccadilly. He was uncle of Linnell's first wife, Mary Ann Palmer, and was unrelated to the artist's family.[2] Their account, dated 13 August 1827, gives the following details:

For Funeral of Mr Wm Blake

a 5 ft. 9 Elm Coffin covered with black flannel & finished with black varnished Nails, a plate of Inscription, 3 pair handles, lined ruffled & pitched	2	14	0
a Shroud, pillow & Bed		17	0
2 Men carrying in do. and dressing Body		3	0
Use of a best Velvet Pall		5	0
do. of 6 Gents Cloaks		6	0
do. of 6 Crepe Hatbands, & 3 pair Gloves		4	6
2 Men as porters in Gowns & proper dresses . . .		12	
a Hearse & pair & a Coach & pair to Bunhill Fields . .	2	8	0
2 Coachman's Cloaks		2	
4 Men as Bearers		12	
a Man to attend & conduct Funeral		5	
3 crepe Hatbands & Gloves for Porters and Attender . .		13	6
Paid for Lime to make up Coffin		2	

[1] First published in *The Times Literary Supplement* (1958), lvii. 348.
[2] As I am informed by Mr. Raymond Lister.

Paid Mens' Allowance for refreshment on taking in the coffin & on morning of Funeral	6 6
Paid Dues at Bunhill Fields, Clergyman, Grave diggers &c.	1 7 6
	10 18 0

This account together with the receipt for the money paid by Linnell on 28 January 1828 is now in the H. E. Huntington Library and Art Gallery, San Marino, California, having been given by Bryan Palmer in 1952.[1]

'The total', A. H. Palmer added, 'was £10-18-0. Linnell gave this amount to Mrs. Blake, who herself paid the bill, and the amount was afterwards refunded. This funeral was about the same in cost & detail as that which my grandfather ordered in the case of one of his sisters and those of his wife's poor relations who afterwards became (very willingly) almost entirely dependent upon him.' The funeral took place on Friday, 17 August, attended by a few friends.

It is of interest to have the measurements of the coffin—5 ft. 9 in. It has always been stated that Blake was short, but it is now apparent that he cannot have exceeded 5 ft. 5 in. in old age. His wide shoulders and strong build compensated for lack of stature. The exact place of Blake's burial was not marked, but in 1911 the late Herbert Jenkins[2] claimed to have determined the precise position from the available data. Sir William Blake Richmond, the son of Blake's friend, then wrote to *The Times* suggesting the removal of Blake's remains to Westminster Abbey. The fact that the coffin was provided with an inscription plate now makes it more probable that the body could be identified, if that were still to be desired. This seems, however, to be the less desirable now that Blake is so splendidly commemorated in the Abbey by Sir Jacob Epstein's bronze bust unveiled on 24 November 1957.

---

[1] It was Linnell's father-in-law, Thomas Palmer, who signed a receipt as a coal merchant for money due from Linnell on Blake's behalf under the date 25 January 1826:

A Chald^{rn} Coals to Mr Blake 56/ . . .	2 16	
Metage Shoot^{s} &c	5	
	3 1 0	
Deduct for ready money	1 6	
Rec^{d} Jany 31st	£2 19 6	

Thos. Palmer

'Metage' is the duty payable for weighing a load of coal or other goods. The document is now among the Linnell papers.

[2] Writing as 'Herbert Ives' in *The Nineteenth Century* (1911), lxx. 163–9, and in his *William Blake* (1925), pp. 81–96.

Linnell's *Journal* recorded that for several days after Blake's death he was busied about his friend's affairs:

'Aug. 14. To Sir Thomas Lawrence about Mrs Blake.
Aug. 16. Sent Mr Blake's Jerusalem to Mr Ottley.
Aug. 18. To Mrs Blake.
Aug. 21. Mr F. Tatham came and Mrs Blake.
Aug. 22. Mrs Blake to arrange about moving Printing Press &c.
Aug. 29. Mrs Blake's press moved to C[irencester] Place.'

Mrs. Blake herself moved to Cirencester Place on 11 September and acted as Linnell's housekeeper there for nine months. Linnell also wrote to some of Blake's friends about his death, among them to John Constable, who replied as follows:

My dear Sir,
  I am much concerned at the death of poor Mr Blake
  I hope our Charity will do something handsome for the widow as it is now in its power. If the case of the poor widow is urgent an especial meeting of directors can be held immediately & I will make it a point to attend. But you had better lose no time in seeing or writing to Mr Roper our secretary (14 Duke St.) & he will inform you what to do.

Yours truly,
John Constable

35 Charlotte St. Fitzroy Square Aug^st 14 1827

Linnell wrote also to Thomas Griffith Wainewright (later notorious as 'the poisoner'), who had known and admired Blake and his work. From a letter to Linnell, dated 28 March [1826], we now know that Wainewright, in addition to owning a set of the *Job* prints, had also bought from Blake a copy of *Milton*. This is likely to have been the magnificent example (*Census*, copy D) now in the Lessing J. Rosenwald Collection, Library of Congress, Washington, D.C. The early history of this book has not hitherto been known, but as it was certainly the last copy completed by Blake (not before 1815 according to the watermark) it was probably the only one available to Wainewright, who asked also for 'a list of all Mr. B.'s works executed by his own hand'. To Linnell's letter in 1827 Mrs. Wainewright replied:

Dear Sir, Mr. Wainewright is out, but I beg in his name that you will accomplish your intention of favouring us tomorrow. We shall indeed *deeply sympathise* with you in the loss of so great an Artist, & I fear that Mr W.'s regrets will be most poignant that he did not enjoy over again the pleasures of an hour with him.

Yours truly, Dear Sir,
E. F. Wainewright.

In the years 1828 to 1830 Linnell was still visiting Mrs. Blake on amicable terms, though on 27 January 1829 Mrs. Blake said to him 'that Mr Blake told her he thought I should pay 3 gns. apiece for the plates of Dante'. Linnell was still trying to interest people in buying Blake's work from his widow, the names of Augustus Callcott, the painter, Haviland Burke, nephew of Edmund Burke, Dr. Jebb, Bishop of Limerick, and the Princess Sophia being mentioned in the *Journal*. In 1828 Mrs. Blake left Cirencester Place to take charge of Frederick Tatham's chambers, and afterwards moved to 17 Upper Charlotte Street, Fitzroy Square, where she died in October 1831.

It is sad that throughout this year irritation was growing between Linnell on the one side and Tatham and Mrs. Blake on the other, the bone of contention being Blake's last work, the 102 drawings and seven copper-plates for Dante's *Divine Comedy*. Throughout his notes A. H. Palmer drew attention in red ink to anything that might be thought to show that Linnell had a mean and grasping character. Most of his dealings with Blake suggest that he was usually generous and considerate. There is one document, however, shewing that he was in fact extremely careful to safeguard his own interests. Most of the facts concerning the *Job* engravings are well established, and it is known that Blake in 1823 signed an agreement of financial terms and on 14 July 1826 signed in the presence of a witness a receipt for £150 in return for the copyright and plates of *Job*. Linnell was not satisfied with this, and exacted yet another document, signed and witnessed on the same day: 'I hereby Declare That Mr John Linnell has purchased of Me The Plates & Copyright of Job; & the same is his sole Property.' This accompanied a short and friendly letter from Blake, first printed in the Nonesuch edition of the *Complete Writings*, 1957. Blake himself was evidently in no way aggrieved by this hard, commercial attitude, but in 1831 his widow was feeling less confident of Linnell's generosity. Tatham was acting on Mrs. Blake's behalf, and on 9 March 1831 Linnell sent him the following statement:

The sum paid by me to Mr Blake on acc^t of Dante is 103£ & to Mrs B. 47£. 20£, however, I deduct for House Keeping, &c., leaving a clear sum of 130£ to be paid if The Drawings are sold.

This was amplified in the following letter:

Dear Sir, in answer to your request respecting the sum to be refunded to me in the event of the drawings by Mr Blake from Dante being sold, I beg to say that from Decr. 1825 to August 1827 I paid to Mr Blake in various sums (the particulars of which may be seen) 103£ on account of the Drawings from the Poem of Dante's Inferno, Purgatorio, &c., the plates and whatever else he might intend for me—with the distinct understanding, as I can prove by his letters to me at the time, that what he had in hand for me was in return for the money advanced by me; it was left entirely to him to do little or much as most convenient or agreeable, but what was done was considered paid for: as, however, much was done for the time he employed himself upon the Drawings, it is now my intention, as I have intimated, to dispose of the Drawings for any larger sum that may be thought proper to demand & the surplus (after my being repaid) to be handed over to Mrs Blake, for whose benefit alone I desire or consent to part with the drawings. In addition to the sum of 103£ pd. to Mr Blake I paid 47£ to Mrs Blake for the Funeral, the rent of fountain Court &c., 20£ of which, however, I shd. deduct for taking care of house &c. in Cirencester Place, leaving 130£ clear to be paid to me before the drawings are given up.

All arrangements for shewing the Drawings must be made with my consent and anything else can be settled personally.

With sincere regards for Mrs Blake,

I remain, Dr. Sir,

yours truly, J. Linnell.

P.S. The seven copperplates of Dante shall be given up to Mrs B. when the Drawings are sold.

Linnell seems to have told Tatham before this letter was written that he had been making tracings of the Dante drawings, for Tatham replied on 15 March 1831:

Dear Sir, After a week's consideration it occurred to me that I ought not to withold from Mrs Blake (as you requested) that you had made tracings of the Dante. The more I considered of it, the more covetous & unfair it appeared to me, as it depreciates the drawings full 25 per Cent. I could not, therefore, allow a thing that appeared in such a light to me (upon due reflection) to fester in my secresy—Up to that transaction I espoused your cause & frequently to my own great annoyance. Mrs Blake thinks as I do upon it. She has, I now recollect, mentioned her suspicions to me upon several occasions, but I would not hear them. I received your note & mentioned to her the contents. I think it is better you should see her, or rather, she wishes you to do so. Would you, therefore, make an early appointment to meet her here. She wishes [me] to be present at the interview.

I remain, Dr Sir, Yours Truly,

Frederick Tatham.

Linnell then drafted a long and somewhat repetitive letter, which need not be given in full. It is not dated.

Dear Sir, Before you had decided against me I think you might have waited until any one who was about to purchase the Dante Drawings had objected to there being any tracings by my children of them (for they are partly done by them).

This reference to the tracings having been made partly by his children (Hannah, aged 13, afterwards Mrs. Samuel Palmer, and Elizabeth, aged 10) was somewhat disingenuous, for he had recorded in his *Journal* on 10 January that he was occupied 'every morning & evening with tracings of Mr Blake's drawings from Dante; began them ten days back or thereabouts', and then on 13 January: 'tracings of Dante. Do. 18, 27, Feb. 2, 7, 19'. There is no mention of the children having taken part. The letter then continues:

I consider that I am very ill used in the whole affair & I shall feel it my duty to myself and family to consult with other friends than yourself before anything more is done respecting the drawings. If, however, Mrs Blake can procure any friends who will advance what they cost me viz. 130£ I will give them up to her with the plates & she can make what she pleases of them. . . .

It can answer no end but to create irritation on both sides for me to meet either yourself or Mrs Blake upon the subject of the Dante. I cannot afford the time which such discussions take up or, what is more, the time lost through the agitation they create in the mind. I have endured much already from Mrs B. & yourself upon the subject & must now decline any further personal intercourse until this affair is settled.

I will inform Mrs Blake when I hear from anyone respecting the Dante and will receive any written communication from her upon the subject. I have volunteered from conscientious motives to part with the Drawings upon being remunerated the price they cost me. I cannot perceive that it is my duty to submit to everything you or Mrs B. may think fit to impose upon me. . . .

Besides, the sum paid by me for the Dante Drawings & Plates was, I can prove fully, in proportion to what I had been in the habit, & others also, of paying Mr Blake for other Drawings, which he did willingly & considered himself sufficiently paid for by me, situated as I am with a large family; he did not expect me to pay him like a nobleman: he knew that it was from no covetous feeling that I laid out above 300£ with him, for which I did not receive anything in return in money (the Job only paid the expenses of printing & paper). When you have done as much for anyone you will know better how to consider the subject.

A mention is made of the drawings having been offered to Lord Egremont, who had already bought others of Blake's works, but that nobleman did not on this occasion respond.

The dispute dragged on until Tatham wrote on 18 October 1831:

Dear Sir, I have the unpleasant duty of informing you of the death of Mrs Blake, who passed from death to life this morning at ½ past 7; after bitter pains, lasting 24 hours, she faded away as the whisper of a breeze.

Mrs Tatham & myself have been with her during her suffering & have had the happiness of beholding the departure of a saint for the rest promised for those who die in the Lord. That we all may thus die transferred from wretchedness to ioy, from pain to bliss,

Is Sir, the sincere desire of
Your obliged servant,
Frederick Tatham

After a night of painful anxiety & watching I write this hardly knowing whether to rejoice or tremble.

After Mrs. Blake's death Tatham became possessed of her and her husband's effects, though the dispute about the Dante remained unsettled. Tatham returned to the attack on 1 March 1833:

Dear Sir, If convenient to you I will attend upon you to-morrow to come to some settlement concerning the Dante &c. I have no doubt we shall be able to settle it satisfactorily to both.

Any time from 2 to 4 I will be with you if it suits you.

I am, dear Sir, Yours truly,
Frederick Tatham

He only received, however, another rebuff, and wrote again on the same day:

Dear Sir, It is not my intention in any way to commit myself in writing; therefore, if you will give me the name of your Solicitor, mine shall confer with him, but upon this consideration, that, as you have refused to see me, you must pay the costs of such arrangement.

I am, Dear Sir, your obt. sert.,
Fredk Tatham

In the event, both drawings and copper-plates remained in Linnell's keeping, though he did not, as far as we know, ever again attempt to dispose of them. Apart from a few working proofs made by the artist himself no further prints were made during Blake's lifetime. It was left to Linnell's grandchildren to realize a sum far greater than he could have ever foreseen, though the unjustified accusation has sometimes been made that he exploited Blake for his own advantage. When the Blake collection was sold in 1918 the Dante drawings made £7,665. The tracings made by Linnell and his children were not sold with the main collection, but were disposed of at some other time and are now in the Art Gallery at Yale University.

A Note on the Later History of the Dante Engravings

Other than the working proofs of the engravings taken by Blake no prints were made until 1838, when 120 sets were struck for Linnell by the firm of Dixon & Ross. The firm's day-books have been examined by Mr. Iain Bain and the record is there. On 26 September 1838 twenty-five sets were printed on India paper laid down on (French) Colombier plate paper, and on 29 September a further ninety-five were printed, the total cost being £4. 5s. The receipts for two sums of £2. 15s. and £1. 10s. are now among the Linnell family papers, together with charges for the paper amounting to £5. 6s. 3d. Dixon & Ross, who are still in business, were 'fine art' printers, providing work of very high quality. In 1838 they operated on a modest scale, employing only four men and three apprentices working for thirteen customers besides Linnell. Some of these early proofs can be identified. Thus a set from the collection of the Marquess of Crewe, sold at Sotheby's on 8 May 1943 (lot 312, Edwards, £68), was bound in hard-grained green cloth lettered BLAKE'S DANTE on the front cover; on the flyleaf was the inscription: 'A few copies may be had of Mr Chance, 28 London Street, Fitzroy Square, W. Artist's Proofs £3-13-6. Only 25 copies printed.' A similar set of great beauty in the same binding is in my collection and another one was until recently in the possession of a member of the Linnell family. The dealer who sold these copies was James H. Chance, a nephew of Linnell through his elder sister and a younger brother of Edward J. Chance, who witnessed Linnell's agreement with Blake concerning the copyright of the *Job* engravings (see p. 208). The date of their sale is fixed by a letter from James Chance to his uncle dated 30 December 1856, stating that his taking twenty-five sets was entirely his own speculation because he liked them. At different times he marketed a number of copies of the *Job* prints and further sets of Dante.

John Linnell did not himself have any further prints made, but his sons had another working done in 1892. A statement to this effect was written to Bernard Quaritch by John Linnell, jr., on 6 May, though he did not specify the number of sets printed. These were, however, enough to satisfy the limited demand, and unbound sets of prints could be bought from the trustees for 7 guineas up to the time of the sale of the whole collection in 1918. On this occasion one set of early proofs, probably those made by Blake himself, was sold (lot 179), followed by two lots of five sets each, unbound. The trustees had deposited the copper-plates of the *Illustrations of the Book of Job* in the British Museum, but the Dante plates seem to have been regarded as of less importance. After the death of Herbert Linnell, the last surviving trustee, they were discovered in an outhouse and were soon afterwards sold through Messrs. Robinson to Mr. Lessing J. Rosenwald. They are consequently now in the Rosenwald Collection in the keeping of the National Gallery of Art, Washington, D.C. In 1954 a reprint of twenty sets, with three extra prints of the first plate, was made for Mr. Rosenwald in Philadelphia on very thick paper. In 1968 a further working was made after the plates had been carefully cleaned. Twenty-five sets were printed in very black ink on soft Japanese paper with interesting, and in some respects satisfactory, results. Yet neither of these reworkings can compare in beauty with the impressions on India paper made in 1838. Though the main lines of the engravings show no obvious sign of wear, the dry-point has inevitably almost all disappeared, and the very black ink, sometimes too liberally applied, has an adverse effect on the balance of the compositions. Mr. Rosenwald has inscribed each print certifying that it was made for him in 1968. There is no intention of making any further prints in the future.

XXIX

GEORGE CUMBERLAND AND
WILLIAM BLAKE[1]

THE name of George Cumberland, virtuoso and amateur artist, 1754–1848, is well known chiefly because of his long association with Blake. He was one of the few friends whose relations with Blake remained unclouded over many years, and he played an important part in Blake's life. Cumberland was also an author, publishing fourteen books from 1793 to 1829, in three of which Blake had a hand. The following account of the two friends is based on a recent survey of the Cumberland papers in the British Museum. It provides evidence of the reasons for Blake's lasting regard for a man who clearly did not fully appreciate the qualities of his eccentric friend.

George Cumberland was descended from a money-scrivener who came to London early in the seventeenth century. George and his younger brother, Richard Denison, were the sons of a ship-builder, George Cumberland, and Elizabeth Balchen, who belonged to a distinguished naval family. Their father died in 1771, leaving the two boys, then aged 19 and 17, in rather poor circumstances. Their older and more prosperous cousin, Richard Cumberland, the dramatist, expressed his goodwill towards them after their father's death, though his relations with them remained somewhat formal. Richard Denison was, nevertheless, able to enter Magdalene College, Cambridge, and later obtained preferment as Vicar of Driffield, near Cirencester. George, on the other hand, was compelled to seek salaried employment at an early age and became a clerk in the Royal Exchange Assurance Company.

Richard Denison Cumberland was a quiet, unenterprising man and remained Vicar of Driffield until his death in 1825. George, by contrast, was of a restless temperament, with many intellectual and artistic interests, eager to take an active part in everything that attracted him. He chafed under the restrictions of his life as a clerk, and in 1783, after he had been disappointed by not gaining advancement in his office, which he thought was his due, wrote to his brother that nevertheless he was not sure that he would not submit to the disgrace and misery of

---

[1] First printed in *The Book Collector*, Spring, 1970, with a check-list of Cumberland's books.

remaining at the Royal Exchange. 'Who knows but in time I may come to be plodding, avaricious, and mean, a man of the world, a submissive Hypocrite.'[1] Yet by the end of the same year he announced that he had reached the end of his 'fourteen years' servitude' and had resigned his place.[2] This did not, however, take effect, as his letters shew, until the beginning of 1785.

The Cumberland brothers, though of differing temperaments, remained affectionate friends, and the sixteen volumes of the Cumberland papers, now in the British Museum, bear ample evidence of this in the large number of letters that passed between them. George was a great hoarder of documents, which form a rich source of information concerning both of their lives, one that might also throw light on his relations with his friend William Blake. It has long been known that these volumes contain five letters in Blake's hand to Cumberland, two to the Reverend, though eccentric, Dr. Trusler, and one returned from Cumberland to Blake. There must have been many more to Blake, which have not survived. Cumberland kept everything and insisted on the return of his letters to his brother, but he was not in the habit of making preliminary drafts of his ordinary correspondence. Moreover, many of his later dealings with Blake were conducted through his sons, George and Sydney, both employed as clerks in the Army Pay Office.

These documents seemed to offer hope of discovering when Cumberland and Blake first met. Blake's earliest letter to him is dated 6 December 1795, though its terms indicate that they had been friends for some time before this date. I pointed out in 1921[3] that there was a possibility that they had met as early as 1784, since a reference in Blake's satire, *An Island in the Moon* (c. 1784), to printing off 2,000 copies of a text by a new method of engraving or etching it on copper instead of ordinary printing agrees with Cumberland's own proposal described in a letter to his brother dated 3 January 1784 and later published in Henry Maty's *New Review* 1784 (vi. 318).[4] He had first mentioned 'multiplying copper plates' in a letter of 29 September 1783.[5] In January 1784 he wrote:

The occasion of my writing today is to send you the enclosed specimen of my new mode of Printing—it is the amusement of an evening and is capable of Printing 2000 if I wanted them—you see here one page which is executed as easily as writing and the cost is trifling, for your Copper is worth at any rate near as much as it cost, besides you are not obliged to print any more than you want at one time, so that if the work dont take you have nothing to do but to cut the copper

[1] B.M. Add. MS. 36494, f. 81.　　　　　　　　　　　　　　　　[2] Ibid., f. 225.
[3] *Bibliography of Blake*, New York: Grolier Club, 1921, p. 10.
[4] Reprinted in Mona Wilson's *Life of Blake*, London, 1948, p. 330.　　[5] B.M. Add. MS. 36494, f. 165.

to pieces, or clean it—but if it does you may print 4 editions, 2000 and then sell the Plate as well—all this would be . . . can only be read with the help of a looking glass as the letters are reversed—I know that would be none to you or to anyone who reflects & knows that glasses are always at hand—but it will be *none to the crowd* by and by, for we may begin with printing Debates or great news and then they will condescend to the Mirror for information and so discover there is no trouble; however we have a remedy for this defect also, for in printing 20 we can have 20 more right by only taking the impressions while wet, in fact this is only etching words instead of Landscapes, but nobody has yet thought of the utility of it that I know of. The expense of this page is 1/6 without reckoning time which was never yet worth much to authors and the Copper is worth 1/6 again when cut up. In my next I will tell you more and make you also an engraver of this work—til then keep it to yourself.[1]

With this letter Cumberland sent a print of the poem, 'To the Nightingale', made as a counterproof and therefore the right way round for reading as described in the letter. Two similar counterproofs are contained in scrap-books compiled by Cumberland himself and now in my library.

Writing to his brother on 26 November 1784 Cumberland again referred to 'a new method of engraving' and to making plates from 'my late views', that is, from drawings made on his travels in Great Britain. He had done three plates in three days. Had he perhaps been having lessons from Blake in the technique of etching? He also wrote that he had learnt 'that inflammable air may now be made very reasonably by an invention of Dr Priestly, and has discovered that a Frenchman, Hoffman, was practising his art of writing on copper; he will therefore write an account of it for Gentleman's Magazine'. 'Everlasting lamps', he said, had been invented by a Mr. Taylor, a modest young man of much learning, a great admirer of the doctrines of Plato and was translating Plotinus. 'He has lent me a Poem composed from *Diotima's* speech in Plato's Banquet on the subject of *Love*, which has given me a higher idea of these ancient Metaphysics than I ever had, as well as a great opinion of his talents for Poetry.'[2] These echoes of Blake's Inflammable Gass (Dr. Priestley) and Sipsop the Pythagorean (perhaps Thomas Taylor the Platonist) suggest that Cumberland had been meeting Blake socially at the house of the Revd. Anthony Stephen Mathews or elsewhere. He was also referring to 'my friend Stothard' as early as March 1783; Blake had been closely associated with Stothard certainly since 1780. We learn from Cumberland's article in Maty's *New Review* that he had employed the engraver, W. S. Blake, of Exchange Alley

---

[1] B.M. Add. MS. 36494, f. 232.   [2] Ibid., ff. 371–2.

to print his copper-plates, but during the next ten years his relations with William Blake became much closer. He had been active on Blake's behalf in October 1791, when he persuaded Willey Reveley to ask him to engrave some plates for the third volume of Stuart and Revett's *Antiquities of Athens*.[1] He had bought the first three of the four volumes in May 1808 and reminded himself of his part in the book by writing in his memorandum book: 'Got Blake to Engrave for Athens.'[2] Blake's four plates are dated 3 April 1792. In 1793 he turned to Blake for help in etching and lettering plates for his *Thoughts on Outline*.

Cumberland had finally left the Royal Exchange Assurance Company by 1785 and in March of that year was in Paris. He had acquired a modest competence by inheritance and was now free to pursue his own interests. In 1788 he married, though against the wishes of his family, and was, as he said, 'virtually banished' to Rome. There he learnt to speak Italian and became deeply interested in Italian art, particularly in Raphael's paintings and in the engravers Bonasoni and Marc Antonio Raimondi. In 1790 he returned to England and lived for a time at Lynd-hurst, near Southampton. On 27 January 1791 he wrote to his brother: 'The fruits of my Travels has been that my wants are considerably lessened, insomuch that my chief pleasure consists in studying simplicity, as I am sensible that with it are compatible both beauty of Form, and elegance of Life, together with Ease, health and usefulness in Society.'[3]

As a gentleman of leisure he could now afford to adopt a style of comfortable simplicity with time to spend in cultivation of the arts. He was soon to begin his modest career as author and virtuoso and to consolidate his friendships with artists and other persons who could share his interests. He could never be content to remain merely a spectator and his letters covering the next fifteen years shew that he took an active part in politics, education, the study of psychology and occult faculties, metaphysics and ontology, archaeology, and practical farming, with special attention to mechanical devices for its improvement. An interest in Egyptian antiquities and hieroglyphics led to a steady correspondence with Francis Douce, the antiquary and Keeper of Manuscripts in the British Museum. Cumberland naturally became an assiduous collector of Italian prints, coins, and other antiquities, with cabinets of minerals and fossils.

An influential friend from early days was the politician Charles Long, Member of Parliament from 1789, Secretary of State for Ireland in 1806, Paymaster-General in 1810, and raised to the peerage as Lord Farnborough in 1826. Long was an

---

[1] See *Blake's Letters*, ed. Keynes, 1968, p. 25.   [2] B.M. Add. MS. 36519H, f. 355.
[3] Ibid., 36496, f. 260.

authority on pictures, sculpture, and architecture and was always ready to help Cumberland in forwarding his various interests. Another constant correspondent was Thomas Johnes of Hafod, landowner and cultivator of the arts. Cumberland had visited his Welsh estate in 1794 and two years later celebrated its beauty in a small book. In 1791 Cumberland mentioned in his letters his Anecdotes of Bonasoni and a Poem on Landscape Painting. Both subjects were soon to take shape in books. His first publication was *A Poem on the Landscapes of Great Britain* written in 1780 during the first flush of his aesthetic enthusiasms. His taste in book production is immediately seen in this slim quarto published in 1793, his personal influence being evident in the typography of the title-page. It is set for the most part in upper-case letters, producing a lapidary effect, a style maintained by Cumberland in almost all the books published under his name. The poem is illustrated with one plate drawn and etched by the author. A note states that if the book met with 'the approval of the judicious' he hoped to issue a reprint with more illustrations, but this hope was not fulfilled. On page 19 of the *Poem* Cumberland expressed his hatred of his years of servitude as a clerk in the lines:

> Bold is the man that dares attempt a rhyme,
> Where tasteful talents are almost a crime.

with a footnote, 'The Author refers to two or three wretched individuals on whom, at the period of writing, he had the misfortune to be dependent, and who, as he fears is but too often the case among mere men of business, endeavoured to render his liberal pursuits an obstacle to his advancement in life.'

Many years later Cumberland gave his last copy of *A Poem on Landscapes* together with his next publication, *Lewina, The Maid of Snowdon*, to a Bristol friend, John Eagles, inscribing it as follows:[1]

To Rev Jn. Eagles with G.C.'s best regards

These two Poems were my earliest productions and were rather passed by Reviewers. Robinson the Publisher paid me £56 for the Profits of the Sale, and offered to buy the Copy right for £50 more which I refused, being dissatisfied with them and resolved never to republish them—but at the persuasion of Dr Warner, I did at the end of my 2ᵈ vol. of Tales correct & republish the Lewina written on the model, as I thought, of Dryden's fables.

This is the only copy left me, and as you are the only Poet I was ever acquainted with except S. Rogers, I send it you—I did not quite turn my back on the Muses however, and when, in great solitude at Weston super Mare (before it was a watering place) they came and solaced me between the showers of misfor-

---

[1] B.M. Library, 11630, f. 68.

tune—I finished that Poem on *Home* when I was once *near* shewing you—and which I am not likely ever to Print as I don't think it better than either of these.

G.C.

N. When I wrote these I had never been beyond Wales—but I had loved the fine arts from almost infancy and sought them out alone!

Cumberland's cultivation of the arts was combined with high ideals in the conduct of life. In January 1792 he wrote in a letter to his brother, 'Follow Reason, follow Truth and never ask what their Society will cost—if we lose the pleasure that one hour of their applause confers on the human mind, we lose all the sweets and all the happiness that Life can bestow. Money is dross in that Scale, Power a painful prominence and Long Life a disgrace.'[1] This sounds high-flown and he did in fact worry throughout his life about financial affairs, but this was because he never had quite enough money even for his modest extravagances. His morals and general integrity were above reproach. His family life was happy and nothing could dim his affection for his four children, however badly they behaved.

In the year 1792 Cumberland acquired a small estate at Bishopsgate, near Egham, in Windsor Great Park, and here two more books were taking shape for publication in 1793. One, entitled *Lewina, The Maid of Snowdon*, is illustrated with three copper-plates, and it seems likely that he was before this date calling on Blake for help with his drawings and etchings. Egham was near enough to London for visits to Blake's house in Lambeth to be easily made. The third book published in 1793 was perhaps the most important of all Cumberland's works. Although primarily concerned with the life and art of Julio Bonasoni, he prefixed 'A Plan for the improvement of the Arts in England', containing a suggestion for the formation of a public art gallery, which was ultimately realized by the foundation of the National Gallery in 1824. In an address printed with the Plan, Cumberland claimed that Sir William Hamilton, diplomatist and authority on Greek sculpture, had given it his 'Hearty and impartial Approbation'.

A letter to Cumberland from Arthur Champernowne, a picture collector, dated 7 February 1792, is a reminder that this friend acquired ten years later a copy of *Songs of Innocence* (copy O in the *Census*) and that Benjamin Heath Malkin gave a copy of the same book to Thomas Johnes of Hafod (copy P). Cumberland himself bought copies of *Thel* (copy A), *The Marriage of Heaven and Hell* (copy A), *Songs of Innocence and of Experience* (copy F), *The Book of Urizen* (copy F), and *Europe* (copy D), and was active in bringing Blake's works to the notice of his

[1] B.M. Add. MS. 36497, f. 108.

friends whenever he had the opportunity. In his copy of *Europe* he wrote a number of glosses, the majority derived from Bysshe's *Art of English Poetry* and regarded by some critics as explanatory of political references in the poem and probably supplied by Blake himself.[1]

AN ATTEMPT TO DESCRIBE

HAFOD,

AND THE NEIGHBOURING SCENES ABOUT THE BRIDGE OVER THE FUNACK, COMMONLY CALLED THE DEVIL's BRIDGE, IN THE COUNTY OF CARDIGAN.

AN ANCIENT SEAT BELONGING TO THOMAS JOHNES, ESQ. MEMBER FOR THE COUNTY OF RADNOR.

BY GEORGE CUMBERLAND.

> Unvex'd with quarrels, undisturb'd with noise,
> The country king his peaceful realm enjoys;
> Cool grots, and living lakes, the flow'ry pride
> Of meads, and streams that thro' the valley glide,
> And shady groves, that easy sleep invite,
> And, after toilsome days, a soft repose at night.
>
> *Dryden's Virgil.*

LONDON:
Printed by W. Wilson, St. Peter's Hill, Doctors' Commons,
And sold by T. Egerton, Whitehall.

———

M DCC XCVI.

In 1793 Cumberland told his brother that his *Poem on Landscapes* had brought a very polite note of appreciation from Thomas Johnes, and this was followed in August 1794 by an invitation to stay at Hafod. This led to the friendship already mentioned and to Cumberland's very attractive little volume, *An Attempt to Describe Hafod*, 1796. This was dedicated to Charles Long, then M.P. for Rye, and contains

[1] See Damon's *Blake's Philosophy and Symbols*, 1924, pp. 347-51.

a folding engraved map of the Hafod estate by Blake, hitherto unrecognized as his work. The identification was made recently by Professor David Erdman, who noticed that the lettering contained Blake's peculiar lower-case *g* with a leftward directed upper serif, used only by him at this period. Cumberland was himself pleased with the book and wrote to his brother on 23 March 1796, 'I have published my account of Hafod and if you think you can dispose of 20 at Cirencester I will order them to be sent. They are 4° large Paper, which is really a beautiful book and 2° [8°] smaller. I have secured 12 of *the large* for myself and friends and bound them—the rest of the large are, I believe, nearly all gone, having only printed 50—and 450 small.'[1]

Thomas Johnes was so impatient to see the book that he wrote to the publisher, Egerton, asking him to send a copy in sheets,[2] and soon afterwards told Cumberland, 'I wish my six to be neatly bound, tho' not in the highest extravagance of the mode.'[3]

In January 1795 Cumberland had written to his brother, 'I am writing on Art and engraving my own designs. One must do something.'[4] This was no doubt in reference to his best-known book, *Thoughts on Outline*, 1796, which discusses the value of outline to the artists of Greek vases and later to painters, in particular Michelangelo and Raphael, as compared with the moderns. The importance of outline was a favourite theme of Blake's and Cumberland's views may have owed some of their immediacy to converse with him. In this connexion Cumberland protested against the fig-leaf prudery of his time, and in an appendix paid a tribute to Blake, who had taken upon himself the labour of engraving eight of the twenty-four plates from the author's own 'inventions'. In addition he thanked Blake 'for the instruction which encouraged me to execute a great part of the plates myself, enabling me thereby to reduce considerably the price of the book'. All the plates were lettered by Blake in the same style as the Hafod map.

---

[1] B.M. Add. MS. 36498, f. 74.
[2] Ibid., f. 68.
[3] Ibid. 36497, f. 98 (misplaced among letters of 1791).
[4] Ibid. 36498, f. 8.

On 29 December 1795 the artist Richard Cosway had written to Cumberland:

I have contemplated with pleasure the Outline you was so good as to leave with Mrs C. of the Picture of Leonardo & do not hesitate to pronounce it one of the most beautiful Compositions I ever beheld of that Great Man. I hope it will not be long before I shall be able to request a sight of the Picture—why do you not get Blake to make an engraving of it? I shou'd think he wou'd be delighted to undertake such a Work & it wou'd certainly *pay him very well* for whatever time & pains he may bestow upon such a Plate, as we have *so very few* of Leonardo's Works well engrav'd & the composition of this Picture is so very graceful & pleasing I am convinc'd he might put almost any Price on the Print & assure himself of a very extensive Sale.[1]

Cumberland did not fall in with this suggestion which Blake would have been unlikely to refuse, but it shews how much Blake's burin was in the minds of his friends.

It was at this time (6 December 1795) that Blake wrote the first of his extant letters to Cumberland, giving instructions for waxing a plate for etching. On 5 July 1796, just before the publication of *Thoughts on Outline*, a friend, W. Lucas, wrote to Cumberland on behalf of the printer Richard Wilson, ' . . . his Brother, the young Oxonian, keeps him so poor that he is under the necessity of asking a Favour of you. What he wishes is that you would have the Goodness to let him have fifty Pounds—on account I mean of "Hafod" and "Outlines". You may afterwards settle it with Egerton, who will otherwise he fears be rather long-winded.'[2] On 6 July 1796 Cumberland wrote to his brother, 'My Book called *Thoughts on Outline* will be published next Thursday by Robinson, Paternoster Row, & Egerton, Charing Cross—the price will be a guinea, but it has cost me a great deal of Money. A learned Critic writes me word that the arguments are incontrovertibly Just, the illustrations surprisingly happy and the style equally strong and unaffected—So that I hope my Friends will now take out their guineas with pleasure to buy it.'[3]

Cumberland was to be disappointed, for the book did not sell readily. The number of copies printed is not recorded, but it was probably small, the book being printed in large type on Whatman paper, so that the cost of each copy must have been high. Eleven years later a note from Longman's (12 May 1807), who appear to have taken over some of the stock, stated that they still had 159 copies in hand, of which ninety-three belonged to the author; they declined considering the issue of a

---

[1] B.M. Add. MS. 36498, f. 53.   [2] Ibid., f. 108.   [3] Ibid., f. 110.

THOUGHTS ON OUTLINE, SCULPTURE, AND THE SYSTEM THAT GUIDED THE ANCIENT ARTISTS IN COMPOSING THEIR FIGURES AND GROUPES:

ACCOMPANIED WITH FREE REMARKS ON THE PRACTICE OF THE MODERNS, AND LIBERAL HINTS CORDIALLY INTENDED FOR THEIR ADVANTAGE.

TO WHICH ARE ANNEXED TWENTY-FOUR DESIGNS OF CLASSICAL SUBJECTS INVENTED ON THE PRINCIPLES RECOMMENDED IN THE ESSAY BY GEORGE CUMBERLAND.

AINSI IO SON PITTORE.

LONDON. PRINTED BY W. WILSON, ST. PETER'S-HILL, DOCTORS'-COMMONS; AND SOLD BY MESSRS. ROBINSON, PATERNOSTER-ROW; AND T. EGERTON, WHITEHALL. MDCCXCVI.

second edition.[1] Further efforts to sell copies through his son George in October 1813 succeeded in disposing of only seven copies out of seventy-four.[2] Blake did not thank Cumberland for his copy until 23 December 1796, when he had some 'pricks of conscience'. At the same time he sent six plates he had procured for Cumberland 'to be transmuted',[3] but their identity among the many etched or engraved by him is not known.

Early in 1797 Cumberland was involved in an altercation with a neighbour, Henry Griffiths, who had objected to his allowing two poor families to settle, or 'squat', as would now be said, on waste land close to their two houses. This charitable action resulted in the publication of a pamphlet printed at Windsor in Cumberland's characteristic style and sold in Egham and Reading. A reply by Griffiths was issued by the same printer. Copies of both pamphlets are preserved in the British Museum,[4] but no others are known to me.

Cumberland's tireless efforts for the 'improvement of the arts in England' led to his making a curious suggestion to the potter Josiah Wedgwood the younger. On 3 December 1796 Wedgwood, writing from Etruria, thanked him for his 'ingenious idea of converting portraits into vases', but declined making the attempt as 'our hands are fully occupied'.[5] Cumberland's letter may be now in the Wedgwood archive at Keele University.

Cumberland had distributed copies of *Thoughts on Outline* to a number of friends and in October sent one to the Society of Arts. Thomas Taylor, recently appointed assistant secretary to the Society, wrote to thank him for the gift, prefacing his letter with his opinion of another book sent by Cumberland, which he called 'your novel'. This was *The Captive of the Castle of Sennaar*, an allegory of life in a Utopian valley in Africa. Taylor wrote:

I thank you for your present of the two books. With respect to your novel, since you desire me to give you my opinion freely of its merit, I must own that I think it more entertaining than instructive, more ingenious than moral. I will not, indeed, I cannot suppose that you would undertake to defend lasciviousness publickly & yet to me it appears that it is as much patronized by the conduct of your Sophians, as by the works of Mrs Woolstoncraft [sic]. You will doubtless excuse the freedom of this Opinion, when you consider that as I am a professed Platonist, love is with me *true* only in proportion as it is *pure*; or in other words in proportion as it rises above the gratification of our brutal part. Hence, I consider the

[1] B.M. Add. MS. 36501, f. 79. [2] Ibid. 36514, f. 97.
[3] *Blake's Letters*, ed. Keynes, 1968, p. 26. [4] B.M. Library, 1414, h. 11.
[5] B.M. Add. MS. 36498, f. 151.

delight which lovers experience when in poetic language they drink large draughts of love thro' the eyes as far superior to that arising from copulation, because the union is more incorporeal; since in the former case there is a conjuction of the pure *image* of the lover with that of the beloved, but in the other there is nothing, but a union of *bodies*. This notion will doubtless appear to you as eccentric as it is novel—I wish, however, you may at length become as much a convert to it as I am.[1]

Cumberland is not known to have possessed a copy of *Visions of the Daughters of Albion*, but had he read it he would not have understood the spiritual nature of love as conceived by Plato and by Blake, though neither does Taylor appear to have understood the position of Mary Wollstonecraft, who had lodged for a time in his house and to whom Blake is usually believed to have addressed his poem 'Mary'.[2]

In 1801 Cumberland left his Bishopsgate residence and searched for somewhere to live in the neighbourhood of Bath or Bristol. For a few years he stayed in various places, first at Clevedon, near Bristol, and then for some time at Axbridge in Somerset, or at Weston-super-Mare. By 1808 he had settled in a house in Culver Street, Bristol. Meanwhile his two sons, George and Sydney, were growing up and each, as he reached a suitable age, was placed as a clerk in the Army Pay Office, doubtless by favour of Charles Long, the Paymaster-General. Cumberland himself was now too far from London to be able to transact his business as he had formerly done by personal visits to Blake and other friends. He therefore habitually used as intermediary his elder son, George, who became very familiar with Blake, first in his second-floor room at 17 South Molton Street and afterwards in his brother-in-law's house in Fountain Court.

On 2 December 1808 Cumberland wrote to George, 'I send Blake the drawings by Georgiana [one of his two daughters] . . . I send Mr Blake a few old Tracings from Raffael's Pictures in Fresco—I shall keep a great many for you—and when you come to draw a little send them up to you a few at a time—send them to Blake the first opportunity as things of little value to him, being rude sketches only. Those I keep for you are the best.'[3] George answered two days later, 'Mr Blake was very much pleased with the traicings. I thought it a good opportunity to ask him for the Holy Family he gave very readily.'[4] On 12 December, after admonishing George, 'tracings not traicings', Cumberland, feeling somewhat

---

[1] Ibid., f. 244.

[2] Blake's *Complete Writings*, ed. Keynes, p. 428. See also Kathleen Raine, *Blake and Tradition*, 1969, i. 71.

[3] B.M. Add. MS. 36501, f. 300.　　　　　　　　　　　　　[4] Ibid., f. 302.

guilty about having asked Blake for his water-colour of 'The Holy Family', added, 'I hope you did not ask Blake for the Picture very *importunately*. I must send him more of these heads.'[1] On 18 December he wrote his well-known, but only surviving, letter to Blake, sending it by George with instructions to get an immediate answer. This was duly written by Blake on the 19th and included his somewhat cryptic statement that, 'I have Myself begun to print an account of my various Inventions in Art, for which I have procured a Publisher.'[2] It appears from Cumberland's letter that Blake had talked of this plan, presumably when visited by Cumberland in London not long before. Nothing is now known of this project, though the suggestion has been made that it referred merely to the *Descriptive Catalogue* of 1809. There is, however, a memorandum book used by Cumberland in 1808 containing an undated entry, 'Blake N 17 South Molton St.', and on the other side of the leaf, 'Blake's new mode of engraving to be Published by me at his desire'.[3] This request was made, it seems, during their conversation, and establishes the project as a definite work on Blake's technique, which Cumberland was to see through the press. Later, however, a pencil note was added below, 'He will publish it', this being added when Cumberland received the letter of 19 December. Yet Cumberland's mind was still worrying about this, since six leaves further on he made another note, 'Blake N 17 South Molton St.' There the matter ended. The drawing of 'The Holy Family' is probably the same as a picture of 'The Holy Family with John the Baptist and a Lamb', afterwards in the collection of Alexander A. Weston. Its present owner is not known. The old tracings from Raphael's paintings in fresco had presumably been made from murals while Cumberland was living in Rome, 1789–90. Blake would certainly have been delighted with them.

Blake's exhibition of his pictures was opened at his brother's house in Broad Street in May 1809. Cumberland is not known to have visited this himself, but on 14 October his son George wrote, 'Blakes has published a Catalogue of Pictures being the ancient method of Frescoe *Restored*—you should tell Mr Barry [a bookseller in Bristol] to get it, it may be the means of serving your friend, it sells for 2/6 and may be had of J. Blake 28 Broad St. Golden Square at his Brother's—the Book is a great curiosity. He as given Stothard, a compleat set down.'[4] Cumberland answered on 5 November, 'send by Mr Grindon 2 vols. of Blake's work & make my regards to Blake—Mr G. will pay you the 5/- for me'.[5] Later, on

---

[1] B.M. Add. MS. 36501, f. 310.
[3] B.M. Add. MS. 36519, vol. for 1808, f. 385.
[5] Ibid., f. 95.

[2] *Blake's Letters*, ed. Keynes, 1968, p. 134.
[4] Ibid. 36502, f. 83.

13 November, he wrote, 'Blake's Cat. is truly original—part vanity part madness —part very good sense—is this the work of his you recommended, and of which I gave you a Comm[n]. to buy *two* sets one for me and one for Mr Barry's Library? —did he sell many Pictures? and had he many subscribers to the Wife of Bath?— Tell him with my best regards if I was not among the Subscribers it was because I literally cannot afford to lay out a shilling in any thing but *Taxes & necessaries of Life*.'[1] His son replied to this, 'Mr Blake has nothing but the remarks on his Chaucer—have you seen the etching of Mr Stothard Pilgrims—it is finished.'[2]

In 1810 George Cumberland, jr., was sent to Lisbon by Charles Long to carry on his work as an official in the Paymaster-General's office and there he remained for several years. The young man was, however, too fond of spending his time sketching in Portugal and Spain and insufficiently fond of performing his duties. In 1812 his idleness resulted in his being set to the menial task of copying documents for Lord Wellington at army headquarters. There his behaviour reached the point of incurring the displeasure of the Commander-in-Chief. His father was alarmed lest his son should be dismissed from the service in disgrace and on 13 November 1813 he drafted a letter to Lord Wellington[3] appealing for leniency and sent it to Charles Long to be forwarded, but it was never sent and presumably Long, as Paymaster-General, was able to intercede with the authorities in Spain, so that George was forgiven. At the same time, in 1812, Sydney was giving trouble in London, his dissolute habits repeatedly landing him in debts which his father had to meet. Charles Long solved this problem by sending Sydney to join George in Lisbon, so that for a long time the father had no one to do his business in London, and his dealings with Blake were reduced to occasional visits. Thus in 1813 he recorded on 12 April in his memorandum book, 'I saw Blake who recommended Pewter to scratch on with the prints. He is doing L[d] Spencer.'[4] Blake's advice about using pewter probably relates to his own memorandum made *c.* 1807 in his *Notebook* 'To woodcut on Pewter'.[5] The reference to his engraved portrait of Lord Spencer supplies a date for its execution two years later than the only other clue given by the watermark, 1811, in the paper used for the two impressions known.[6]

Again, while Cumberland was in London in June 1813 he made calls on the 3rd on Cosway, Blake, and Stothard, dining with Praed, his banker. He wrote in his memorandum book, 'Called Cosway by *Dayley* N 51 South Molton St facing

[1] Ibid. 36514, f. 216. [2] Ibid. 36515, f. 84.
[3] Ibid. 36504, f. 184. [4] Ibid. 36520, f. 155.
[5] *Complete Writings*, ed. Keynes, p. 440. [6] Keynes, *Blake's Separate Plates*, 1956, p. 80.

Poor Blake where he has been 3 Years—(Eagles Cousin) Called Blake—still poor still Dirty—got to Praeds to Dinner at 6 o'clock passed even^s with Stothard New-man St—still more dirty than Blake yet full of Genius.' Eagles, whose name recurs in the letters, was a poet living in Bristol. It was Cosway who had been in South Molton Street for three years. Blake had gone there after leaving Felpham late in 1803.

There are no letters from Blake to Cumberland during this long period of separation. Blake was passing through his worst time of neglect and poverty, while Cumberland was going about his own affairs in Bristol and occasionally bringing out a book. In 1810 Cumberland printed an elegant double leaf, now very uncommon, carrying a birthday ode to his admired friend Horne Tooke, politician and scholar, to be placed under a bust of Tooke executed by Thomas Banks in 1800. Cumberland had himself etched a lively portrait of his friend.[1] Tooke's name occurs in a list of Blake's friends compiled by John Linnell for Gilchrist,[2] though no record remains of any intercourse between them.

In 1811 Cumberland sought to do honour to his old friend, the Right Hon. Charles Long, M.P., by publishing a hastily composed description of his country seat at Bromley-Hill, printed in good Cumberland style by Bulmer. The edition was probably small and a second revised edition was printed, this time by Bensley, in 1816, part of the issue being on large paper in quarto. A letter from the publisher, Robert Triphook, dated 13 February 1813 shews that negotiations began a long time before publication. It was proposed that 500 copies would be enough and that a frontispiece would much assist the sale, though this suggestion was not carried out.

George and Sydney Cumberland returned to England after the end of the Peninsular War and resumed their visits to Blake. On 21 April 1815 George wrote to his father:

We call upon Blake yesterday evening, found him & his wife drinking Tea, durtyer than ever—however he received us well & shewed his large drawing in Water Colors of the last Judgement; he has been labouring at it till it is nearly as black as your Hat—the only lights are those of a *Hellish Purple*—his time is now intirely taken up with Etching & Engraving—upon which subject I shall ask his advice if I do not shortly Succeed more to my wishes—I have made some pretty things but not worth send you—Blake says he is fearful they will make too great

---

[1] Reproduced in *The Book Collector*, Spring, 1970, plate xiii.
[2] G. E. Bentley, jr., *Blake Records*, 1969, p. 319 n.

a Man of Napoleon and enable him to come to this Country—Mrs B. says that if this Country does go to War our K-g ought to loose his head.[1]

Blake was still in South Molton Street and was living precariously on the money earned by engraving Flaxman's designs for *Hesiod's Works and Days*, published in 1816, together with a few plates for Rees's *Cyclopaedia* and Wedgwood's private catalogue of their crockery. His picture of 'The Last Judgement', a replica of the one executed for the Earl of Egremont in 1808, was evidently spoiled by over-working and it has not survived. His grinding poverty, reflected by the dirty state in which the young men found him living, was duly noted, but seemingly not pitied. Their father replied in an undated letter with no more sympathy, 'You have a free estimate of Blake—& his devilish Works—he is a little Cracked, but very honest—as to his wife she is maddest of the Two—He will tell you any thing he knows.'[2] George jr. was clearly determined to get all the help he could from Blake in order to transfer his drawings to copper. His father had never succeeded in having more than a very few of his drawings published as illustrations in his books. Although he had announced in 1798 the impending publication of *Letters from Italy, with Seventy Views*, no such work ever appeared. His son was more successful. The British Museum has a copy of *Views in Spain and Portugal, taken during the Campaigns of his grace the Duke of Wellington by George Cumberland Jr. only 30 Copies Printed.* The flimsy marbled paper boards enclose twelve plates, 24·5 × 37·5 cm., with a handwritten label on the front cover. Some of the incidents recorded by these quite competent drawings are dated 1811 or 1813, evidence of the artist's inattention to his official duties. There is no date of publication but it presumably appeared before 1820. I have also a note of *Forty Views from Nature by G.C. Jun. 1821*, but have not found a copy.

In 1818 George Cumberland, jr., was instrumental in effecting a change in Blake's life and fortunes. In an undated letter of this year he told his father, 'I have introduced him [John Linnell] to Blake—they like one another much [and are likely to assist one another *del.*] and Linnel has promised to get him some work.'[3] Linnell fulfilled his promise by immediately employing Blake to work on an engraving from one of his portraits and from this introduction flowed the steady stream of Linnell's care for Blake's welfare until his death in 1827.

In a letter to his son dated 22 January 1819, Cumberland wrote, 'Tell Blake a Mr Sivewright of Edinburg has just claimed in some Philosophical Journal of

---

[1] B.M. Add. MS. 36505, ff. 63-5.   [2] Ibid. 36514, f. 97.
[3] Ibid. 36515, f. 118.

Last month As his own invention Blake's method—& calls it Copper Blocks, I think.'[1] The year of this letter has hitherto been read as 1809, thereby creating something of a mystery, the identity of 'Mr Sivewright of Edinburg' being uncertain. It seems, however, now to be clear that he was Thomas Sivright of Meggetland (now a suburb of Edinburgh), a well-known collector of works of art of all kinds, particularly prints, and experimentor.[2] The first volume of the *Edinburgh Philosophical Journal*, June to October 1819, contains an article by William Home Lizars, who executed the first ten plates of Audubon's *Birds of America*. This article gives an 'Account of a new style of Engraving on Copper in Alto Relievo, invented by W. Lizars.' It describes a method, very similar to Blake's, of making copper-plates for surface printing by deep etching with 'diluted acid (commonly called Aquafortis)', the design having been drawn on the copper with pen or pencil using turpentine varnish as medium. At the end of the article Lizars acknowledged 'Mr Sivright of Meggetland, a gentleman well known in this city for his scientific acquirements, and to whom, during these experiments, I was much indebted, used with very great success the same kind of limestone which is employed in lithography.'[3] The date on Cumberland's letter might be read as 22 June 1819, though it looks more like 22 Jan. The year is, I think, not in doubt. If Sivright had himself already described this method of etching copper, the publication remains to be discovered.[4]

Cumberland visited Blake on 6 June 1820 and recorded in his memorandum book:

Went to Blake's and read the Courier to him about the Queen's arrival. Mr Linel came in & I recommended to him the Subject of Spring on a large scale—viz. the whole of That Season from the first budding to the full leaf with many [word illegible] to Introduce fly Fishing Barking Trees, Lambing in watered vallies—late leaping on exposed Hills, Horses fighting for mares &c. with showers. He liked the ideas as does Blake.[5]

[1] This reference was first noticed by Arthur Symons in the *Saturday Review*, 25 August 1916, p. 231.

[2] His collections were sold at auction in Edinburgh at Tait's rooms in February 1836.

[3] I am indebted to Dr. Isabel Henderson of the National Library of Scotland for help in making this identification. Mr. Iain Bain tells me that the article by Lizars was reprinted in the *Gentleman's Magazine*, 1821, pp. 625-7.

[4] A commentary on the article by Lizars was contributed to W. Newton's *London Journal of Arts and Sciences* (1820), i. 55-8, by Charles Pye. He described 'a new Process of engraving on Metal and Stone', his experiments having been made five years earlier. He agreed that Lizars was the first to publish his process of engraving on 'Copper Blocks in alto relievo'. The process described by Pye must have produced results almost exactly like Blake's.

[5] B.M. Add. MS. 36520H, f. 384.

Views from Nature did not really interest Blake, but he no doubt wished to encourage his new friend.

Cumberland had been engaged for many years on a catalogue of the works of the early Italian engravers and in 1816 was negotiating with Robert Triphook as publisher. In a letter dated 27 May Triphook proposed that the edition should be 250 ordinary copies and 50 on large paper. Cumberland would receive one-fifth of the impression and would etch the monograms, furnishing the publisher with 300 prints. The book was eventually published in 1827 by three other firms, one being Colnaghi. Meanwhile Cumberland lent his catalogue to various friends, sending it in November 1823 to Blake who returned it a few days later.[1]

Another project occupying Cumberland's mind over a number of years was a volume of 'Outlines', eventually published in 1829 as *Outlines from the Ancients*. The publisher was to be Septimus Prowett. Young George conducted negotiations with him in 1824, reporting on 24 May that, 'Mr Prowet after calculating the expense of publishing your Outline makes an offer of 50 guineas & 12 copies of the work.'[2] His father replied on 9 May saying that, 'young [Charles] Stothard would do the outlines, I think, well—Blake a few'.[3] Their correspondence has many other references to Blake's part in the work, which was to repair four of the plates he had engraved for *Thoughts on Outline* in 1793–5. On 17 June Cumberland wrote to his son that he had sent these plates to be 'carefully repaired by Blake if they are worn by printing. *He* understands me, and how to keep a free and equal outline which is always best.' After other instructions he added, 'I send you with this one from Blake's etching from my own design backgrounded so as to imitate the Greek vases—shew it to Mr Prowett and perhaps he may think it worth while to go the expense of aquatinting the back ground . . . he may then do them on red paper.'[4] He eventually accepted the offer of 50 guineas. By a coincidence Richard Denison Cumberland on 8 May 1825 told his brother that he had paid nearly £500 to another Blake; this concerned a lease, and soon afterwards George jr. was having dealings with a house decorator of the same name, Blake.[5] Later in May Richard Denison died at Driffield and much of his brother's time thereafter was spent dealing with his affairs.

In October 1825 George Cumberland was in London and recorded in his memorandum book under Saturday, 15 October, that Thomas Taylor had breakfast with him and in talking of old friends noted that 'The Duke of Sussex is also

[1] Ibid., f. 412.   [2] Ibid. 36510, f. 89.
[3] Ibid., f. 92.   [4] Ibid., f. 113.
[5] Ibid., f. 244.

Taylor's friend—memo to see Blake'.¹ This conjunction of Blake's name with Taylor and his friend helps to strengthen the probability that they too were more than acquaintances, though there is still no direct documentation of this.

It is likely that during this period, 1826–7, Blake was visited by his two sons, but there is no evidence that their father ever saw him again. He was, however, doing his best to find customers in Bristol for his *Book of Job*. In an undated letter of 1827 to his son he wrote, 'for Blake I have spared no pains but have no success. They seem to think his prices above their reach, yet they seemed very anxious to have his works. My best regards to him. His Job I have placed with a third book-seller Mr Lewis of Clifton.'² Blake's last letter to Cumberland is well known. It was written on 12 April when he was very ill and is filled with gratitude to Cumberland for what he had done on his behalf. Near the end of the letter he remarked, 'The Little Card I will do as soon as Possible but when you Consider that I have been reduced to a Skeleton from which I am slowly recovering you will I hope have Patience with me.'³ The 'Little Card' was a small copper-plate with an allegorical design surrounding the name 'Mr. Cumberland' in Gothic lettering. It was the last engraving that he made before his death, and is the subject of most of the remaining references found in Cumberland's letters.

Blake died on 12 August in Fountain Court, but it was not until 3 November that Cumberland wrote to his son, 'Tell me of what Blake died & how, & how he has left his widow—*all you can learn of him*. I have the *Job* to sell and if she *wants* the money, *must*, if I cannot sell it, take it myself.'⁴ George replied, without a date, 'I can tell you nothing as yet about your old friend Blake, for Mr Linnell is living at Hampstead & as promised to see me when he comes to town. All I know is that your card is ready for you, I suppose finished according to your request.'⁵

It was Sydney who next reported to his father in an undated letter, 'Geo: has seen the widow of Blake, but knows no particulars yet of his death—She is living with Mr Linnell the artist: she told Geo: that he died like an angle [angel]—you are expected to take the Job.'⁶

Soon afterwards, on 12 November, Linnell wrote to George Cumberland, jr.:

I take it for granted that you are acquainted with the death of our friend Mr Blake and I now wish to inform you that Mrs Blake is living with me here [Cirencester Place] and has the small card plate ready for you whenever you will call for it. Will you have the goodness to inform your Father respecting it & also to

¹ B.M. Add. MS. 36520, ff. 471–2.
² Ibid. 36512, f. 10.
³ *Blake's Letters*, ed. Keynes, 1968, p. 163.
⁴ B.M. Add. MS. 36512, f. 41.
⁵ Ibid., f. 64.
⁶ Ibid., f. 52.

say that it will be expected that he will pay for the Book of Job he had of Mr Blake at the same time—an early attention to the above will be esteemed a favour.[1]

George did not send this on to his father at once.

On 25 November Cumberland wrote to Mrs. Blake:

My dear Madam.

It was only very lately that I heard of the death of my excellent friend, your departed husband; and this week by an enclosure from my Son I find a Lett to him from Mr Linell stating that the card plate was ready for me, and that it will be expected that I pay for the Book of Job at the same time—I have in consequence written to him, by this conveyance, to call for the Card Plate, and now assure you, that if I do not succeed in Selling the Job (which was sent to me for that purpose from Mr Blake,) I shall certainly take it for myself and remit you the money as soon as I conveniently can.

That elaborate work, I have not only shewn to all our amateurs and artists here without success but am now pushing it through Clifton, by means of *Mr Lane* the Bookseller there, having previously placed it with Mr *Tyson*, Mr *Trimlet*, and another of our Print Sellers here without success—and as that is the case, and that even those who desired me to write to my friend for a List of his works and prices (among whom were his great admirers from having seen what I possessed—viz. Dr King of Clifton & Mr Rippengale the Artist.) declined giving him any orders, on account, as they said, of the prices—I should not recommend you to send any more here—but rather to fix a place in London where all his works may be disposed of, offering a complete set for Sale to the British Museum Print room, as that will make them best known—better even than their independant author who for his many virtues most deserved to be so—a Man who has stocked the english school with fine ideas,—above trick, fraud, or servility.

With my best wishes for your happiness

I am My dear Madam

Yours very truly

G. Cumberland

PS.

The reason I did not continue to purchase everything Mr Blake engraved, was that latterly I have not only been unable to continue Collecting but have even sold all I had Collected—yet still preserving all I possessed of his graver.

If you have occasion to write, let the Lett be left for me with my son George at the army Pay Office and he will get it franked.[2]

[1] Ibid., f. 45.
[2] Linnell family papers in the custody of Miss Joan Ivimy.

On 3 December he wrote to his son:

When *Linell* calls on you, he will probably bring an answer to my Lett^r to Mrs Blake & bring the Plate which I sent up to have a few ornaments engraved or etched round my name—as to the Job, it was sent to me to get sold, and they have no right to demand me to take it—I will, however inconvenient it may be, do so, if I cannot sell it for the sake of my old friend's widow—who leaves me this Legacy, to pay not to receive—I have tried all shops & acquaintances in vain hitherto—it is a sad work yet full of imagination.[1]

George then sent to his father Linnell's rather abrupt note of 12 November, which brought the following reply dated 26 December:

Your always welcome Lett^r I read on Xmas Day and Mr Linnell's polite Christmas Box enclosed which I only think ignorant not impudent, your Cockneys are all so almost and having had probably little intercourse with gentlemen are *brusque* and unreflecting. If I really in the Lett^r I wrote to poor honest Blake, who always acted and meant well, I have said [*sic*] I would take it if it did not sell here he may think I want now he is gone to evade that proposal or promise—but I much doubt if he can shew you any thing of the sort, not because I was not at all times affectionate to our simple honest friend and willing to serve him as my former purchase of nearly all his singular works will prove, will shew—and I might in feeling it was a delicate way of serving him have indicated such intention as the taking the Job—although I never could consider it as equal to his other performances. I therefore, without entering into any discussion with Mr L., could which [wish] you would take the 2.12.6 wh. she asks for the Job and £3.3— making £5.15.6, of Sydney as part of my Quarter's rent—and call on Mrs Blake herself to explain every thing clearly to her—taking the copper Plate and her receit for the same on a proper Stamp—for we must be so careful to shew it is settled properly in form—as to the Plate you will say I have never received it or any proof of it or notice, till Mr Linel demanded the money I knew not if it was ever done at all, at the same time let her know that I have always taken every measure to promote the sale of Mr B's works among my friends here without the smallest success, the prices having always been a hindrance—That I heartily wish her every success and shall still do all I can to serve her, but take no more Prints of any one to sell here by the Booksellers, as nothing does here, and if sold it is difficult to get the money without a long while—I suppose by her charging 3 gns. he has made a new Plate instead of my old one which I sent to be ornamented on the margin—and if so you will take that I sent back, as a plain one may be more useful—I long much to see what he has done—but if it is ever so trifling take it

[1] B.M. Add. MS. 36512, f. 57.

at her price as it is the last call I shall have on that feeling—which I often was forced to restrain—and now in particular, not having £10 to last me here till my Quarterage comes.[1]

The rather peevish tone of this long letter is perhaps accounted for by the fact that the writer was in bed with gout.

Cumberland paid Mrs. Blake the whole amount through his son, Sydney, taking it out of the quarter's rent due to his father, who made a note that this had been done on 16 January 1828.[2] Young George then wrote in an undated letter to his father:

Mrs Blake sends her Compts with many thanks. She tells me that the card would have been more finished if Mr B. had lived—that it was the last thing he attempted to engrave—that the Job is Mr Linnell's property now—her late husband's works she intends to print with her own hands and trusts to their sale for a livelihood—I saw Mr Linnell this morning & am sorry to say he is in a very bad state of health, a nervous affliction from over application. Dr Thornton whose card I enclose was with him.[3]

A few days later George wrote again to say, 'The card which I had not time to get printed represents the Seasons. I shall only give them to those likely to serve Mrs B.—it might be as well to reserve them till the Widow has printed her late husband's works which she intends to do and then send it to your friends.'[4] This probably crossed with his father's next letter of 7 January 1828:

As you have sent no proof of Blake's engraving I cannot tell what to make of it and here we have no one who could make a proof without spoiling the Engraving. I expected you would have taken off a few for yourself and shall give you some when I can get them printed off—as I wish by means of it to spread my old friend's fame and promote his wife's Interest by making him thus the subject of conversation and his works—which by the bye I think, as well as that of another friend C. Stothard, I fear I must sell for want of Money as I never in my life was before so bare of Cash as just now[5]—could not Colnaghis sell them think you by private contract, as might not the Museum be glad of such singular works which are so rare.[6]

On 1 February Cumberland added a postscript to a letter to George, 'I send you and Syd half a Dozen of the Cards—I could only get 20 Printed since I got it—

---

[1] Ibid., ff. 60–1.   [2] Ibid. 36521, f. 164.
[3] Ibid. 36512, f. 62.   [4] Ibid., f. 66.
[5] Cumberland nevertheless kept most of his Blake collection until he sold it at Christie's, 6 May 1835.
[6] B.M. Add. MS. 36512, f. 74.

they cost near 1d each here for fast Prints—do you know what it means?'[1] Blake's lovely little allegory of Innocence and Experience, Life and Death, had conveyed nothing more than 'the Seasons' to young George's mind. His father probably had more idea of Blake's intention. He was certainly pleased with it and attached one of the prints to Blake's last letter, now to be seen in the Fitzwilliam Museum.

Cumberland's recorded thoughts about Blake end with a letter to his son, George, dated 17 July 1830. 'I have read Blake's Life in the Family Library of Allan Cunningham and it seems he died amusing himself harmlessly in his own way. I think it is pretty true and suspect it was written by Mr Linnell. I could add a creditable anecdote or two and you perhaps several.'[2] It is certain that both the Cumberlands could have added much detail to our knowledge of Blake's life, but the father died at the age of 94 in 1848, too soon to be able to help Alexander Gilchrist in gathering information for his *Life of Blake*. Gilchrist may have talked with the son, but he did not always name his informants and George is not known to have been one of them.

R. H. Cromek, when sending Cumberland a copy of Blair's *Grave*, wrote on 14 August 1808, 'You are the only Person in Bristol who thoroughly understands the Inventions of Blake.'[3] Bristol certainly held few people who understood Blake's art at all, but it must be doubted whether even Cumberland's understanding was thorough. It is probably true that he had known Blake for upwards of forty years and clearly had great respect for his qualities and character, yet he was one of those who thought him 'a little mad', and his attitude, though always kind, was slightly condescending. He was grateful for the technical instruction that Blake could give him and was always active in forwarding his interests among his friends, but his understanding of Blake's mind was very imperfect. When Dr. Trusler sent Cumberland the two letters from Blake to himself, Cumberland wrote on the back of one of them, 'Blake, dim'd with superstition'.[4] This note has often been attributed to Trusler, but it is in Cumberland's hand. He truly sensed Blake's quality as a creative artist and leaned heavily on him as a technician. Though he remained puzzled by his eccentricities, he never wavered in his friendship for 'poor honest Blake', and Blake never found any cause for doubting his loyalty.

---

[1] B.M. Add. MS. 36512, f. 76.   [2] Ibid., f. 260.   [3] Ibid. 36501, f. 254.
[4] Ibid. 36498, f. 328.

INDEX

PRINTED IN GREAT BRITAIN
AT THE UNIVERSITY PRESS, OXFORD
BY VIVIAN RIDLER
PRINTER TO THE UNIVERSITY